Art of War: Then and Now

ART OF WAR: THEN AND NOW

Major (Retd.) S.K. Sharma

PRASHANT PUBLISHING HOUSE
DELHI-110094

Published by :
Prashant Publishing House
C-34, 28 Foota Road, Gali No.-3,
West Karawal Nagar, Delhi-110094
Phone : 011-22963970, Mob. : 9810396373

Art of War: Then and Now

First Published 2012

ISBN 978-93-80565-32-3

PRINTED IN INDIA
Published by Mr. R.K. Jha M/s Prashant Publishing House and Published at **Dynamic Printers, Delhi**

Preface

In many East Asian countries, The Art of War was part of the syllabus for potential candidates of military service examinations. Various translations are available. During the Sengoku era in Japan, a daimyo named Takeda Shingen (1521-1573) is said to have become almost invincible in all battles without relying on guns, because he studied The Art of War. The book even gave him the inspiration for his famous battle standard "Furinkazan" (Wind, Forest, Fire and Mountain), meaning fast as the wind, silent as a forest, ferocious as fire and immovable as a mountain.

The Art of War is one of the oldest books on military strategy in the world. Like a work of mathematics or science, much of the work is dedicated to defining its concepts in what has been described as a series of formulas. It is the first and one of the most successful works on strategy and has had a huge influence on Eastern and Western military thinking, business tactics, and beyond. Sun Tzu was the first to recognize the importance of positioning in strategy and that position is affected both by objective conditions in the physical environment and the subjective opinions of competitive actors in that environment. He taught that strategy was not planning in the sense of working through a todo list, instead it requires quickly responding appropriately to changing conditions. Planning works in a controlled environment, but in a competitive environment, competing plans collide creating situations that no one plans.

The 20th century has seen veritable successive 'revolutions' in warfare, starting with the advent of air power in World War I, and cemented by aircraft carriers further extending this reach across the oceans by World War II. This was followed by the introduction of nuclear weapons, development of nuclear warfighting doctrines, growth of missile and electronic warfare, and a move towards increasing coordination and jointness between the single Services. In the last two decades, technological advances have provided near real-time situational awareness and minimal sensor-shooter cycle, even as the reach, accuracy and lethality of modern weapons have attained unprecedented levels. Over this period, the 'ways and means' of war have undergone constant transformation. The ends for which war was waged have also expanded, from territorial ambitions to increasing geostrategic spheres of influence, to pursuit of religious-ideological conflicts, and again a reversion towards safeguarding of territorial and socioeconomic interests. The nature of war, as seen through its ways, means and ends, has probably traversed its largest arc of change in the last 100 years. The evolutionary trends of war led to several assessments, even before 9/11, of the emerging nature of 21st century warfare. This was appreciated as being more diverse and divisive, with the ways, means and ends of war continuing to change, along with traditional rationale and actors, and expectations of a transmutation of conflict, from total to limited war, from inter-state to intra-state war, and from regular, structured warfare to irregular warfare.

This book concludes that the only way to bring about a lasting peace and prevent more insurgencies rising up in the future is to build a state that attends equally to the interests of Art of War.

—Editor

Contents

1

Introduction

The Art of War is one of the oldest books on military strategy in the world. Like a work of mathematics or science, much of the work is dedicated to defining its concepts in what has been described as a series of formulas. It is the first and one of the most successful works on strategy and has had a huge influence on Eastern and Western military thinking, business tactics, and beyond. Sun Tzu was the first to recognize the importance of positioning in strategy and that position is affected both by objective conditions in the physical environment and the subjective opinions of competitive actors in that environment. He taught that strategy was not planning in the sense of working through a todo list, instead it requires quickly responding appropriately to changing conditions. Planning works in a controlled environment, but in a competitive environment, competing plans collide creating situations that no one plans.

The book was first translated into a European language in 1782 by French Jesuit Jean Joseph Marie Amiot, and had possibly influenced Napoleon, and even the planning of Operation Desert Storm. Leaders as diverse as Mao Zedong, General Pervez Musharraf, Vo Nguyen Giap, and General Douglas MacArthur have claimed to have drawn inspiration from the work. The Art of War has also been applied, with much success, to business and managerial strategies.

ANNOTATIONS

Before the bamboo scroll version was discovered by

archaeologists in April 1972, the most cited version of The Art of War was the Annotation of Sun Tzu's Strategies by Cao Cao, the founder of the Kingdom of Wei. In the preface, he wrote that previous annotations were not focused on the essential ideas. Other annotations cited in official history books include Shen You (1762-04)'s Sun Tzu's Military Strategy, Jia Xu's Copy of Sun Tzu's Military Strategy, Cao Cao and Wang Ling's Sun Tzu's Military Strategy. The Book of Sui documented seven books named after Sun Tzu. An annotation by Du Mu also includes Cao Cao's annotation. Li Jing's The Art of War is said to be a revision of Sun Tzu's strategies. Annotations by Cao Cao, Du Mu and Li Quan were translated into Tangut language before 1040 AD.

After the movable type printer was invented, The Art of War (with Cao Cao's annotations) was published as a military text book, known as Seven Military Classics with six other strategy books. A book named Ten Schools of The Art of War Annotations was published before 1161 AD. As a required reading military textbook since the Song Dynasty, Seven Military Classics has many annotations. More than 30 differently annotated versions of this book exist today. Vernacular Chinese became increasingly popular in the late 1920s. Annotations in Vernacular Chinese began to appear after this time. Some of these works were translated from other languages, such as Japanese.

The two most common traditional Chinese versions of the Art of War, (the Complete Specialist Focus and Military Bible versions) were the sources for early translation into English and other languages. It was not until the 1970s that these works were compiled with more recent archeological discoveries into a single more complete version in Taipei. The resulting work is known as the Complete Version of Sun Tzu's Art of War for the National Defence Research Investigation Office has been the source for more recent and complete translations.

Quotations

So it is said that if you know your enemies and know yourself, you will fight without danger in battles.

If you only know yourself, but not your opponent, you may win or may lose.

If you know neither yourself nor your enemy, you will always endanger yourself. This has been more tersely interpreted and condensed into the modern proverb: If you know both yourself and your enemy, you can come out of hundreds of battles without danger.

Many people interpret this sentence as 'If you know both sides, you will win a hundred times in one hundred battles. This translation is incorrect. The word '?' in Chinese means 'danger'. '?' in this sentence is better interpreted as 'numerous' rather than 'hundred'.

Furthermore, knowing both sides doesn't guarantee winning. Since in the beginning paragraph of chapter four, Sun Tsu wrote 'Hence, we can well predict who would win but there is no strategy guaranteeing winning'. The reason of the uncertainty is quite simple. How about dealing with the opponent who knows both sides better than you do? Similar verses have also been borrowedin a manner construing skilfulness as victory "without fighting" for example: Therefore one hundred victories in one hundred battles is not the most skilful. Seizing the enemy without fighting is the most skilful. And, the most famous quotation: All warfare is based on deception.

Military Applications

In many East Asian countries, The Art of War was part of the syllabus for potential candidates of military service examinations. Various translations are available. During the Sengoku era in Japan, a daimyo named Takeda Shingen (1521-1573) is said to have become almost invincible in all battles without relying on guns, because he studied The Art of War. The book even gave him the inspiration for his famous battle standard "Furinkazan" (Wind, Forest, Fire and Mountain), meaning fast as the wind, silent as a forest, ferocious as fire and immovable as a mountain.

The translator Samuel B. Griffith offers a chapter on "Sun Tzu and Mao TseTung" where The Art of War is cited as influencing Mao's On Guerilla Warfare, On the Protracted War, and Strategic Problems of China's Revolutionary War and includes Mao's quote: "We must not belittle the saying in the book of Sun Wu Tzu, the great military expert of ancient China, 'Know your enemy and know yourself and you can fight a thousand battles without disaster.'"

During the Vietnam War, some Vietcong officers studied The Art of War, and reportedly could recite entire passages from memory. The Department of the Army in the United States, through its Command and General Staff College, has directed all units to maintain libraries within their respective headquarters for the continuing education of personnel in the art of war. The Art of War is specifically mentioned by name as an example of works to be maintained at each individual unit, and staff duty officers are obliged to prepare short papers for presentation to other officers on their readings.

Applicability Outside the Military

Since at least the 1980s, The Art of War has been applied to fields well outside the military. Much of the text is about how to fight wars without actually having to do battle: it gives tips on how to outsmart one's opponent so that physical battle is not necessary. As such, it has found application as a training guide for many competitive endeavours that do not involve actual combat. The book has gained popularity in corporate culture; there have been a variety of business books written applying its lessons to "office politics" and corporate strategy. Many Japanese companies make the book required reading for their key executives. The book is also popular among Western business management, who have turned to it for inspiration and advice on how to succeed in competitive business situations.

The Art of War has also been the subject of various law books and legal articles on the trial process, including negotiation tactics and trial strategy. It has also crept its way into sport: Australian cricket coach John Buchanan handed out excerpts from the book to his players before a match against England in 2001, and the book is allegedly a favourite of University of South Carolina football head coach Steve Spurrier.

Former Brazilian football coach, and current coach of the Portuguese national football team Luiz Felipe Scolari uses the book to plot his football strategy. In the 2002 FIFA World Cup he gave each of his players copies. In the recent 2006 FIFA World Cup in Germany he used the book to plan his team's win against England.

On the popular reality television show Survivor: China, participants were given copies as a source of strategy and advice. It has found use in political campaigning as well; Republican election strategist Lee Atwater claimed he travelled everywhere with it. Some have also interpreted The Art of War as providing methods for developing social strategies, such as social relationships, maintaining romantic relationships, and seduction. The book stresses subtlety and always making it appear like one is trying to achieve something other than one's actual intention. The use of individual quotations from the book as a source of fortune cookielike proverbs and not seeing the general coherence of the text has been criticized by many scholars of Chinese history. The book has also gained influence among players of strategy games, including TCGs, collectible miniatures games, and realtime strategy games.

MODERN WAR MILITARY STRATEGY

Military strategy is a collective name for planning the conduct of warfare. Derived from the Greek strategos, strategy was seen as the "art of the general". Military strategy deals with the planning and conduct of campaigns, the movement and disposition of forces, and the deception of the enemy. The father of modern strategic study, Carl von Clausewitz, defined military strategy as "the employment of battles to gain the end of war." Liddell Hart's definition put less emphasis on battles, defining strategy as "the art of distributing and applying military means to fulfil the ends of policy" Hence, both gave the pre-eminence to political aims over military goals, ensuring civilian control of the military. Military strategy was one of a triumvirate of "arts" or "sciences" that govern the conduct of warfare; the others being tactics, the execution of plans and manoeuvring of forces in battle, and logistics, the maintenance of an army.

The border line between strategy and tactics is blurred and sometimes categorisation of a decision is a matter of almost personal opinion.

FUNDAMENTALS OF MILITARY STRATEGY

Strategy and tactics are closely related. Both deal with distance, time and force but strategy is large scale while tactics are small scale. Originally strategy was understood to govern the prelude to a battle while tactics controlled its execution. However, in the world wars of the 20th century, the distinction between maneuver and battle, strategy and tactics, became blurred. Tactics that were once the province of a company of cavalry would be applied to a panzer army. It is often said that the art of strategies defines the goals to achieve in a military campaign, while tactics defines the methods to achieve these goals. Strategic goals could be "We want to conquer area X", or "We want to stop country Y's expansion in world trade in commodity Z"; while tactical decisions range from "We're going to do this by a naval invasion of the North of country X", "We're going to blockade the ports of country Y", all the way down to "C Platoon will attack while D platoon provides fire cover". In its purest form, strategy dealt solely with military issues. In earlier societies, a king or political leader was often the same person as the military leader. If he was not, the distance of communication between the political and the military leader was small. But as the need of a professional army grew, the bounds between the politicians and the military came to be recognized. In many cases, it was decided that there was a need for a separation. As French statesman Georges Clemenceau said, "war is too important a business to be left to soldiers." This gave rise to the concept of the grand strategy which encompasses the management of the resources of an entire nation in the conduct of warfare.

In the environment of the grand strategy, the military component is largely reduced to operational strategythe planning and control of large military units such as corps and divisions. As the size and number of the armies grew and the technology to communicate and control improved, the difference between "military strategy" and "grand strategy" shrank. Fundamental to grand strategy is the diplomacy through which a nation might forge alliances or pressure another nation into compliance, thereby achieving victory without resorting to combat. Another element of grand strategy is the management of the postwar peace. As Clausewitz stated, a successful military strategy may be a means to an end, but it is not an end in itself. There are numerous examples in history where victory on the battlefield has not translated into long term peace, security or tranquility.

PRINCIPLES OF MILITARY STRATEGY

Many military strategists have attempted to encapsulate a successful strategy in a set of principles. Sun Tzu defined 13 principles in his The Art of War while Napoleon listed 115 maxims. American Civil War General Nathan Bedford Forrest required only one: "to git thar furst with the most men". The fundamental concepts common to most lists of principles are:

1. The Objective
2. Offense
3. Cooperation
4. Concentration (Mass)
5. Economy
6. Manoeuvre
7. Surprise
8. Security
9. Simplicity.

Which are reflected in the United States Army's United States Army Field Manual (FM3) of Military Operations (sections 432 to 439) as:

1. Objective (Direct every military operation towards a clearly defined, decisive, and attainable objective)
2. Offensive (Seize, retain, and exploit the initiative)
3. Mass (Concentrate combat power at the decisive place and time)

4. Economy of Force (Allocate minimum essential combat power to secondary efforts)
5. Maneuver (Place the enemy in a disadvantageous position through the flexible application of combat power)
6. Unity of Command (For every objective, ensure unity of effort under one responsible commander)
7. Security (Never permit the enemy to acquire an unexpected advantage)
8. Surprise (Strike the enemy at a time, at a place, or in a manner for which he is unprepared)
9. Simplicity (Prepare clear, uncomplicated plans and clear, concise orders to ensure thorough understanding).

Some strategists assert that adhering to the fundamental principles guarantees victory while others claim war is unpredictable and the general must be flexible in formulating a strategy. Field Marshal Count Helmuth von Moltke expressed strategy as a system of "ad hoc expedients" by which a general must take action while under pressure. These underlying principles of strategy have survived relatively unscathed as the technology of warfare has developed. Strategy (and tactics) must constantly evolve in response to technological advances. A successful strategy from one era tends to remain in favour long after new developments in military weaponry and material have rendered it obsolete. World War I, and to a great extent the American Civil War, saw Napoleonic tactics of "offense at all costs" pitted against the defensive power of the trench, machine gun and barbed wire. As a reaction to her WWI experience, France entered World War II with a purely defensive doctrine, epitomized by the "impregnable" Maginot Line, but only to be completely circumvented by the German blitzkrieg.

DEVELOPMENT OF MILITARY STRATEGY

Early Military Strategy

The principles of military strategy can be found as far back as 500 BC in the works of Sun Tzu and Chanakya. The campaigns of Alexander the Great, Chandragupta Maurya, Hannibal, Qin Shi Huang, Julius Cæsar, Zhuge Liang, and

Khalid ibn alWalid demonstrate strategic planning and movement. Mahan describes in the preface to The Influence of Sea Power upon History how the Romans used their sea power to effectively block the sea lines of communication of Hannibal with Carthage; and so via a maritime strategy achieved Hannibal's removal from Italy, despite never beating him there with their legions.

In 1520 Niccolò Machiavelli's Dell'arte della guerra (Art of War) dealt with the relationship between civil and military matters and the formation of the grand strategy. In the Thirty Years' War, Gustavus Adolphus of Sweden demonstrated advanced operational strategy that led to victories in Holy Roman Empire area. It was not until the 18th century that military strategy was subjected to serious study. In the Seven Years' War (1756-1763), Frederick the Great improvised a "strategy of exhaustion" to hold off his opponents and conserve his Prussian forces. Assailed from all sides by France, Austria, Russia and Sweden, Frederick exploited his central position which enabled him to move his army along interior lines and concentrate against one opponent at a time. Unable to achieve victory, he was able to stave off defeat until a diplomatic solution was reached. Frederick's "victory" led to great significance being placed on "geometric strategy" which emphasized lines of manoeuvre, awareness of terrain and possession of critical strongpoints.

Genghis Khan and the Mongols

As a counterpoint to European developments in the strategic art, the Mongol Emperor Genghis Khan provides a useful example. Genghis' successes, and those of his successors, were based upon manoeuvre and terror. The point of Genghis' strategic assault was nothing less than the psychology of the opposing population. By a steady and meticulous implementation of this strategy, Genghis and his descendants were able to conquer most of Eurasia. The building blocks of Genghis' army and his strategy were his tribal levies of mounted archers and (just as important) the vast horseherds of Mongolia. Each archer had at least one extra horse; (it was an average five horses per man) thus the entire army could move with incredible rapidity. Moreover since horse milk and horse blood were the staples of the Mongolian diet, Genghis' horseherds functioned not just as his means of movement but also as his logistical tail. All other necessities could be foraged and plundered. It was not until well into the 20th century that any army was able to match the rapidity of deployment of Genghis' armies. Compared to the armies of Genghis, all other armies were heavy and comparatively immobile. Through manoeuver and continuous assault, Chinese, Persian, Arab and Eastern European armies could be stressed until they broke, and then annihilated in pursuit.

When confronted with a fortified city, the Mongol imperatives of manoeuver and speed required that it be quickly subdued. Here the fear engendered by the awful reputation of the Mongolians helped. So too did primitive biological warfare. A trebuchet or other type of ballista weapon would be used to launch dead animals and corpses into a barricaded city, spreading disease and death among the inhabitants. If a particular town or city displeased the Mongolian Khan, everyone in the city would be killed to set an example for all other cities. This could be called a form of psychological warfare. Note that of the above list of strategic terms, even this elementary summary indicates that the Mongols strategy was directed towards an objective (that schwerpunkt (main focus) being nothing less than the psychology of the opposing population) achieved through the offensive; the offensive was characterized by concentration of forces, manoeuvre, surprise and simplicity.

Napoleonic Strategy

The French Revolution and the Napoleonic Wars that followed revolutionized military strategy. The impact of this period was still to be felt in the American Civil War and the early phases of World War I. With the advent of cheap small arms and the rise of the drafted citizen soldier, armies grew rapidly in size to become massed formations. This necessitated dividing the army first into divisions and later into corps. Along with divisions came divisional artillery; lightweight, mobile and with great range and firepower. The rigid formations of pikemen and musketeers firing massed volleys gave way to light infantry fighting in skirmish lines. Napoleon I of France took advantage of these developments to pursue a brutally effective "strategy of annihilation" that cared little for the mathematical perfection of the geometric strategy. Napoleon invariably sought to achieve decision in battle, with the sole aim of utterly destroying his opponent, usually achieving success through superior manouevre. As ruler and general he dealt with the grand strategy as well as the operational strategy, making use of political and economic measures.

While not the originator of the methods he used, Napoleon very effectively combined the maneuver and battle stages into one event. Before this, General Officer had considered the approach to battle a separate event. However, Napoleon used the maneuver to battle to dictate how and where the battle would progress. The Battle of Austerlitz was a perfect example of this maneuver. Napoleon withdrew from a strong position to draw his opponent forward and tempt him into a flank attack, weakening his centre. This allowed the French army to split the allied army and gain victory. Napoleon used two primary strategies for the approach to battle. His "Maneuver De Derrière" was intended to place the French Army across the enemy's lines of communications. This forced the opponent to either march to battle with Napoleon or attempt to find an escape route around the army. By placing his army into the rear, his opponents supplies and communications would be cut. This had a negative effect on enemy morale. Once joined, the battle would be one in which his opponent could not afford defeat. This also allowed Napoleon to select multiple march routes into a battle site. Initially, the lack of force concentration helped with foraging for food and sought to confuse the enemy as to his real location and intentions. This strategy, along with the use of forced marches created a morale bonus that played heavily in his favour.

The "indirect" approach into battle also allowed Napoleon to disrupt the linear formations used by the allied armies. As the battle progressed enemy committed their reserves to stabilize the situation, Napoleon would suddenly release the flanking formation to attack the enemy. His opponents, being suddenly confronted with a new threat and with little reserves, had no choice but to weaken the area closest to the flanking formation and draw up a battle line at a right angle in an attempt to stop this new threat. Once this had occurred, Napoleon would mass his reserves at the hinge of that right angle and launch a heavy attack to break the lines. The rupture in the enemy lines allowed Napoleon's cavalry to flank both lines and roll them up leaving his opponent no choice but to surrender or flee.

The second strategy used by Napoleon I of France when confronted with two or more enemy armies was the use of the central position. This allowed Napoleon to drive a wedge to separate the enemy armies. He would then use part of his force to mask one army while the larger portion overwhelmed and defeated the second army quickly. He would then march on the second army leaving a portion to pursue the first army and repeat the operations. This was designed to achieve the highest concentration of men into the primary battle while limiting the enemy's ability to reinforce the critical battle. The central position had a weakness in that the full power of the pursuit of the enemy could not be achieved because the second army needed attention. So overall the preferred method of attack was the flank march to cross the enemies logistics. Napoleon used the central position strategy during the Battle of Waterloo Hundred Days. Napoleon masked Arthur Wellesley, 1st Duke of Wellington and massed against the Prussian army, and then after the Ligny battle was won, Napoleon attempted to do the same to the Allied/English army located just to the south of Waterloo. His subordinate was unable to mask the defeated Prussian army, who reinforced the Waterloo battle in time to defeat Napoleon and end his domination of Europe. It can be said that the Prussian Army under Gebhard Leberecht von Blücher used the "maneuver de derrière" against Napoleon who was suddenly placed in a position of reacting to a new enemy threat.

Napoleon's practical strategic triumphs, repeatedly leading smaller forces to defeat larger ones, inspired a whole new field of study into military strategy. In particular, his opponents were keen to develop a body of knowledge in this area to allow them to counteract a masterful individual with a highly competent group of officers, a General Staff. The two most significant students of his work were Carl von Clausewitz, a Prussian with a background in philosophy, and AntoineHenri Jomini, who had been one of Napoleon's staff officers. Clausewitz's On War has become the bible of strategy, dealing with political, as well as military, leadership. His most famous assertion being:

> "*War is not merely a political act, but also a real political instrument, a continuation of policy carried out by other means.*"

Clausewitz dismissed "geometry" as an insignificant factor in strategy, believing instead in the Napoleonic concept of victory through battle and destruction of the opposing force, at any cost. However, he also recognized that limited warfare could influence policy by wearing down the opposition through a "strategy of attrition". In contrast to Clausewitz, AntoineHenri Jomini dealt mainly with operational strategy, planning & intelligence, the conduct of the campaign, and "generalship" rather than "statesmanship". He proposed that victory could be achieved by occupying the enemy's territory rather than destroying his army. As such, geometric considerations were prominent in his theory of strategy. Jomini's two basic principles of strategy were to concentrate against fractions of the enemy force at a time and to strike at the most decisive objective.

One notable exception to Napoleon's strategy of annihilation and a precursor to trench warfare were the Lines of Torres Vedras during the Peninsular campaign. French Armies lived off the land and when they were confronted by a line of fortifications which they could not out flank, they were unable to continue the advance and were forced to retreat once they had consumed all the provisions of the region in front of the lines.

The Peninsular campaign was notable for the development of another method of warfare which went largely unnoticed at the time, but would become far more common in the 20th century. That was the aid and encouragement the British gave to the Spanish to harass the French behind their lines which led them to squander most of the assets of their Iberian army in protecting the army's line of communications. This was a very cost effective move for the British, because it cost far less to aid Spanish insurgents than it did to equip and pay regular British army units to engage the same number of French troops. As the British army could be correspondingly smaller it was able to supply its troops by sea and land without having to live off the land as was the norm at the time. Further, because they did not have to forage they did not antagonise the locals and so did not have to garrison their lines of communications to the same extent as the French did. So the strategy of aiding their Spanish civilian allies in their guerrilla or 'small war' benefited the British in many ways, not all of which were immediately obvious.

STRATEGY IN THE INDUSTRIAL AGE

The evolution of military strategy continued in the American Civil War (1861-65). The practice of strategy was advanced by generals such as Robert E. Lee, Ulysses S. Grant and William Tecumseh Sherman, all of whom had been influenced by the feats of Napoleon (Thomas "Stonewall" Jackson was said to have carried a book of Napoleon's maxims with him). However, the adherence to the Napoleonic principles in the face of technological advances such as the longrange infantry rifle generally led to disastrous consequences. The time and space in which war was waged changed as well. Railroads enabled swift movement of large forces but the manoeuvring was constrained to narrow, vulnerable corridors. Steam power and ironclads changed transport and combat at sea.

There was still room for triumphs of strategy of manoeuvre such as Sherman's March to the Sea in 1864, but these depended upon an enemy's unwillingness to entrench. Towards the end of the war, especially in defence of static targets as in the battles of Cold Harbour and Vicksburg, trenches between both sides grew to a World War I scale. Many of the lessons of the American Civil War were forgotten when in wars like the

AustroPrussian War or the FrancoPrussian War manoeuvre won the day. In the period preceding World War I, two of the most influential strategists were the Prussian generals, Helmuth von Moltke and Alfred von Schlieffen. Under Moltke the Prussian army achieved victory in the Austro-Prussian War (1866) and the Franco-Prussian War (1870-71), the latter campaign being widely regarded as a classic example of the conception and execution of military strategy. In addition to exploiting railroads and highways for manoeuvre, Moltke harnessed the telegraph for control of large armies. He recognised the increasing need to delegate control to subordinate commanders and to issue directives rather than specific orders.

Moltke is most remembered as a strategist for his belief in the need for flexibility and that no plan, however well prepared, can be guaranteed to survive beyond the first encounter with the enemy.

Field Marshal Schlieffen succeeded Moltke and directed German planning in the lead up to World War I. He advocated the "strategy of annihilation" but was faced by a war on two fronts against numerically superior opposition. The strategy he formulated was the Schlieffen Plan, defending in the east while concentrating for a decisive victory in the west, after which the Germans would go on to the offensive in the east. Influenced by Hannibal's success at the Battle of Cannae, Schlieffen planned for a single great battle of encirclement, thereby annihilating his enemy. Another German strategist of the period was Hans Delbrück who expanded on Clausewitz's concept of "limited warfare" to produce a theory on the "strategy of exhaustion". His theory defied popular military thinking of the time, which was strongly in favour of victory in battle, yet World War I would soon demonstrate the flaws of a mindless "strategy of annihilation".

At a time when industrialisation was reaping major advances in naval technology, one American strategist, Alfred Thayer Mahan, almost single-handedly brought the field of naval strategy up to date. Influenced by Jomini's principles of strategy, he saw that in the coming wars, where economic strategy could be as important as military strategy, control of the sea granted the power to control the trade and resources needed to wage war. Mahan pushed the concept of the "big navy" and an expansionist view where defence was achieved by controlling the sea approaches rather than fortifying the coast. His theories contributed to the naval arms race between 1898 and 1914.

STRATEGY IN WORLD WAR I

At the start of World War I strategy was dominated by the offensive thinking that had been in vogue since 1870, despite the more recent experiences of the Second Boer War (1899-1902) and RussoJapanese War (1904-05), where the machine gun demonstrated its defensive capabilities. By the end of 1914, the Western Front was a stalemate and all ability to manoeuver strategically was lost. The combatants resorted to a "strategy of attrition". The German battle at Verdun, the British on the Somme and at Passchendaele were among the first widescale battles intended to wear down the enemy. Attrition was timeconsuming so the duration of World War I battles often stretched to weeks and months. The problem with attrition was that the use of fortified defenses in depth generally required a ratio of ten attackers to one defender, or a level of artillery support which was simply not feasible until late 1917, for any reasonable chance of victory. The ability of the defender to move troops using interior lines prevented the possibility of fully exploiting any breakthrough with the level of technology then attainable.

Perhaps the most controversial aspect of strategy in World War I was the difference among the British between the "Western" viewpoint (held by Field Marshal Haig) and the "Eastern"; the former being that all effort should be directed against the German Army, the latter that more useful work could be done by attacking Germany's allies. The term "Knocking away the props" was used, perhaps an unfortunate consequence of the fact that all of Germany's allies lay south of (i.e. 'beneath') her on the map. Apologists and defenders of the Western viewpoint make the valid point that Germany's allies were more than once rescued from disaster or rendered capable of holding their own or making substantial gains by the provision of German troops, arms or military advisers, whereas those allies did not at any time provide a similar function for Germany. That is, it was Germany which was the prop, and her allies (particularly Bulgaria and AustriaHungary) did not suffer significant reverses until Germany's ability to come to their aid was grossly impaired.

On other fronts, there was still room for the use of strategy of manoeuver. The Germans executed a perfect battle of annihilation against the Russians at the Battle of Tannenberg (1914). In 1915 Britain and France launched the well-intentioned but poorly conceived and ultimately fruitless Dardanelles Campaign, combining naval power and an amphibious landing, in an effort to aid their Russian ally and knock the Ottoman Empire out of the war. The Palestine campaign was dominated by cavalry, which flourished in the local terrain, and the British achieved two breakthrough victories at Gaza (1917) and Megiddo (1918). Colonel T.E. Lawrence and other British officers led Arab irregulars on a guerrilla campaign against the Ottomans, using strategy and tactics developed during the Boer Wars.

World War I saw armies on a scale never before experienced. The British, who had always relied on a strong navy and a small regular army, were forced to undertake a rapid expansion of the army. This outpaced the rate of training of generals and staff officers able to handle such a mammoth force, and overwhelmed the ability of British industry to equip it with the necessary weapons and adequate highquality munitions until late in the war. Technological advances also had a huge influence on strategy: aerial reconnaissance, artillery techniques, poison gas, the automobile and tank (though the latter was, even at the end of the war, still in its infancy), telephone and radio telegraphy.

More so than in previous wars, military strategy in World War I was directed by the grand strategy of a coalition of nations; the Entente on one side and the Central Powers on the other. Society and economy were mobilized for total war. Attacks on the enemy's economy included Britain's use of a naval blockade and Germany employing submarine warfare against merchant shipping.

Unity of command became a question when the various nation states began coordinating assaults and defenses. Under the pressure of horrendously destructive German attacks beginning on March 21, 1918, the Entente eventually settled under Field Marshal Foch. The Germans generally led the Central Powers, though German authority diminished and lines of command became confused at the end of the war.

World War I strategy was dominated by the "Spirit of the Offensive" where generals resorted almost to mysticism in terms of a soldiers personal "attitude" in order to break the stalemate, this led to nothing but bloody slaughter as troops in close ranks charged machineguns. Each side developed an alternate thesis. The British under Churchill developed tank warfare with which they eventually won the war.

The Germans developed a "doctrine of autonomy" the forerunner of both blitzkrieg and modern infantry tactics using groups of Stormtroopers who would advance in small mutually covering groups from cover to cover with "autonomy" to exploit any weakness they discovered in enemy defenses. Almost all the blitzkrieg commanders of WWII, particularly Rommel were stormtroopers in World War 1. After the Treaty of BrestLitovsk. Germany launched and almost succeeded in a final offensive, however the new tactics of autonomy revealed a weakness in terms of overall coordination and direction. The March offensive, intended to drive a wedge between the French and British armies, turn on the latter and destroy it, lost direction and became driven by its territorial gains, its original purpose neglected.

World War I ended when the ability of the German army to fight became so diminished that Germany asked for peace conditions. The German military, exhausted by the efforts of the March offensives and dispirited by their failure, was first seriously defeated during the battle of Amiens (11 August 1918) and the German homefront entered general revolt over a lack of food and destruction of the economy. Victory for the Entente was almost assured by that point, and the fact of Germany's military impotence was driven home in the following hundred days. In this time, the Entente reversed the gains the

Germans had made in the first part of the year, and the British Army (spearheaded by the Canadians and Australians) finally broke the Hindenburg defensive system.

Though his methods are questioned, Britain's Field Marshal Haig was ultimately proved correct in his grand strategic vision: "We cannot hope to win until we have defeated the German Army." By the end of the war, the best German troops were dead and the remainder were under continuous pressure on all parts of the Western Front, a consequence in part of an almost endless supply of fresh American reinforcements (which the Germans were unable to match) and in part of industry at last supplying the weakened Entente armies with the firepower to replace the men they lacked (whilst Germany wanted for all sorts of materials thanks to the naval blockade). Interior lines thus became meaningless as Germany had nothing more to offer its allies. The props eventually fell, but only because they were themselves no longer supported.

The role of the tank in World War One strategy is often poorly understood. Its supporters saw it as the weapon of victory, and many observers since have accused the high commands (especially the British) of short-sightedness in this matter, particularly in view of what tanks have achieved since. Nevertheless, the World War I tank's limitations, imposed by the limits of contemporary engineering technology, have to be borne in mind. They were slow (men could run, and frequently walk, faster); vulnerable (to artillery) due to their size, clumsiness and inability to carry armour against anything but rifle and machine gun ammunition; extremely uncomfortable (conditions inside them often incapacitating crews with engine fumes and heat, and driving some mad with noise); and often despicably unreliable (frequently failing to make it to their targets due to engine or track failures). This was the factor behind the seemingly mindless retention of large bodies of cavalry, which even in 1918, with armies incompletely mechanised, were still the only armed force capable of moving significantly faster than an infantryman on foot. It was not until the relevant technology (in engineering and communications) matured between the wars that the tank and the airplane could be forged into the coordinated force needed to truly restore manoeuvre to warfare.

STRATEGY DEVELOPMENT BETWEEN WORLD WARS

In the years following World War I, two of the technologies that had been introduced during that conflict, the aircraft and the tank, became the subject of strategic study. The leading theorist of air power was Italian general Giulio Douhet who believed that future wars would be won or lost in the air. The air force would carry the offensive and the role of the ground forces would be defensive only. Douhet's doctrine of strategic bombing meant striking at the enemy's heartlandhis cities, industry and communications. Air power would thereby reduce his willingness and capacity to fight. At this time the idea of the aircraft carrier and its capabilities also started to change thinking in those countries with large fleets, but nowhere as much as in Japan. The UK and USA seem to have seen the carrier as a defensive weapon and their designs mirrored this, the Japanese Imperial navy seem to have developed a new offensive strategy based around the power projection these made possible.

British general J. F. C. Fuller, architect of the first great tank battle at Cambrai, and his contemporary, B. H. Liddell Hart, were amongst the most prominent advocates of mechanization and motorization of the army in Britain. In Germany, study groups were set up by Von Seekt, commander of the Reichwehr Truppenamt, for 57 areas of strategy and tactics to learn from WW1 and to adapt strategy to avoid the stalemate and then defeat they had suffered. All seem to have seen the strategic shock value of mobility and the new possibilities made possible by motorised forces. Both saw that the armoured fighting vehicle demonstrated firepower, mobility and protection. The Germans seem to have seen more clearly the need to make all branches of the Army as mobile as possible to maximise the results of this strategy. It would negate the static defences of the trench and machine gun and restore the strategic principles of manoeuvre and offense. Nevertheless, it was the British Army which was the only one truly mechanised at the beginning of the Second World War, the Germans still relying on horse traction for a portion of their artillery.

The innovative German Major (later General) Heinz Guderian developed the motorised part of this strategy as the head of one of the Truppenamt groups and may have incorporated Fuller's and Liddell Hart's ideas to amplify the groundbreaking Blitzkrieg effect that was seen used by Germany against Poland in 1939 and later against France in 1940. France, still committed to stationary World War I strategies, was completely surprised and summarily overwhelmed by Germany's mobile combined arms doctrine and Guderian's Panzer Corps.

Technological change had an enormous effect on strategy, but little effect on leadership. The use of telegraph and later radio, along with improved transport, enabled the rapid movement of large numbers of men. One of Germany's key enablers in mobile warfare was the use of radios, where these were put into every tank. However, the number of men that one officer could effectively control had, if anything, declined. The increases in the size of the armies led to an increase in the number of officers. Although the officer ranks in the US Army did swell, in the German army the ratio of officers to total men remained steady.

STRATEGY IN WORLD WAR II

German Strategy

The German strategies of World War II were almost exclusively designed or condoned by Adolf Hitler himself. Though he was an amateur strategist at best, the initial successes of his unconventional and aggressive strategies, both military and political (e.g. Czechoslovakia, Poland, France), combined with the mythical attributes ascribed to him ("Führerprinzip"), led to wide support for his leadership, both among the German population and the traditional military. The main point of Hitler's strategy was the accumulation of "Lebensraum" ("Living space") for the German race. He felt that the German borders were too contained to secure their appropriate position in the geopolitical world relations, and that he needed territories similar to the (British and French) colonies to secure enough economic resources to secure Germany's position as a major power. Furthermore, the current population of these territories needed to be enslaved, migrated, or exterminated, and repopulated by Germanic settlers. He felt that these areas could best be secured in the East (Poland, Ukraine, Russia) because he thought the races populating these territories were inferior.

The intended strategy to achieve these goals was a series of relatively short wars, employing "blitzkrieg" tactics, to defeat one opponent at a time, and thus securing more land step by step. These wars were to be intertwined with periods of peace, or stalemate, when the German army could resupply and accumulate force for the next war. The initial success of this strategy (the remilitarization of the Saarland, the Austrian Anschluss, and the occupation in two stages of Czechoslovakia) stifled critique and gave Hitler great prestige. Hitler didn't realize that the turning point had come with the invasion of Poland. Both France and Britain had frowned upon his expansion, and declared war on Germany on that occasion. Hitler believed that Britain could be appeased by the defeat of France, but he had underestimated the British determination. Even though Britain couldn't do much against Germany at first, a war of attrition had begunsomething that the "blitzkrieg" concept was never designed for.

In the later years of the war, Hitler's strategy became more and more based on intuition, flawed logic, and unrealistic assumptions. However, the strength of his hold on domestic policy remained so strong, that his "brilliance" was not questioned, or was quickly suppressed. In the final stages of the war, his actions and orders had turned into the rambling of a madman rather than any attempt to conduct a coherent strategy.

Anglo-American Strategy

Confronted with the rise of Hitler's power on the continent, and realizing the brutality of his regime, the British gradually turned to a fierce opposition and finally a war declaration over the invasion of Poland. Britain wasn't prepared for war, especially on land, and the initial years were a series of defeats, as they got thrown off the European continent everywhere (France, Norway, Greece). However, the sea ensured their survival, since Germany had no navy to speak of compared to the British. After air superiority over the Channel was secured in the battle of Britain, and the antisubmarine weapons were perfected to win the battle of the Atlantic, Britain itself was not threatened anymore. Strategic plans could turn to the offensive, especially with the USA leaning more and more to a war with Germany. After the USA entered the war, Europe (as opposed to the Pacific) was chosen as the prime theatre of operations by the formulation of the "Germany first" principle at the Arcadia Conference. However, their land armies wouldn't be capable of invading the mainland of Europe for years, even as Stalin pleaded for this to alleviate pressure on the Russian front. Instead, the Allies decided to take an indirect approach by invading Europe from the South. After cleansing North Africa of Axis forces (the invasion of French NorthAfrica and El Alamein), Sicily and southern Italy were invaded, effectively knocking Italy out of the war. Given that the terrain circumstances in this area were unviable to turn this route into the main thrust on Germany itself, the main purpose of these operations weren't mainly territorial, but focused on tying up as many German forces in southern Europe as possible, thereby alleviating pressure from the Soviets as well as thinning the garrison forces in France, where the main Allied force was still planned to invade.

In the air war, superiority was gained pretty early. After that, the Allies launched a strategic bombing campaign against Germany. After initial emphasis on economic targets (factories, infrastructure, etc), the Allies turned more and more towards terror bombing of German cities.

Soviet Strategy

Early Soviet strategy intended to avoid war for as long as possible. After the cleansing of the Red Army officer corps, the army was seen as unfit to conduct any kind of serious war, and this proved to be true by the Finnish winter war. With the signing of the Molotov Ribbentrop pact, Joseph Stalin believed he had secured peace for as long as he needed to rebuild the Soviet military force. The Barbarossa campaign of 1941 came as a complete surprise to the Soviets. Nevertheless, they reacted swiftly, particularly in the civilian aspect. As the army was being defeated and gave ground at an amazing speed, a gigantic operation was staged to move the economic capacity from the Western areas that were about to be overrun, to Eastern regions that were out of reach for the Germans, like the Ural. Entire factories, including their labour force, were simply moved out of reach from the Germans, and what couldn't be taken was destroyed ("Scorched earth"). Thus, even though huge territories were captured by the Germans, the production potential was relatively unharmed, and the factories shifted to mass production of military equipment quickly, outproducing the German economy soon.

After achieving numerical superiority, the Soviets were still qualitatively inferior. To compensate this, they emphasized on gaining an even larger quantitative edge. The later offensive Soviet campaigns all saw a massive employment of manpower, often resulting in extremely bloody battles. It wasn't unusual that Soviet "victories" inflicted far larger casualties on themselves than on the Germans. However, the total national manpower pool was so much larger than the German one, that this still led to success.

Japanese Strategy

Japanese World War II strategy was driven by two factors: the desire to expand their territories on the mainland of Asia (China and Manchuria), and the need to secure the supply of raw resources that they didn't have themselves, particularly oil. Since their quest after the former (conquest of Chinese provinces) endangered the latter (an oil boycott by the USA and its Allies), the Japanese government saw no other option than to conquer the oil sources in Southeast Asia. Since these were controlled by American allies, war with the USA was also inevitable; and given that fact, they decided it would be best to deal a big blow to them first. This was executed in the Pearl Harbour strike, crippling the American battle fleet.

Japan hoped that it would take America so long to rebuild, that by the time they were back in force in the Pacific, they would consider the new balance of power a "fait accompli", and barter for peace. They had underestimated the psychological effect of the Pearl Harbour strike; the USA wouldn't negotiate with an enemy that had struck them in this way. Even though Southeast Asia was quickly conquered (Philippines, Indochina, Malaya, Dutch East Indies), the early sea battles in the Pacific were tied. After the vital aircraft carrier force was destroyed in the Battle of Midway, the Japanese had to revert to a stiff defence that they kept up for three years after that.

American Pacific Strategy

Since the American economic force was much larger than the Japanese, even considering their effort in the European theatre, the numerical inferior US forces remaining in the area after Pearl Harbour weren't afraid to battle the Japanese; they knew they could replace battle losses faster than the Japanese. In several aircraft carrier battles, the initiative was taken from the Japanese, and after the Battle of Midway, the Japanese navy was rendered helpless, effectively giving the Americans the possibility to sail wherever they wanted. As the Japanese offensive died down in the second half of 1942, the Americans saw themselves confronted with an endless amount of fortified garrisons on small islands in the ocean. They decided on a strategy of "leapfrogging", leaving the strongest garrisons alone, just cutting their supply, and securing bases of operation on the lightly defended isles instead. They kept up this strategy until they were in the Japanese waters themselves, allowing the aerial bombing of the Japanese mainland.

Australian Strategy

Australia's historical ties with Britain meant that with the commencement of World War II her armies were sent overseas to contribute to battles in Europe. Fear from the north was so understated that at the outbreak of open warfare with Japan, Australia itself was extremely vulnerable to invasion (possible invasion plans were considered by the Japanese high command). Australia's policy became based entirely on domestic defence following the attacks on Pearl Habour and British assets in the South Pacific. Defying strong British opposition, Australian Prime Minister John Curtin recalled most troops from the European conflict for the defence of the nation.

Australia's defensive doctrine saw a fierce campaign being fought along the Kokoda track in New Guinea, which was the first land defeat upon the Japanese in the Pacific Theatre. This policy sought to further stretch Japanese supply lines, preventing the invasion of the Australian mainland until the arrival of fresh American troops and the return of seasoned Australian soldiers from Europe. This can be seen as a variant of the war of attrition strategy, where the defenderout of necessityhad to hold the aggressor at a semistatic defensive line, rather than falling back in the face of superior numbers. This method is in stark contrast to the Russian scorched earth policy against Napoleon in 1812, where the defenders yielded home territory in favour of avoiding open battle. In both cases the lack of supplies was successful in blunting the assaults, following exhaustive defensive efforts.

Cold War Strategy

The Cold War was the last time period dominated by the threat of total world annihilation through the use of nuclear weapons, a policy known as mutually assured destruction. As a consequence it was also a war in which attacks were not exchanged between the two main rivals, the United States and the Soviet Union. Instead, the war was fought through proxies. Instead of mainly being confined to Europe or the Pacific, the entire world was the battlefield, with countries rather than armies acting as main players. The only constant rule was that troops of the Soviet Union and the United States could not overtly fight with each other. The difference between tactics, strategy and grand strategy began to melt during the Cold War as command and communication technologies improved to a greater extent, in first world armed forces. The third world armed forces controlled by the two superpowers found that grand strategy, strategy and tactics, if anything, moved further apart as the command of the armies fell under the control of super power leaders.

American cold warriors like Dean Acheson and George C. Marshall quickly recognized that the key to victory was the economic defeat of the Soviet Union.

The Soviet Union had adopted an aggressive posture of Communist expansionism following the end of World War II, with the United States and its strong navy quickly finding that it had to aggressively defend much of the world from the Soviet Union and the spread of communism. Strategies during the Cold War also dealt with nuclear attack and retaliation. The United States maintained a policy of limited first strike throughout the Cold War. In the event of a Soviet attack on the Western Front, resulting in a breakthrough, the United States would use tactical nuclear weapons to stop the attack.

The view from Moscow was to adapt to the prevailing changes in the NATO strategic policies that are divided by periods as:

- Strategy of massive retaliation (1950s)
- Strategy of flexible reaction (1960s)
- Strategies of realistic threat and containment (1970s)
- Strategy of direct confrontation (1980s) one of the elements of which became the new highly effective high precision targeting weapons.
- Strategic Defence Initiative (also known as "Star Wars") during its 1980s development which became a core part of the strategic doctrine based on Defence containment.

Soviet Union responded by adopting a policy of no first use, involving massive retaliation resulting in mutual assured destruction. So, if the Warsaw Pact attacked using conventional weapons, NATO would use tactical nukes. The Soviet Union would respond with an all out nuclear attack, resulting in a similar attack from the United States, with all the consequences the exchange would entail. This did not happen. The United States continues to maintain a policy of limited first strike to the present (October 2006).

Post Cold War Strategy

Strategy in the post Cold War has come to be defined by the hyperpower status of the United States. It is increasingly relying on advanced technology to minimize casualties and improve efficiency. The technological quantum leaps brought by the Digital Revolution are essential for this strategy. The gap in strategy today (from a western viewpoint) is in what the Americans call "asymmetric warfare": the battle against guerrilla forces by conventional national armed forces. The classical strategic triumvirate of politics/military/populace is very weak against protracted warfare of paramilitary forces such as the Provisional Irish Republican Army, Hezbollah, ETA, and AlQaeda.

The ability of conventional forces to deliver utility (effect) from their hugely powerful forces is largely nullified by the difficulties of distinguishing and separating combatants from the civilian populace in whose company they hide. The use of the military by the politicians to police areas seen as bases for these guerrillas leads to them becoming targets themselves which eventually undermines the support of the populace from whom they come and whose values they represent.

The primary effect of insurgent elements upon conventional force strategy is realized in the twofold exploitation of the inherent violence of military operations. Conventional armies face political attrition for each action they take. Insurgent forces can cause harm and create chaos, whereby the conventional army suffers a loss of confidence and esteem; or they can drive the conventional elements into an attack which further exacerbates the civilian condition. The militaries of today are largely set up to fight the 'last war' and hence have huge armoured and conventionally configured infantry formations backed up by airforces and navies designed to support or prepare for these forces. Many are today deployed against guerrillastyle opponents where their strengths cannot be used to effect. The mass formations of Industrial War are often seen as much less effective than the unconventional forces that these organisations also possess. The new opponents operate at a local level whereas Industrial armed forces work at a much higher 'theatre' level.

The nervous system of these new opponents is largely political rather than military hierarchical and adapted to the local supporting populace who hide them. The centre provides the political idea and driving logic perhaps with overall direction and some funding. Local groups decide their own plans, raise much of their own funds and may be more or less aligned to the centre's aims. Defeat of forces when revealed does not disable this type of organisation, many modern attack strategies will tend to increase the power of the group they are intended to weaken. A new more political strategy is perhaps more appropriate here with military backing. Such a strategy has been illustrated in the war between the IRA an adoption and codification is unclear.

Netwar

An extra issue concerning asymmetric warfare concerns the nature of some paramilitary organizations which are involved in guerrilla military actions, but which are not traditional organizations with a central authority defining their military and political strategies. These organizations (such as Al-Qaeda) may exist as a sparse network of groups lacking central coordination, making them extremely difficult to confront following standard strategic approaches. This new field of strategic thinking is tackled by what is now defined as Netwar.

2

Art of War: Principle and Theory

Now that dramatic improvements in weaponry, communications, sensors and even the utility of individual combatants have been demonstrated in Afghanistan and Iraq, it is clear that America must revise and expand its principles of war to effectively plan and execute the more expansive and complex warfare of the future battlefield. Before redefining the principles of war for future conflicts, three questions must be answered. First, how has the revolution in military affairs (RMA) affected military capability, and how will it affect capability in the future? Second, what types of conflicts and enemies should America expect to confront over the next quarter-century? And third, who will be cooperating with America in military operations of the future? Even these seemingly simple questions have complex answers and significant caveats that must be recognized.

With regard to the effects of the RMA, some historical perspective is necessary. The current principles of war have remained essentially unchanged since at least 1921, when in the wake of World War I, there was a push in the U.S. military to codify doctrine based on the lessons of that conflict. Going into the future, great benefits for, and changes to, conventional military power are expected from the RMA. The Global Information Grid promises to be a leap forward for communications and the collection, analysis and distribution of information. Developing systems will allow a commander on one platform to electronically execute offensive or defensive action using the sensor data from a second platform and weapons from a third. The net-centric battle space will allow for seamless interservice communication, information-sharing, and the rapid fulfilment of support requests. A mistake can be made, though, in assuming that the RMA has an endpoint and the military will return to a static structure following transformation. Therefore, the first assumption when drafting new principles of war is: A new set of principles of war must be broad enough to readily accommodate the fast pace of development in military doctrine, technology and capabilities.

With respect to threats, most observers of the events of the past decade point out that America is facing a new enemy. But in this observation, critics of America's current force usually are only half right. Yes, America is in an ongoing war with a dispersed, low-tech, nonstate, adaptive and resourceful enemy. But in truth, the terrorist threat is an additional threat, not a replacement for old threats.

China continues to modernize its military to challenge American hegemony in the Pacific, and the possibility of war at sea still looms large, even if it appears to be over the horizon for the time being. In addition, most of the rogue states of the world, like Syria, North Korea and Iran, still have significant conventional military forces that may need to be defeated to achieve American objectives. The lines between different levels of war in the range of military operations are also blurring. In the past, casualties and destruction of property in low-intensity conflict were small. Now, a small, well-funded and organized group of irregulars or terrorists could execute extraordinarily destructive attacks. Therefore, the second assumption underpinning the reassessment of the principles of war is: The types of conflicts America will face will continue to broaden, and new principles must be equally applicable when raiding a terrorist safe house, when confronting a large, conventional force on land or sea, or when planning for nuclear deterrence and response.

When considering potential U.S. partners in conflict, political and military realities become apparent from examining a number of recent conflicts. There is no doubt that military and political objectives are easier to justify when support and participation in a military operation is multilateral and broad. In addition, there are many aspects and consequences of war that are uniquely nonmilitary, such as humanitarian relief and care of refugees, which require careful consideration and planning. When America encourages the participation of allies — other governmental agencies and nongovernmental organizations — these actors must not only be integrated into the coalition force, their participation also must be meaningful. As a result, the third assumption in this process is: American forces are not likely to be the only important actors in a conflict, and any updated principles of war must be flexible enough to integrate all the participating forces and organizations.

Given these observations and assumptions, the current principles of war require considerable revision and expansion. But they cannot be discarded wholesale. All of the current principles represent timeless, essential elements of warfare that will continue to be relevant in the future, although most are applicable now in more limited circumstances. Instead, the current principles must be developed into more complex principles that represent a better approach to the future of war.

Without a clear, achievable objective, the threat cannot be adequately assessed, courses of action cannot be developed, and consequences and contingencies cannot be identified.

1. Objective is focusing all efforts toward the decisive achievement of an obtainable end state and is the only current principle of war to emerge unscathed by the changes of the past few decades. Clearly defining an achievable end state remains critical to successful military operations. This was reinforced in the Weinberger Doctrine after evaluating American experiences in Vietnam and Lebanon, and confirmed by America's experiences in Somalia and Iraq.
2. Speed is the rapid execution of all functions and operations related to war. Implied in speed are the current principles of offensive and maneuver. The practice of seizing the initiative, striking an enemy and striking him again before he has a chance to reorient

and act has proven successful time and time again. Speed enables a force to seize the initiative, deliver time-critical strikes and plan and decide on the fly. The need for speed, however, doesn't begin and end when the first and last shots are fired. America must rapidly deploy and build up forces prior to combat operations and rapidly redeploy once the end state is achieved. A moderate force that is in position to act 10 days after the start of a conflict can be just as effective as a large force that takes 30 days to arrive. In addition, enemies will always seek to exploit periods when America seems occupied with one conflict and unable to respond, so America must demonstrate that it can reset on a moment's notice and be back in position to act.

3. Concentration of effects, which replaces mass, is the focusing of conventional fires and other useful tools, such as electronic attack and information operations, to defeat the enemy. Today, the battle line is difficult to identify as operations are conducted on a dispersed, in-depth battlefield. The range and precision of advanced weapons, capability of long-range sensors, employment of space systems and unmanned vehicles, and proven utility of nondestructive tactics such as electronic attack, deception and information operations leaves mass with increasingly narrow utility. The rising cost of technology and platforms — and necessary decrease in the numbers of platforms — further devalues the principle of mass. Going forward, the rapid evolution of combat forces and technology, combined with the smaller size of future forces, demands planners think not in terms of force but in terms of effects.

With effects now taking primacy over forces, successful military operations require a commander to focus first on how the areas of effect of systems and weapons overlap, and second on the positioning of platforms. In truth, areas of effect have always been the first consideration in the positioning of forces. Military formations were developed to concentrate the effects of weapons, and the dispersal of forces and combatants beginning in the 20th century was designed to counter massing of fires and area effect weapons. Just how secondary the position of platforms has become was demonstrated in the Kosovo war, in which heavy bombers based in the central U.S. routinely serviced targets halfway around the globe. It may be wise to forward deploy or concentrate such platforms in particular scenarios to increase availability and utility, but it is not always necessary — and in some circumstances deployment or concentration may result in an asset being unavailable in a concurrent conflict.

4. Economy of effects is employing the right number and combination of effects to neutralize or destroy an enemy and achieve the objective. Economy of force, which is replaced by economy of effects, has been debated for decades. The first major re-evaluation of economy of force began during the Vietnam War, when some drew the conclusion from evaluating the forces deployed to Southeast Asia that America was not committed to winning the war. The first high-profile refutation of economy of force was spoken by Gen. Colin Powell, a combat veteran of the Vietnam War, during the run-up to the 1991 Persian Gulf War when he proposed that America should, in the future, employ overwhelming force in military conflict rather than a strictly economical force. The RMA dealt the final, fatal blow to economy of force with its shift in focus from forces to effects.

   In the future, planners must employ a systems-thinking process to evaluate and address a commander's minimum requirements. By this process, planners may sequence the effects of systems, platforms and weapons synergistically to produce the desired result with a minimum of destruction and casualties. One note of caution is required when considering economy of effects, however; when requesting forces for an operation, planning must include some definition of required tasks and corresponding effects for contingencies and the unlikely and worst-case scenarios.

5. Pervasive awareness is building an exploitable, in-depth knowledge of the battle space, the opponent, and his centres of gravity and vulnerability. One of the lessons of recent conflicts is that decision-makers, planners and operators up and down the chain of command must have access to comprehensive, timely and actionable intelligence. Poor intelligence resulted in America bombing the Chinese Embassy in Belgrade during the Kosovo conflict in 1999. Inadequate or excessively time-late intelligence led America to miss several opportunities to apprehend or kill Osama bin Laden and a number of the Sept. 11 hijackers. Poor integration and dissemination of intelligence have also been blamed as factors in America's failure to recognize Islamist terrorists as a grave threat to national security before 9/11.

   Information is increasingly critical to the effective planning and execution of combat operations, and this awareness must extend beyond the battle space awareness provided by multispectrum sensors. Decision-makers, operators and planners must have access to much more than the standard laundry list of military positions, equipment, training and tactics. Information and intelligence on the enemy's communication and power grids, transportation and public works infrastructure, and even social structure, institutions and political actors can and should be collected, analysed, disseminated and exploited when possible.

6. Continuous planning is the ongoing development and redevelopment of courses of action, for the current situation and contingencies, to rapidly achieve the objective. Given the complexities of modern warfare, the old axiom that no plan survives first contact with the enemy is even more salient. Planning for conflict must begin at the first hint of a crisis, continue apace with the progress of the conflict, and include detailed planning for post-conflict operations up to and including turnover to the host nation or nongovernmental and

international organizations and withdrawal of coalition forces. In the age of net-centric warfare, simplicity is the first casualty of war — Napoleon's corporal is dead. No longer is the simplest plan necessarily the best plan, and no longer can we expect anyone to understand all of the details of the plan. Unnecessary complexity should still be avoided, but an increasing level of complexity in plans should be expected.

Planning must also expand to give adequate attention to unlikely, worst-and best-case scenarios. For instance, the Iraq war has brought an interesting caveat of success to light: The unexpected success and rapid advance of coalition forces created an environment in which coalition forces could not adequately control the territory they had gained. Armed with this lesson in success, planners in the future must anticipate potential successes as well as potential failures.

7. Flexibility is rapidly adapting to new or different requirements or situations. Underpinning economy of effects, concentration of effects and continuous planning is flexibility. Many of America's current and future systems offer the capability to deliver similar effects. In addition, the useful effects of systems are often discovered in times of emergent need when innovation is at its peak. The focus of planners and commanders must be on performing mission-essential tasks in a timely, efficient manner, and they must be encouraged to consider their options carefully and be creative in employing weapons and systems.
8. Sustainment is ensuring the persistence of forces to see the conflict through, from entry to withdrawal. Forces have depended upon supply and logistics for ages. The armies of the First Crusade failed to reach the Holy Land because they could not forage enough to subsist en route. The teeth of America's force racing across Iraq in 2003 were required to slow their pace of advance and wait for their logistics tail to catch up. A force in the field, no matter how well equipped or trained, is useless

if it cannot be sustained, and in the future, sustainment is an indispensable principle of war.

9. Efficiency of command is ensuring the force has no more divisions and layers of command than necessary, and implies unity of command. War is divided into levels in American doctrine for good reason, and the speed and scope of future conflicts argue for more authority in the hands of unit-level commanders, not less. Unnecessary review of target lists and interference in tactical decisions must be eliminated. In situations in which political concerns are significant, higher levels of command must provide clear guidance to subordinate commanders and trust them to act with good judgment. Commanders must resist the temptation to allow loyalty to their parent service or community to influence the development of the best plan or force structure. Likewise, political leaders must resist the temptation to let everyone play and unnecessarily widen the field of actors in the name of jointness.
10. Security is ensuring the safety and integrity of forces and certain noncombatants during all phases of the operation. The principle of security expands somewhat with the nature of war. If there is one lesson America has learned the hard way in the wars in Iraq and Afghanistan, it is that security remains an essential consideration in planning and executing future operations. In addition, security of NGO and other-agency personnel, persecuted minorities and refugees, politically and legally, may need to be provided, as well. During the Bosnia conflict, the inability of a Dutch force to protect the civilian population of Srebrenica proved politically disastrous for the Netherlands and NATO.
11. Integration of actors is allowing appropriate participation in planning, and assigning useful tasks to all forces, agencies and NGOs taking part in an operation. Unilateral military action by the U.S., except on the small scale, is becoming less and less likely. The current principles of war were essentially defined in an era

when joint operations were unheard of and combined operations were a recent innovation. Major international conflicts now demand the participation of coalition partners and are arguably more successful because of international participation. As a result, the principle of integration of actors must be adopted to ensure planning is executed not only for joint and combined military forces, but also for the participation of other government agencies and NGOs.

12. Surprise is acting in an unpredictable fashion to leverage the utility of effects, and it retains some value in the updated principles of war. Strategic surprise is increasingly difficult in the information age when around-the-clock news on troop movements and the political process is available to anyone with a satellite dish or Internet connection. In addition, in exercising the Bush Doctrine to pre-empt threats, it may be necessary to show America's hand by laying out the causes and urgency of the conflict to gather political support and coalition partners before military action is executed. However, operational and tactical surprise remain undiminished, and by exploiting pervasive awareness, a flexible, creative military commander should always find opportunities to strike at a time, in a place and in a manner that an opponent cannot predict.

Finally, feedback and evaluation are what brings it together. The collecting and analyzing information from the force, during operations and for immediate application, are already familiar to the American military. Every evolution, exercise and operation conducted by the U.S. military today concludes with debrief and identifying lessons learned. In the future, the rapid execution of operations requires ongoing feedback from operators to planners on what did and did not work. Planners and commanders must then identify and incorporate lessons into revised planning to maximize the effectiveness of forces in the field, reduce the duration of the conflict and minimize the effect of the war on civilians. Transformation and technology expand and complicate the battlefield of the future, and to remain useful, the principles of war must expand and become more complex. The independence of individual principles is now a thing of the past, as well. Like the actors and systems in this new method of war, most of the new principles of war are interdependent. For example, flexibility, pervasive awareness, and feedback and evaluation are key to continuous planning — feedback and evaluation depend on the integration of actors and pervasive awareness, and economy of effects and concentration of effects depend on flexibility.

Most who argue that the principles of war should remain unchanged begin by pointing to the timeless nature of war mentioned earlier. However, they then usually go on to propose an extensive overhaul of the meanings of individual principles. Retaining the current terms, even if they could adequately be reinterpreted to fit the evolving conduct of war, is a half-measure that fails to communicate the transformation in progress. The elements of successful military operations have evolved and will continue to evolve with the nature of war, and it is time the American military acknowledges these changes in official doctrine.

PRINCIPLES FOR WAR IN GENERAL

1. The theory of warfare tries to discover how we may gain a preponderance of physical forces and material advantages at the decisive point. As this is not always possible, theory also teaches us to calculate moral factors: the likely mistakes of the enemy, the impression created by a daring action,... yes, even our own desperation. None of these things lie outside the realm of the theory and art of war, which is nothing but the result of reasonable reflection on all the possible situations encountered during a war. We should think very frequently of the most dangerous of these situations and familiarize ourselves with it. Only thus shall we reach heroic decisions based on reason, which no critic can ever shake.

   Any person who may present this matter differently to Your Royal Highness is a pedant, whose views will only be harmful to you. In the decisive moments of your life, in the turmoil of battle, you will some day feel that this view alone can help where help is needed most, and where a dry pedantry of figures will forsake you.

2. Whether counting on physical or moral advantages, we should always try, in time of war, to have the probability of victory on our side. But this is not always possible. Often we must act against this probability, should there be nothing better to do. Were we to despair here, we would abandon the use of reason just when it becomes most necessary, when everything seems to be conspiring against us. Therefore, even when the likelihood of success is against us, we must not think of our undertaking as unreasonable or impossible; for it is always reasonable, if we do not know of anything better to do, and if we make the best use of the few means at our disposal.

   We must never lack calmness and firmness, which are so hard to preserve in time of war. Without them the most brilliant qualities of mind are wasted. We must therefore familiarize ourselves with the thought of an honourable defeat. We must always nourish this thought within ourselves, and we must get completely used to it. Be convinced, Most Gracious Master, that without this firm resolution no great results can be achieved in the most successful war, let alone in the most unsuccessful.

   Certainly this thought frequently occupied the mind of Frederick II during his first Silesian wars. Because he was familiar with it he undertook his attack near Leuthen, on that memorable fifth of December, and not because he believed that his oblique formation would very likely beat the Austrians.

3. In any specific action, in any measure we may undertake, we always have the choice between the most audacious and the most careful solution. Some people think that the theory of war always advises the latter. That assumption is false. If the theory does advise anything,

it is the nature of war to advise the most decisive, that is, the most audacious. Theory leaves it to the military leader, however, to act according to his own courage, according to his spirit of enterprise, and his self-confidence. Make your choice, therefore, according to this inner force; but never forget that no military leader has ever become great without audacity.

TACTICS OR THE THEORY OF COMBAT

War is a combination of many distinct engagements. Such a combination may or may not be reasonable, and success depends very much on this. Yet the engagement itself is for the moment more important. For only a combination of successful engagements can lead to good results. The most important thing in war will always be the art of defeating our opponent in combat. To this matter Your Royal Highness can never turn enough attention and thought. I think the following principles the most important:

General Principles For Defence

1. To keep our troops covered as long as possible. Since we are always open to attack, except when we ourselves are attacking, we must at every instant be on the defensive and thus should place our forces as much under cover as possible.
2. Not to bring all our troops into combat immediately. With such action all wisdom in conducting a battle disappears. It is only with troops left at our disposal that we can turn the tide of battle.
3. To be little or not at all concerned about the extent of our front. This in itself is unimportant, and an extension of the front limits the depth of our formation (that is, the number of units which are lined up one behind the other). Troops which are kept in the rear are always available. We can use them either to renew combat at the same point, or to carry the fight to other neighbouring points. This principle is a corollary of the previous one.
4. The enemy, while attacking one section of the front,

often seeks to outflank and envelop us at the same time. The units which are kept in the background can meet this attempt and thus make up for the support usually derived from obstacles in the terrain. They are better suited for this than if they were standing in line and extending the front. For in this case the enemy could easily outflank them. This principle again is a closer definition of the second.

5. If we have many troops to hold in reserve, only part of them should stand directly behind the front. The rest we should put obliquely behind.

   From this position they in turn can attack the flank of the enemy columns which are seeking to envelop us.

6. A fundamental principle is never to remain completely passive, but to attack the enemy frontally and from the flanks, even while he is attacking us. We should, therefore, defend ourselves on a given front merely to induce the enemy to deploy his forces in an attack on this front. Then we in turn attack with those of our troops which we have kept back. The art of entrenchment, as Your Royal Highness expressed so excellently at one time, shall serve the defender not to defend himself more securely behind a rampart, but to attack the enemy more successfully. This idea should be applied to any passive defence. Such defence is nothing more than a means by which to attack the enemy most advantageously, in a terrain chosen in advance, where we have drawn up our troops and have arranged things to our advantage.

7. This attack from a defensive position can take place the moment the enemy actually attacks, or while he is still on the march. One can also, at the moment the attack is about to be delivered, withdraw he troops, luring the enemy into unknown territory and attacking him from all sides. The formation in depth-i.e., the formation in which only two-thirds or half or still less of the army is drawn-up in front and the rest directly or obliquely behind and hidden, if possible-is very suitable for all

these moves. This type of formation is, therefore, of immense importance.

8. If, for example, some one had two divisions, one would prefer to keep one in the rear. If some one had three, he would keep at least one in the rear, and if four probably two. If some one had five, he should hold at least two in reserve and in many cases even three, etc.
9. At those points where we remain passive we must make use of the art of fortification. This should be done with many independent works, completely closed and with very strong profiles.
10. In our plan of battle we must set this great aim: the attack on a large enemy column and its complete destruction. If our aim is low, while that of the enemy is high, we will naturally get the worst of it. We are penny-wise and pound-foolish.
11. Having set a high goal in our plan of defence (the annihilation of an enemy column, etc.), we must pursue this goal with the greatest energy and with the last ounce of our strength. In most cases the aggressor will pursue his own aim at some other point. While we fall upon his right wing, for example, he will try to win decisive advantages with his left. Consequently, if we should slacken before the enemy does, if we should pursue our aim with less energy than he does, he will gain his advantage completely, while we shall only half gain ours. He will thus achieve preponderance of power; the victory will be his, and we shall have to give up even our partly gained advantages. If Your Royal Highness will read with attention the history of the battles of Ratisbon and Wagram, all this will seem true and important.

In both these battles the Emperor Napoleon attacked with his right wing and tried to hold out with his left. The Archduke Charles did exactly the same. But, while the former acted with great determination and energy, the latter was wavering and always stopped half-way. That is why the advantages which Charles gained with the victorious part of his army were without consequence, while those which Napoleon gained at the opposite end were decisive.

12. Let me sum up once more the last two principles. Their combination gives us a maxim which should take first place among all causes of victory in the modern art of war: "Pursue one great decisive aim with force and determination."
13. If we follow this and fail, the danger will be even greater, it is true. But to increase caution at the expense of the final goal is no military art. It is the wrong kind of caution, which, as it has been said already in my "General Principles," is contrary to the nature of war. For great aims we must dare great things. When we are engaged in a daring enterprise, the right caution consists in not neglecting out of laziness, indolence, or carelessness those measures which help us to gain our aim. Such was the case of Napoleon, who never pursued great aims in a timid or half-hearted way out of caution.

If you remember, Most Gracious Master, the few defensive battles that have ever been won, you will find that the best of them have been conducted in the spirit of the principles voiced here. For it is the study of the history of war which has given us these principles. At Minden, Duke Ferdinand suddenly appeared where the enemy did not expect him and took the offensive, while at Tannhausen he defended himself passively behind earthworks. At Rossbach, Frederick II threw himself against the enemy at an unexpected point and an unexpected moment. At Liegnitz, the Austrians found the King at night in a position very different from that in which they had seen him the previous day. He fell with his whole army upon one enemy column and defeated it before the others could start fighting. At Hohenlinden, Moreau had five divisions in his front line and four directly behind and on his flanks. He outflanked the enemy and fell upon his right wing before it could attack. At Ratisbon, Marshal Davout defended himself passively, while Napoleon attacked the fifth and sixth army-corps with his right wing and beat them completely.

Though the Austrians were the real defenders at Wagram, they did attack the emperor on the second day with the greater part of their forces. Therefore Napoleon can also be considered a defender. With his right wing he attacked, outflanked and defeated the Austrian left wing. At the same time he paid little attention to his weak left wing (consisting of a single division), which was resting on the Danube. Yet through strong reserves (i.e., formation in depth), he prevented the victory of the Austrian right wing from having any influence on his own victory gained on the Rossbach. He used these reserves to retake Aderklaa. Not all the principles mentioned earlier are clearly contained in each of these battles, but all are examples of active defence.

The mobility of the Prussian army under Frederick II was a means towards victory on which we can no longer count, since the other armies are at least as mobile as we are. On the other hand, outflanking was less common at that time and formation in depth, therefore, less imperative.

PRINCIPLES OF WAR IN A CHANGING WORLD

The 20th century has seen veritable successive 'revolutions' in warfare, starting with the advent of air power in World War I, and cemented by aircraft carriers further extending this reach across the oceans by World War II. This was followed by the introduction of nuclear weapons, development of nuclear warfighting doctrines, growth of missile and electronic warfare, and a move towards increasing coordination and jointness between the single Services. In the last two decades, technological advances have provided near real-time situational awareness and minimal sensor-shooter cycle, even as the reach, accuracy and lethality of modern weapons have attained unprecedented levels. Over this period, the 'ways and means' of war have undergone constant transformation. The ends for which war was waged have also expanded, from territorial ambitions to increasing geostrategic spheres of influence, to pursuit of religious-ideological conflicts, and again a reversion towards safeguarding of territorial and socioeconomic interests. The nature of war, as seen through its ways, means and ends, has probably traversed its largest arc of change in the last 100 years. The evolutionary trends of war led to several assessments, even before 9/11, of the emerging nature of 21st century warfare. This was appreciated as being more diverse and divisive, with the ways, means and ends of war continuing to change, along with traditional rationale and actors, and expectations of a transmutation of conflict, from total to limited war, from inter-state to intra-state war, and from regular, structured warfare to irregular warfare.

Wars of choice were assessed to more likely dominate the 21st century, with significant effort required to keep them limited amidst a danger of cascading effect upon wider areas in the world. The tragic events of 9/11 and the ensuing wars against (and by) terrorism have exemplified these earlier estimates and the wider spectrum of modern war. In the constant evolution of the nature of war, it is reasonable to expect that changes would be reflected in revision of not only the doctrines of warfighting, but also the underlying Principles of War (PoW). However, whilst warfighting doctrines have undergone significant changes in the last two decades, there has been little debate on the corresponding evolution of the PoW, which provide the (conceptual) foundation for building these warfighting doctrines. Areview of the prevailing PoW, in the light of the current nature and spectrum of war, would reveal significant deficiencies and point out the revisions necessary for the principles to have continued relevance in the 21st century. The PoW have been codified from the time of Sun Tzu, and evolved/refined by Napoleon, Clausewitz, J.F.C. Fuller, and thence given institutionalised definition and interpretation by various nations and militaries. The fact that there is still no consensus on a single list of PoW underscores the complexities in addressing war across time and space.

A glance at the table shows there is a fair degree of commonality in the list and understanding of the PoW amongst the various nations, though some emphases and nuances would naturally vary. In the modern spectrum of war, however, some of these principles appear excessively focused on conventional, unlimited, war, and do not adequately cover the imperatives of other forms of significant changes in the last two decades, there has been little debate on the corresponding war, such as limited conventional war and sub-conventional war, which are both more widespread and more likely in the post-Cold War geostrategic environment. Conventional limited wars are restricted in aim, scope and methods, and may require a broader canvas and interpretation of the PoW to meet their specific requirements. Sub-conventional war, where at least one actor is a nonstate and the war is characterised by an irregular and covert fabric such as for terrorism, militancy, insurgency, proxy war and civil war, may also need a more flexible interpretation of the PoW, especially since such warfare may take place in own territory and impose limitations on the applicability of the PoW.

However, even this would be more relevant for fighting against sub-conventional forces, rather than in the waging of such form of warfare, since the latter is the domain of mostly non-state actors who do not follow established norms and laws of war. Hence, full application of the PoW to them would remain tenuous. Some of the existing PoW, with slight amendments, would retain their validity in this context, even whilst others may be seen to suffer from limitations in addressing the wider spectrum of modern war. The principle of Selection and Maintenance of Aim is the primary PoW, which entails that the desired 'end-state' must be clearly defined and selection of the attainable aim done after careful cost-benefit analysis, keeping in mind the resources available. More often than not, this principle has been interpreted in purely military terms (since it is, after all, a principle of 'war'). But, accepting the Clausewitzian precept that war is an extension of politics by other means, the issue of politics can never be separated from the military objective.

Military aims would have to be situated in the political purpose for the use of force. In the era of 'total wars,' the selection and maintenance of aim/objective was relatively simpler, with full national resources being devoted to the war and all costs deemed acceptable, since the purpose was survival on one side and 'unconditional surrender' or annihilation on the other. But the nature of war itself has been changing, with total, unlimited war becoming a considerably lesser viable option. In an increasingly globalised and interdependent world, political restraints (including those of domestic pressures) would have a an increasingly globalised and interdependent world, political restraints (including those of domestic pressures) would have a major influence in the way war can be waged, and what sort of end-state can be achieved.

This is even more critical for countries that possess nuclear weapons. It can be argued that 'asymmetric warfare' has emerged primarily because of the politico-military restraints in an information age. The problem is that the 'endstate' is becoming less easy to define. For example, the war against global terrorism might seek to rid the world of the scourge of terrorism. But it obviously remains unachievable without a major political-ideological campaign of ideas. Nuclear weapon states, in particular, have to seriously rethink the issue of military objectives and aims. Warfighting with nuclear weapons would defeat the very logic of war as a rational instrument of policy since it would destroy the very object it seeks to gain. Similarly, even a conventional war between nuclear weapon states would require redefinition of the traditional concepts of victory and defeat. Risk of escalation to nuclear weapons use can nullify what might have been seen as a 'decisive' military victory in a non-nuclear weapon environment. This has wide-ranging implications for the way wars can be fought. But, from the point of view of this examination, the critical point is that the very concept of 'victory' would need to be redefined in a war using conventional weapons and forces under a nuclear overhang. Countries placed in such situations would either have to avoid a direct war (as indeed the two superpowers did during the Cold War), or plan and fight a limited war (e.g. Sino-Russian border war 1969, and Indo-Pak Kargil War 1999). The former, avoidance of direct war, had led to the use of proxy wars; while the latter permits only a war with limited objectives. It is not surprising, therefore, that China has adopted a military doctrine of "local, border war under high-tech conditions." This, in turn, would require far greater synergy between political aims and military goals.

The military aim of modern war may accordingly require refinement, with consequent shift in focus onto attaining key objective areas that signify political victory or provide the post-war political leverage for conflict resolution, rather than seeking 'decisive' military victory as defined in the past. In the case of fighting insurgency/militancy/terrorism, the military objective may need to be similarly attuned to the political purpose, and limited to providing the modicum of security necessary for generating movement towards a politico-economic solution. An excessively ambitious aim, such as "stamping out all violent opposition" or "overthrow of the state" through the use of military force is more likely to fuel that very violence, and also provide non-state actors with an image of victory even if they merely survive or avoid total military defeat. This has been evinced in the ongoing Iraq War, where the desire to crush militant opposition has been faulted as an inappropriate and inapplicable politico-military aim and military strategy, and has probably instead contributed to deterioration of the security environment, rather than provide stability for attaining the political objectives.

The nature of modern warfare emphasises the need to synergise military objectives with political goals, with an inherent recognition of the fact that the latter could change frequently and demand similar readjustment of military objectives and strategy. Such continued synergy was demonstrated in the Indo-Pak Kargil War 1999, where Indian political desire to limit the war to the Indian side of the Line of Control (LoC) was supported by a military strategy to "contain-evict-deny," and included political clearance for use of air power in India's own territory. Inversely, political goals may also be affected by the military situation, and require reorientation according to the military gains or losses in order to derive the best 'end-state' possible, as seen in the India–Pakistan War 1971, where the capture of Dhaka was reportedly not part of the original aim. Hence, while "Selection and Maintenance of Aim" as a PoW remains at the core of modern warfare, its application has undergone significant change with the need for maintaining greater and constant synergy with the political purpose of the war, particularly in the case of limited and sub-conventional wars. Accordingly, the "aim" in the earlier Principle of War needs a more comprehensive and representative interpretation to encompass both political and military aims and, most importantly, the maintenance of synergy between them. The revisions in interpretation warrant a more appropriate term, such as Maintenance of Synergy in Politico-Military Aims.

The principle of Offensive Action, which is often held as the chief means of achieving victory, entails control over the purpose, scope, intensity and pace of operations, and retention of initiative at all times. This places a premium on early action, even preemption. But the nature of sub-conventional warfare, especially terrorism, inherently provides early initiative to the non-state actor. Preemptive action here is difficult, and may well prove counter-productive, such as in the case of faulty intelligence, or due to collateral damage in the apparent absence of adequate justification. This would push the civil populace to favour the non-state actors, as partly experienced in the current Iraq War, and provide strategic-level backlash for tactical actions. In such cases, a higher level of own security and rapid response capability would serve the war aims better than focus on offensive action per se. In the case of conventional limited war, with an inherently higher premium on preemption, there may be less scope for regaining the offensive or dictating fresh parameters against preemptive strike, within the limitations of time, area, scale and methods available.

This was seen in the Indo-Pak War in Kargil, 1999, wherein any Indian attempt to develop military offensive action beyond the tactical level purely on military logic could have escalated the war to the detriment of the war's politico-strategic objective. Hence, the view that offensive action per se is the means to attaining the initiative and freedom of action, and positive results thereby, needs adjustment. In the available technological environment, and ongoing techno-doctrinal focus on rapid response capability, the requirement is not so much on maintaining offensive action, but rather on the maintenance and exploitation of Freedom of Action (FoA) by a variety of measures, since the latter would provide broader options and initiative for decisive, including offensive, action. Freedom of Action has, accordingly, become a core principle across the spectrum of modern warfare, with the requirements extending from its attainment and maintenance for own forces, across all levels and dimensions of war, to the disruption and denial of similar freedom to the opponent. Freedom of Action would need to cover the various dimensions of war, viz. land, sea, air and information.

This would also entail the exploitation of own Freedom of Action by the employment of offensive doctrines, such as attainment and utilisation of favourable situation or air superiority, sea control, command of the air/sea, information superiority, escalation control/dominance, etc. The development and exploitation of Freedom of Action in all dimensions and theatres/battlefields would require the support of robust physical and information security, sound logistics and administration, exercise of mobility, maintenance of initiative, suitable deployment of offensive forces, etc. Each of these aspects would need to be addressed in the military doctrines flowing from the overarching PoW, of maintenance and exploitation of Freedom of Action. It stands to reason that the side losing freedom of action would thereby lose its ability to influence the conduct of the war, and be forced to constantly react to the exercise of corresponding freedom by the opponent.

The principle of Mass/Concentration of Force is viewed as the concentration of combat power at the decisive time and place, to achieve decisive results. This principle has been highly valued, from Sun-Tzu through Napoleon to World War II, wherein it denoted the destructive power of a force. The principle of mass providing a distinct advantage is perhaps embedded in Napoleon's supposed remarks that even God is on the side of the bigger battalions! Mass, no doubt, denoted the killing power of a force, seen essentially in terms of quantity. This was the logic that gave the Roman Phalanx its distinct advantage in battle, and why modern militaries still look at a 3:1 favourable ratio of forces as a doctrinal parameter for successful offensive action. But, if viewed more closely, what we can observe is that killing power as a function of mass was true when the quantum of killing power in a unit element of force was limited. Hence, to maximise the overall impact of killing power, mass and concentration of force became a necessary principle.

In substance, since the accuracy, rate of fire, and range of the manmachine combination that produced the weapon system was limited, this was sought to be compensated by concentrating combat power, so that the friendly force could kill the maximum number of enemy forces/weapon systems. In battlefields that were concentrated in space, mass also provided enhanced moral power because of the emotional-psychological support derived from a greater number of friendly forces. Generation of mass, whether by massing more soldiers or by dispensing more projectiles onto the target, remained intrinsically important because of the limitations of range, target location and acquisition, accuracy and lethality of weapons, and the friction in war (that Clausewitz talked of). This also placed limits on the quantum of combat power that could be concentrated in time and space. In reality, however, the foundations of this principle started getting eroded with the advancement of technology. For example, the carnage at Verdun in World War I demonstrated how even a single machine gun could concentrate more firepower in the hands of a single soldier than what was possible earlier. Advances in military technology have been rapidly altering the traditional aggregative relation between quantum of forces and their combat power. Nowhere has this been more obvious than in the advent of air power, which provided the means to outflank the enemy from the third dimension. This changed the battlefield completely, and rendered the surface forces vulnerable except through acquiring a counter-outflanking capability with their own air power.

Even here, technological changes have determined a continuous expansion of the 'engagement zone', which itself challenges the traditional concept of concentration of force, as brought about by advances in air power. One element of this was air-to-air warfare becoming all-weather with beyond-visual-range (BVR) capability soon after the end of World War II. However, employment of air power against surface targets remained limited to what was essentially 'line-of-sight' targeting till recently, when improvements in targeting technology have enabled the application of combat power by diverse and geographically separated force elements. Space capabilities are expected to further expand this envelope, and in fact have already done so in the form of surveillance and information warfare, e.g. target spotting by an unmanned aerial vehicle (UAV), its classification and targeting by a centre possibly in another continent, and prosecution by a cruise missile launched from a submarine in another theatre, more than 1,000 km away. Expansion of the battlefield along with compression of time has provided a totally different dimension to concentration of combat power in time and space compared to what the principle of mass/concentration of force conveys. In determining the nature of change in this principle, we need to revisit the purpose of concentration of force and augmentation of combat power. Simply, this was to attain a certain destructive effect, wherein the massing of force appeared to provide the best means for attaining this end.

Consequently, this assumed the status of a PoW. The impact of advanced weapon technologies in terms of range, accuracy and lethality, synergised with parallel advancements in sensor and command and control (C2) technologies, has led to a situation wherein firepower-effect, as a derivative of cosmbat power, is no longer a summation of the mass of forces. All other things being equal, and leaving the intangibles like morale, etc. out of consideration for the time being, effective combat power could be denoted normatively by the equation:

Combat Power CP = Q x D x M

where Q is Quantity,

D is Destructive Power (a combination of range, accuracy and lethality) per unit weapon, and M is Mobility (or manoeuvre to enable concentration in time and space) It is obvious that if D, the destructive power of the force (weapon/soldier) is low, then Q, the quantity of force needed, would have to be high. In other words, a greater mass would be necessary to maintain the requisite combat power as constant. But, where D is higher, and M is developed, the Q quotient could be much lower, i.e.

concentration of force would not be required, as the requisite combat power was being applied by the other components. The applicability of the above can be seen even in World War II, wherein the combination of German Panzer Divisions and aerial dive bombers in the Blitzkrieg in France, and Allied "thousand bomber raids" over Germany, were examples of augmenting combat power through enhancing Mobility, Destructive Power and Quantity, respectively.

The recent wars in Iraq and Afghanistan have further demonstrated the applicability of the above, wherein requisite combat power was attained with a lesser concentration of forces than would have been the case earlier, by a corresponding increase in precision strike, destructive power and mobility of the forces used. This fact has also been evident throughout military history, where lesser numbers of higher range and accuracy weapons, with higher rates of fire and speed of delivery, have habitually prevailed against larger concentration of opposing forces, due to their relatively higher concentration of firepower. But, since the weapons and systems in most wars, including the Napoleonic and two World Wars, tended to be comparable for the opposing sides, concentration of forces was perceived as providing the decisive edge, whereas it was actually the concentration of firepower enabled by the massing of forces that was responsible for this effect. In other words, it was the Q+Q, that is (Quality +Quantity) paradigm (both of firepower and manpower) that held the key.

The distinction is important today, when advanced military technologies have led to provision of unprecedented levels of discriminate destructive power in small larger concentration of lances, bows and arrows, and similarly for the British-Indian Army Lee Enfields against Indian-rebel forces with lances, muskets and swords in the War of Independence, 1857, and again in the machine-gun based carnage at Verdun in World War I. Throughout military history, lesser numbers of higher range and accuracy weapons, with higher rates of fire and speed of delivery, have habitually prevailed against larger concentration of opposing forces, due to their relatively higher concentration of firepower.

The source of that firepower could be naval, air or land power, which is also the central logic for joint operations. The most recent and dramatic example in support of the need to replace the existing principle of mass/concentration of force to one of concentration of firepower is to be found in the Iraq War where the United States reversed the traditionally accepted force ratios necessary for offensive action completely on their head. Similarly, the United States employed forces widely dispersed across the globe, ranging from home bases to warships and aircraft carriers, and special forces operating with missiles, UAVs, space assets, etc. in the 2001-02 War in Afghanistan, so as to bring firepower concentrated on specific tactical targets—even employing B-52 strategic bombers for close air support missions with the barest minimum military force deployed on land. This did not mean that the principle of concentration of force per se was ignored, but that its effect was attained through concentration of effective firepower, independent of the position and number of weapon firing platforms rather than from the aggregation of combat power platforms in time and space.

Today, two B-2s can provide the same effect, through accurate delivery of firepower, which required 50 B-52s a decade ago, and 1,000 bombers in World War II. Modern battlefields are expanding in space, even as they are contracting in time, due to the speed and reach of modern firepower. Hence, there will continue to be greater dispersion of forces, especially amongst naval and air platforms. This would seem to violate the principle of concentration of force, as understood hitherto. However, there is no contradiction if the principle is viewed instead as Concentration of Firepower, with its components being the emulative effect of the Quantity, Destructive Power and Mobility paradigm.

Economy of Effort is the principle requiring forces to be judiciously employed so as to maximise the effect of available resources, including through apportionment of resources between the main and secondary efforts. This has been seen as an adjunct to the principle of Concentration of Force (or firepower, as suggested above), and the focus is on the availability of forces. The core, however, relies on attaining the maximum effect for available resources, which also provides the conceptual foundation for the modern doctrine of "Effects-Based Operations." Hence, it may be more appropriate to view this principle instead as the Attainment of Effect, i.e. expand the current understanding from merely fullest use of available forces, to production of the desired effect through best employment of these resources, including by development of different strategies/tactics. For example, guerrilla warfare was developed in response to the adversary's superior force and firepower, wherein it neutralised own inferiority by exploiting potential strengths in relation to the prevailing environment (jungles, mountains, and now also urban areas). This, and also terrorist methods of waging war, such as 9/11 or the Madrid bombings, are not adequately covered under the principle of Economy of Force/Effort, but would be well supported by a shift in focus on production of effect using available resources. The relation between "Effect" and 'Force" may be considered as an equation:

$$E = F \times S$$

Where E is Effect, F is Force/Firepower, and S is Strategy

Thus, while the old principle of Economy of Effort sought to maximise the effect for a given force, it inherently accepted that this maximum effect need not correspond to what was required. This was in consonance with wars being 'total' or unlimited, where the emphasis was on maximum effective utilisation, rather than on utilisation for maximum (desired) effect. However, by shifting focus on attaining the desired effect, rather than on economising the effort, we emphasise the goal more than the means. Thus, the earlier 'economy' of effort would correspond to the component of strategy in the above equation, as a means to attaining the goal. However, strategy would also have other components, and not just judicious employment of forces. Effect could also be achieved by enhancing the firepower and other strategy quotients. Hence, attainment of effect would provide a more useful principle. The principle of Flexibility has been replaced by Manoeuvre, Initiative and/or Mobility by some countries. The principle is looked at in both active and reactive manner, leading to different interpretations and terms used by various nations. For example the US definition of manoeuvre is more active, in that it entails placing the enemy at disadvantage through the flexible application of own combat power at the strategic, operational and tactical levels of war. The Indian Army Doctrine is, however, somewhat reactive, in that it deems flexibility as the capability to react appropriately to changing situations. The Indian Maritime Doctrine is a mix of both, and views flexibility as the capacity to cope with a rapidly changing situation and seize fleeting opportunities, wherein it entails both physical mobility and reaction capability, with the latter accruing from planning, staff-work and the commander's mental outlook. In the various definitions/interpretations, we can see two themes: first, the ability to respond to change and, second, the ability to impose change. In essence, the principle of Flexibility/Manoeuvre/Initiative/Mobility all look at the Management of Change, both in imposition upon the enemy, by the use of manoeuvre and 'flexible' application of combat power, and in reacting to change that is imposed by the enemy or that occurs otherwise. The purpose, in both cases, is to derive advantage from a change in situation that could occur or be created by either side. The change may occur in the various dimensions of war, i.e. through forces arrayed on land, sea or air, and also at the various levels of warfare, viz. tactical, operational or strategic.

Thus, change may be introduced by the application or redeployment of physical forces in the three dimensions, by the timing of executing change, and also by the very rate of change. In fact, the rate of change or pace/tempo of battle is increasingly being recognised as a key factor in introducing and exploiting vulnerabilities in the enemy's Information-Decision-Action (IDA) Cycle, also leading to suggestions of time becoming an independent dimension of war. The 'manoeuvrist' concept of warfare, espoused in the UK Joint Warfare Doctrine, also envisages application of multiple lines of operation, in physical dimensions, at a higher speed and tempo, so as to overwhelm the enemy's mental and moral capability to cope/respond. It may be seen, therefore, that the current principle of flexibility, whilst constituting a valid concept, is inadequate as it does not address the advantages provided in imposing change on the enemy, which are inherent in the corresponding principles of initiative, manoeuvre, and mobility.

However, these latter principles on their part do not address the value of flexibility in enabling rapid and appropriate response to changes in situations that occur or are imposed by the enemy, or the developments in using time/tempo in unsettling the enemy's management of change. Hence, this principle needs to be expanded in scope, and the concepts of Flexibility, Initiative, Manoeuvre, and Mobility all subsumed into a more inclusive term, such as the Management of Change.

Cooperation/Unity of Command has been viewed as the coordination of efforts to attain a common goal. In India and UK, this is seen as emanating from 'jointness', wherein cooperation is the vehicle by which the necessary coordination is sought to be delivered. In the US interpretation of this PoW, coordination is sought to be attained by vesting a single commander with the requisite authority, viz. unity of command, which would allow him to direct all forces in coordinated action. The moot and common point here is in the need for coordination of effort and actions by multiple forces, of the same and also allied nations, so as to avoid mutual interference and synergise their effect upon the opponent. This clearly brings out that the principle is simply Coordination, as already adapted by Russia and China. The concepts of unity of command or cooperation are, thus, not principles in themselves, but merely the tools used to comply with the core, common principle and organisational method of attaining coordination. In an era of growing joint and combined complex and specialised operations, there is increasing focus on effective coordination, through a variety of means. This becomes even more valid in the case of limited conventional wars, where limitations in time, space or methods employable necessitate synchronisation of efforts, as also in subconventional wars, where there is likely to be a larger number of actors and resources involved, including non-military resources. In these cases, unity of command per se may not be feasible and is less likely to provide the result by itself.

Additional tools to strengthen coordination, through joint planning training, perspective and organisations, and experience of combined, multinational operations have accordingly become increasingly important. The principle of Security refers to protection of own forces from enemy action. In essence this points to the factor of vulnerability, in turn, therefore, this is aimed at enhancing own freedom of action. The utility of this concept is certainly evident, but not as an independent principle in the light of the arguments made earlier for replacing the principle of offensive action by Freedom of Action (FoA). It follows that this latter new principle of FoA would subsume the principle of security as well, wherein the concept of maintaining security is inherent in the maintenance of own FoA. The converse of the principle of security is also covered in FoA, viz. attacking the enemy's security through denying him FoA through manoeuvre and offensive counter-FoA operations. The principle of security is, thus, deemed limited in scope, and not worthy of categorisation as an independent principle. Its replacement and absorption by FoA would provide a more robust and inclusive principle.

The principle of Surprise has long been seen as a necessary force multiplier, to provide the decisive edge at strategic, operational and tactical levels of warfare. It entails catching the enemy off-balance and thereby forcing him to give battle in circumstances unfavourable to him. There is a growing realisation, however, that surprise is increasingly difficult to attain at the strategic and operational levels, as a result of the increasing transparency of the battlespace and effect of the Information Age. The reduced attainability of this condition in modern warfare would lead to its reduced applicability as a principle, which gravitates against its viability and status as an independent Principle of War. It is important to examine the purpose and limitations of surprise, in relation to modern warfare, to identify and rectify the flaw.

The purpose of surprise is, very evidently, to provide an advantage, by pushing the enemy 'off-balance'. The purpose itself indicates that surprise is only 'a', and not necessarily 'the', means to an end, let alone being considered as an end/

goal in itself, even though it has been hitherto a primary means in attaining the above purpose. But, in the modern techno-tactical environment, the attainability and sustainability of surprise is coming increasingly under question, whereby combat power would still need to be applied in significant measure to achieve dominance and victory. A great deal would also depend upon a common but frequently ignored aspect of warfare, i.e. the enemy and his ability to cope with surprise. After all, once the initial surprise and possible dislocation due to it is over, the enemy could well convert the disadvantage of being tactically surprised into an advantage of his own, through a technological surprise or a counter-tactical surprise move. Hence, surprise also has to be converted into continuing operational/tactical advantage, rather than be limited to an initial action or early advantage, which has sometimes been deemed adequate. The foregoing does not lend support to the qualification of surprise per se as an independent principle. On the other hand, credible nuclear deterrence relies on reducing surprise and ensuring transparency to allow for successful deterrence.

The excessive focus on surprise as a PoW, and its centrality in avoiding casualties or attrition warfare, appears to have masked the fact that it is merely a tool and not the main principle, as borne out by its stated purpose of "catching the enemy off-balance." The principle, in fact, lies in pushing and then keeping the enemy 'off-balance', rather than in attaining surprise per se. This would require the generation of an asymmetry, which would allow application of combat power in own favour, and then sustaining the same so as to develop a favourable momentum (in other words, a continuing competitive advantage) in the war/battle and thereby attain the overall aims. Hence, it could also be expressed in terms of a 'competitive advantage' in strategic, operational, tactical and also technological terms. Technological asymmetry and surprise is perhaps even more important, but would provide its best value where the doctrine has been developed to support and exploit its potential, so that it can be used in ways superior to that of the enemy, even where the technological level of the opposing forces may be similar. Hence, the key point is the need for a more comprehensive concept, such as Generation and

Sustenance of Favourable Asymmetry, to provide the guidelines in waging of warfare in modern conditions. Surprise, as such, would be one facet of establishing continuing favourable asymmetry in the application of combat power, even while generation and sustenance of favourable asymmetry as a principle would employ a broader range of technical and tactical tools.

The attainment of favourable asymmetry has been the basic theme in warfare through history. The methods used have included use of surprise in terms of time and space, advantages of new technology, exploitation of operational art and environment, use of stratagem, information superiority, etc. Technological tools have arguably been as, if not more, effective than surprise in time and space, for generating favourable asymmetry. The Israeli actions at Beka'a Valley in June 1982 relied on integration of technology with doctrine, leading to spectacular results, and became the forerunner of modern joint operations and the "Revolution in Military Affairs." In World War II, Rommel preparation of the battlefield by RC-135 electronic surveillance aircraft, E-2C Hawkeye AWACS and UAVs, wherein the movement of Syrian forces were constantly tracked. This led to the destruction of 86 Syrian aircraft, 400 tanks and 24 SAM sites, against the loss of only one Israeli aircraft, in 96 hours. The attainment of favourable asymmetry has been the basic theme in warfare through history. The methods used have included use of surprise in terms of time and space, advantages of new technology, exploitation of operational art and environment, use of stratagem, information superiority, etc. marshalled his forces and used them in superior tactical manner to generate local favourable asymmetry against superior forces, mostly by sheer speed of advance.

However, he did not possess the means to sustain that advantage due to poor logistics back-up and inferior air power. The Allied forces, on the other hand, were able to generate sustained favourable asymmetry with air-land cohesion and better logistics, and were thereby able to push Rommel back. This revised approach to the PoW would also recognise logistics as an important ingredient in generating and sustaining favourable asymmetry. The use of pace and tempo of operations, discussed above in the context of flexibility/manoeuvre and the manoeuvrist approach to warfare, also provides another tool for generation of asymmetry, even in the absence of strategic or operational surprise. For example Op Cactus Lily, the Indian military strike through East Pakistan in 1971 in 12 days, led to the collapse of Pakistani defences and capture of 90,000 Pakistani military prisoners of war. It follows, therefore, that the attainment of favourable asymmetry sets the conditions for military victory and is its prerequisite at some stage of the operation. Further, its maintenance enables the avoidance of defeat by denying the enemy the conditions for victory. Asymmetry is not generated automatically through its potential or possession, but by the specific interaction in time and space against the opponent, employing various tools, such as the above. Hence, generation and sustenance of favourable asymmetry deserves to be viewed as an independent PoW, with surprise as its sub-set.

The principle of Administration primarily covers logistics, and also welfare and discipline. The use and value of Logistics in winning wars has been amply demonstrated throughout history, such as its effect on Rommel's operations in North Africa despite tactical superiority, and bears no further reiteration. Based on its time-tested central role in the history of warfare, and its continued relevance today, such as in expanding the reach and reducing the time for response of a force, logistics merits recognition as an independent principle of war. Its inclusion within the principle of administration, as presently done, tends to dilute the value of this concept and limit the scope as long as it is yoked to administration. The aspects of welfare and discipline, which have been dovetailed with logistics in the principle of administration, are certainly important, but need mix up with logistics, which stands on its own merit. In fact, welfare and discipline are more relevant to, and better covered under, the existing, separate principle of Maintenance of Morale, as they are contributory factors to the same. In the practice of maintenance of morale, another aspect that bears recognition is the new challenges thrown against it by the modern techno-tactical environment, where morale has to be maintained for forces spread across different dimensions and separated theatres, amidst higher intensity and increasing opaqueness of operations, and an increasingly deleterious and visible effect of war and its human cost. This is more so in the case of prolonged counter-insurgency and anti-terrorist warfare, in own and foreign lands.

There are a couple of principles that have been enunciated by some countries, but which do not have a parallel amongst other nations. These include "simplicity" in the USA, and "political mobilisation" in China. A closer look at these 'principles' reveals that they do not really merit independent status. Simplicity simply entails avoiding 'complexity' in military operations. In essence, it addresses the need to maintain clarity and cohesion at all levels, and avoidance of unnecessary complications. However, this principle is inherent in the application of the first PoW of aim/objective, and flows from the same, whilst also forming part of the execution of some others, such as "coordination" and "logistics." Hence, its value as an independent PoW is questionable, and it belongs more at the doctrinal level than amongst the higher PoW. Similarly, "political mobilisation" is inherent in the "maintenance of synergy" in politico-military aims.

3

Art of War: Principles and Science

War is an ever changing event. Successful conflict requires innovation, ruthlessness, and surprise. Some strategists debate whether war is a science or an art, but in reality it combines both ideas. There are certain principles that scientifically dominate war—massing troops, supplying them, concentrating forces against an enemy, and surprising the opponent—and they may be mastered through study. By the same token, the application of principles is an artistic process. The same commanders with the same conditions can produce differing results. Inspired and intuitive commanders win battles, if they understand the art of war. Martin van Creveld (1985, pp. 270–273) explains the interplay between art and science. Throughout the history of war, van Creveld says, the most successful commanders have been those who did not turn their troops into automatons.

They selected troops for particular missions and gave them the freedom to make autonomous decisions through the course of a campaign or battle. The result of war is not technological determinism, but freedom to act with innovation as the situation demands. Despite growing communication systems and the desire to exercise control, successful commanders master the principles of war and apply them with artistic freedom.

The art of war is not static, and the years following World War II (1939–1945) brought new meanings to fields of conflict—meanings demanding new and innovative responses. Modern terrorism emerged from this period, beginning with anticolonial revolts and guerrilla wars in the years immediately following the Second World War. Urban terrorism followed the anticolonial phase and it grew into an international affair. These new terrorists encompassed left-wing groups in the West and Latin America and nationalistic terrorists in the West and Asia. Middle Eastern terrorism reemerged in the 1970s in the wake of the leftist and nationalist period. By the 1990s, terrorism was increasingly a religious affair. No matter what form terrorism took, however, successful terrorists did not seek decisive World War II-style confrontations.

They never assumed they were operating in peace time but believed they were perpetually at war. Western democracies, by contrast, made legal distinctions between peace and war. Even when war is undeclared, both governments and terrorists use war as a metaphor for their actions. Terrorists like the metaphor because it glorifies their causes and leaders. In addition, terrorists find military planning convenient.

Governments use references to war because it grants them greater leeway when acting outside the law. Western governments in particular see war as a legal issue producing a code of behaviour distinct from peace. This presents a philosophical problem.

THE NEBULOUS NATURE OF LOW-INTENSITY CONFLICT

Prior to the time of growing terrorism, Americans seemed to know the meaning of conflict. War was an extension of politics fought within the legal framework of the Constitution. Quite simply, the Constitution states that only Congress has the power to declare war, and Congress declares whether America is in a state of war or peace. However, the anticolonial struggles following World War II, the Vietnam War, and battles in Somalia and Serbia confused the issue for the military: American troops were killed in peacetime. To confuse the situation even further, civil agencies responded to a bombing in Oklahoma City, two teenagers on a shooting spree at Columbine High School, and suicide attacks on September 11.

Clearly, the police were not soldiers, but they were being called to military-style attacks. Although criticized in the wake of Germany's defeat in 1945, Western military planning has been influenced by Carl von Clausewitz's military philosophy. Clausewitz cut his teeth during the nationalistic wars against Napoleon (1795–1815). Joining the Prussian Army as a twelve-year-old drummer boy, he fought under the Duke of Brunswick against the French Revolution. Clausewitz noted the Prussians won almost every engagement with the French revolutionary army, but the French always seemed to regroup and stand ready to fight. The French, young Clausewitz thought, were fighting for their nation, while the Prussians were fighting for a king. The French Revolution had produced a new type of war.

Clausewitz began to study war as a philosophical problem. The strength of the French came from their ability to place the nation in arms. To defeat the French, Germany must unite under a democracy and employ its own citizen soldiers. The proof of victory would come when his nation's will could be imposed on its enemies. Clausewitz joined a group of reformers and attempted to modernize the Prussian Army. The Prussians were destroyed, however, in 1806 after the Battle of Jena-Auerstadt, and Clausewitz was carried off to Paris in captivity with a Prussian prince. He began writing—formulating a philosophy of national war. Clausewitz's notions were derived from his study of history, especially the Thirty Years' War (1618–1648) and Frederick the Great (1740–1786). They were also influenced by his decision to join the Russian Army in 1812 to fight Napoleon and the German War of Liberation (1813–1814). Clausewitz's ideas come to us from a book published by his wife Maria the year after he died. *On War* is a philosophical treatise on the nature of total, nationalistic wars. It has also been one of the most influential works on military forces in the twentieth century.

The problem for American law enforcement is not Clausewitz's understanding of the nation-in-arms, but the changing structure of conflict. Victor Hanson (1989) criticizes Clausewitz and the Western way of battle for focusing on warfare in ancient Greece. According to this line of thought, the purpose of military action is to seek a decisive engagement, and Clausewitz's philosophical treatise emphasizes this point. Terrorism is designed to produce the opposite effect, seeking to avoid a direct confrontation with force. In addition, since the emergence of professional, modern warfare in the West after the Peace of Westphalia (1648), the purpose of war has been to impose political will on the defeated party. American law enforcement does not seek a decisive battle with enemy forces, and its purpose can never be the imposition of political will. The goals of terrorism are to create panic and cause social systems to break. While the police have been called to the Clausewitzian paradigm, where America is either at war or at peace, another frame of reference may be more helpful.

Nearly 2000 years ago a Chinese philosopher, Sun Tzu, produced a treatise on the paradoxes of war (Management Analytics, 1995). Rather than conceiving of times when a political realm is at war or at peace, Sun Tzu saw war and peace as two sides of the same coin. War and politics were psychological forces held together by the belief in power. In Sun Tzu's philosophical structure, the highest form of military leadership comes in breaking the enemy's resistance without fighting. Leaders must be able to control their anger and project power.

When military leadership is strong, the state will be strong and have less need to act. If the state appears to be weak, it is vulnerable despite its strength. Clausewitz wrote at a time of emerging nationalism, constitutions, and democracies. It was a time when military victory involved creating mass armies for the delivery of a decisive blow, and even though Communist interpreters of Clausewitz saw peace as another means of war, Clausewitz saw war and peace as legal matters. A nation was either at peace or at war. Writing in another era in another civilization, Sun Tzu saw few dichotomies between war and peace. A state projected power both in war and in peace, and its power could be threatened by public perceptions. In a time of low-level conflict, it may be wise for law enforcement agencies to consider some ancient Chinese concepts of power and warfare.

Nebulous conflicts have become a problem for Western democracies (Howard, 2002). In the face of growing terrorism, domestic unrest, and subnational warfare, one of the greatest challenges to the structure of Western democracies may well be the need to augment military force with civilian police power. Referring to this as a "Security Force" concept, Crozier (1975) argues that combined military and police operations are becoming commonplace. The ironic aspect of this position is that rule through combined police-military power is the norm for totalitarian states. Wilkinson refers to this condition as state terrorism. The paradox is apparent. The extent to which civilian legal authority can be used to counter political threats while maintaining free institutions and individual rights may have been in the minds of the framers of the United States Constitution, and the concept is certainly a dominant topic today.

ASYMMETRICAL WARFARE

Terrorism is based on Sun Tzu's concept of strength-to-weakness, not the strength-to-strength battle as Clausewitz described. In modern military parlance this is called asymmetry. Asymmetry simply means competing forces are out of balance; that is, a weak force fights a much stronger power. A good analogy is to think of a single angry hornet attacking a hiker in the woods. The angry hornet can sting the hiker, and if it is extremely lucky, cause the hiker to panic or maybe induce a fatal allergic reaction. If the hiker stays calm, however, a single swat ends the attack. The odds are in the hiker's favour. Terrorists are much like the imaginary hornet with two exceptions. They tend to be true-believing fanatics who sacrifice the lives of others to carry on a struggle with a superior force, and they have a better chance of striking when avoiding social conventions and societal norms. In other words, terrorists fight outside the rules. Terrorism is a tactic of weakness. When a disadvantaged population strikes a more privileged class, it lacks the ability to confront the other group on an equal level. Just as it lacks economic and political power in the face of the dominant group, it also lacks military power. This is a problem for most revolutionary forces and weak powers attempting to fight a stronger force. A weak power cannot attack a stronger nation directly. It must use unconventional methods of fighting and attack the stronger force indirectly, many times striking nontraditional civilian targets.

The reason terrorists fight outside the norms of society is revealed by the imbalance of power. The major powers hold all the cards in international trade, legal authority, and military power. It does no good to strike them in the open, but they are vulnerable when attacked outside the norms of standard international relations. The lesson is as old as terrorism. The rule is, "If you can't kill their soldiers, kill their civilians." The purpose of asymmetry is to give the impression that powerful economic, military, and political forces cannot protect ordinary people going about daily routines. Terrorists do not seek an open battle but want to show that the norms of civil society cannot protect the population of the superior force. Enemy forces prepared for combat are too strong, but police stations, off-duty military personnel, and schoolchildren make tempting targets.

Asymmetry works only when terrorist infrastructures remain hidden, and concealment gives terrorists strength. If their bases are open or if they overestimate their strength, a superior power is able to reverse the asymmetrical process and engage terrorists on its own terms. This is the reason terrorists fight in the shadows. If state and local police agencies join the asymmetrical fight, their primary strength is the ability to collect information. Information allows security forces to bring terrorists into the open, and it is the key to counterterrorism. Intelligence gathering assumes the most important function in asymmetrical war.

Asymmetry in Afghanistan

Many analysts believe modern terrorism evolved from these colonial revolts. Anticolonialism gave way to left-wing and ethnic violence in the 1960s and 1970s. As left-wing and nationalistic violence swept the Middle East, Asia, Latin America, and the West, an international ethos of revolutionary terrorism seemed to pit itself against the Western world. Carlos Marighella espoused theories of terrorist revolution in *The Minimanual of the Urban Guerrilla* and *For the Liberation of*

Brazil, and some analysts spoke of a terrorist international while others looked for state sponsors. The former Soviet Union's defeat in Afghanistan (1979–1989) introduced a new facet into the logic of asymmetrical war: religion. In essence, the world was experiencing the continually changing nature of war. For the most part, technologically and numerically superior armies were called to fight an illusive enemy in the shadows. In December 1979 the former Soviet Union invaded Afghanistan to support a puppet Communist regime, resulting in a devastating ten year war. Seven differing groups of Islamic holy warriors (mujahadeen) launched a guerrilla war against the Soviets, and young radical Muslims from Morocco to Indonesia flocked to the cause. Osama bin Laden was one of them, and al Qaeda was born in the midst of the guerrilla war. The United States funnelled money and arms to the mujahadeen through Pakistan's Inter-Service Intelligence (ISI) agency.

The ISI, in turn, not only supported the mujahadeen but many violent radical groups with links to the United States, such as al Qaeda and Jamaat al Fuqra. The Soviets left Afghanistan in December 1989, but no single mujahadeen group brought order to the war-torn country. Afghanistan disintegrated into violent anarchy with local warlords vying for control of various portions of the land. Eventually, young puritanical Islamic students known as the Taliban came to power. Bin Laden's mujahadeen reassembled in various guises during the United States' first war with Iraq. Al Qaeda moved to Afghanistan in 1996 and issued a "declaration of war" against the West and the Jewish people. The terrorist organization could survive in Afghanistan because of the country's relative anarchy and because the Taliban was not strong enough to confront al Qaeda. Bin Laden established training bases and terrorist training schools while increasing al Qaeda's strength. United States' military forces destroyed al Qaeda's command structure in the fall of 2001, but autonomous sleeper cells remained in over sixty countries after the fighting wound down.

Asymmetry is not a new concept in war. In fact, the purpose of battle is to bring more resources, troops, and power to a point where the enemy lacks resources, troops, and power. Successful military leaders create asymmetrical situations. It makes little sense for terrorists to fight in the open against a superior force, and the same logic can be applied to troops who fight terrorists. There are times when conventional military tactics can be used to destroy terrorist bases, but there are other times when information gathering, criminal investigation, and arrest are far more effective. Michael Howard (2002) argues this point effectively when discussing counterterrorist operations. Counterterrorism, he says, takes place in quiet intelligence operations, secretive strikes, and the elimination of selected targets. Counterterrorism is asymmetrical by implication. In other words, when an enemy strikes your weakness, learn to fight with your strength and bring the right weapons to the right fight.

PRINCIPLES OF WAR: INITIAL REMARKS

In connection with the planning of the Yalu River river-crossing attack at the beginning of the Russo-Japanese War, General Tamemoto Kuroki, Commander of the [Japanese] First Army, in one paragraph of his instructions to his assembled staff, stated that, "In the military operations of the First Army, particularly the operations at the beginning of the war, if we do not act so that future historians cannot raise even one point of criticism, we should fail in our samurai duty.... Since the plan was made with such care and logic, even if the worst should happen, that would not be a matter for regret; it would be divine will.... and I ask that you perform so that future readers of history will judge that it was with complete dedication."

And France's famous military commander, Marshal Foch, said, "The art of war, like other arts, has its fundamental principles. If that were not the case, war would not be an art. War is learnable and is something that must be learned; it is an understanding of the true nature of war gained through extensive and intensive study of military history that is the basis for study of the art of war." Again, in regard to the principles of war, he also said, "There is a gap between knowing and having ability, but with absolutely no knowledge, it is not possible to move in a single jump to having ability. In contrast, if one has the knowledge, one can have the ability. Knowledge is a necessary condition. If one has knowledge, in a short time one would gain confidence, and confidence brings accurate decisions." These are wise statements presenting suggestions for both the East and the West concerning the principles of war and the development of capability with them; and, in general, for persons studying the art of war, they clarify the principles and rules of warfare (the so-called principles of war) and show the importance of knowing them and developing the ability to apply them.

Particularly for beginning students, it is believed that the essence of improving tactical capability is, first, studying these "principles of warfare" fundamentally and scientifically, then deepening one's understanding of the "knowledge," making this "knowledge" one's guide, accumulating "substantiating evidence" from "military history," developing this base for judgment (capability), and training and improving judgment (capability) through applied tactics.

This book has the objective, from the above viewpoint, of providing beginning students of tactics with deeper understanding of the principles of land warfare and with a basis for future improvement in tactical capability.

THE ESSENCE OF WARFARE AND THE CHARACTERISTICS OF LAND WARFARE

The Essence of Warfare

What is warfare? War is a clash of opposing wills, a struggle between beliefs, and victory goes to the party that crushes the enemy's will and destroys his beliefs. In other words, the warfare discussed here is a struggle for victory, using "power" to cause the opponent's will to yield and our will to prevail. Hence, "the essence of warfare" is "power" and its maximum use. Its objective is to crush the opponent's power of resistance and cause him to submit to our will, and its measures are to use power to destroy the opponent's fighting power (material, spiritual). In other words, it is nothing less than the seizure of victory.

The essence of warfare and its characteristics : The first essential element of warfare is the fact that, "in warfare, there are opponents." Moreover, both parties are characterized by having free will.

The second is that both parties have the will to overthrow the opponent (enemy). War is a struggle between the free wills of both parties, and victory is determined by which one has confidence in it. In other words, it also can be said to be a struggle of faith. The third is that power is used to cause submission of the opponent's will.

The direct instrument for fighting is "power," and when this power is brought to bear against the opponent, it is used for the violent effect of causing submission of the opponent's will. The fourth is the actual battlefield situation, which is extremely important for our study of tactics and is a basic condition. The actual battlefield situation arises from the above essential elements of warfare and varies according to the time period, the place of combat, and the type and scale of warfare, etc.

The most important of these are that, in warfare, the situation always is uncertain, unstable, and unclear, and the normal state is that there is a succession of inconsistencies and mistakes, danger to life is ever-present, mental and bodily difficulties of fear, exhaustion, etc., are encountered, the situation does not develop as expected, etc. In the study of the principles of war and in the study of tactics, if thorough consideration is not always given to the actual battlefield, one will end up in worthless speculation.

Characteristics of Land Warfare

In warfare, the essential role of land warfare (land operations) is the control of persons, and its instrument is the control of land. Hence, the sphere of activity of land units is the land, and the characteristics of the land are the dominant factors governing the character of land warfare. Progress in science and technology contributes greatly to liberation from various limitations of the land, but has not reached the point of changing the basic nature of land warfare.

Also, in the operational environment of land warfare, there are various conditions that affect the handling of troop units and the will of the commander. The principal factors comprising these are national policy (politics, foreign relations, the economy, military affairs, social psychology, etc.), the zone of operations, opposing (enemy) forces, weapon systems, etc., but in this book are treated primarily only matters related to the principles of land-warfare tactics.

Natural Characteristics of the Land and their Effect

The major elements in the natural characteristics of the land are terrain and weather.

It is clear that terrain and weather are closely related to land warfare and that they control the nature of land warfare, but here the discussion is on the general characteristics; special characteristics of terrain and their effect are discussed in Part VII, Operations in Special Terrain, etc.

(1) Terrain, particularly the complexity and diversity of the surface of the earth : The land forms varied and distinctive terrain (regions) that combines various elements of topographic irregularity, the nature of the surface soil, the water system, the vegetation, cultural features, etc., and exerts great influence on land warfare. This effect, in the final analysis, is related to firepower and tactical movement; but it is not limited simply to physical influence, but also exerts great spiritual influence. This effect, through field of view and of fire, trajectory, cover and concealment, ability to withstand bombs and shells, etc., aids or limits the use or effectiveness of firepower, and through the load-bearing capacity of the ground, obstructions, etc., favours or curtails the use of tactical mobility.

(2) Effect of weather : The amount of light, rain and snow, wind, temperature, etc., are related to the circumstances of the ground surface and affect firepower and tactical mobility, as well as exerting a close influence on the combat capability of personnel and the performance of equipment.

Characteristics of Land Warfare

Characteristics of employment of land units :

(a) Sluggishness and the fixed nature of operations : Because of the necessity for an uninterrupted link between the base of operations and the battle front and the sluggishness of movement, the shifting and concentration of combat power, change of direction of operations, etc., are sluggish. In land warfare, special consideration is necessary regarding the "importance of a unit," depending upon the unit's size.

(b) A region's absorption of combat power : Extending the battle line invites a gradual decrease in combat power (personnel, material) because of maintaining of logistics, holding of terrain, etc., and is an important condition making the difference between the offensive and defensive.

(c) Increase in combat capability from the terrain : The value of terrain itself and of fortifications creates the possibility of defence or creates value as an attack objective.

(d) Enduring quality of combat power : The combat power of ground forces—except in cases of panic, the concentration of crushing force, etc.—does not collapse suddenly.

(e) The value of spiritual power is great : With the individual on the battlefield, the mental process at every instant governs the behaviour of his entire body. In particular, the value of command and control is extremely high.

(f) Local independence in military operations (combat) : Military operations of large units also have an integrated character of combat in each independent locality.

Organizational Character of Ground-force Units

(a) Organization of essential elements of combat power into minimal units and the necessity for mass : In order to control a region, it is necessary to control localities. In order to organize the control of these localities, there arises the need for various types of firepower and equipment and various branches of service based in small units. And with the naturally limited, small numbers of elite troops, mass is necessary.

(b) Variety of mobile equipment and necessity for mass : Depending upon distance, or depending upon the characteristics of varied terrain to be traversed on foot, mobile equipment of various types and mass are required.

(c) Complexity and expanding nature of the logistical organization : In land warfare, logistics extends from the country's base of operations to the individual fighting man, and with operational conditions becoming complex and varied, expansion of the battle area, modernization of equipment, etc., its organization is complex and expanding.

In a word, the characteristics of land warfare are the source of the principles of war in land warfare, and in order to understand the principles of war, it is necessary to grasp the characteristics of land warfare.

MEANING AND NATURE OF THE PRINCIPLES OF WAR

The principles of war are "the basic principles of combat in order to obtain victory and the fundamental rules that, to some degree, embody those principles" These are theories and are derived from many military histories. In other words, "the principles of war are theories formed dialectically from accumulated reasoning and corroborative evidence, and they are continually evolving with the passage of time." Hence, the principles of war discussed in this book were obtained up to about the end of World War II and cannot be described as unchanging for all times including the fixture or for all places. However, when consideration is limited to matters of definite time and space, it is believed that the principles of war discussed in this book can be taken as principles and rules for victory. On the other hand, in the present situation where the importance of indirect aggression is increasing, one must not overlook the fact that the principles of war or World War II and earlier are reaching a developmental stage. Also, in one sense, the principles of war are a standard for observing military history and cannot be applied directly in future situations. Only after knowing the principles of war, carefully studying and observing military history with them as a standard, and then improving one's capability (judgment) through applied tactics, etc., can one tackle situations and make accurate decisions. Only at that stage can it be said that the principles of war are completely usable.

RELATIONSHIP BETWEEN THE PRINCIPLES OF WAR AND DOCTRINES

Doctrines are the guiding principles and the embodiment of basic rules for action that should be taken to embody and carry out national defence policies determined on the basis of the organization and equipment of the country's military forces, national character, traditions, terrain, etc., in the country's environment, that is, in the specific geographic, political, and social conditions. Thus, although doctrines are not blindly observed, they must at least be followed. On the other hand, the principles of war are not applied directly but normally are a standard that should be used to improve one's judgment, not something that one should take along during tactical actions. In other words, doctrines are the direct basis for action, whereas the principles of war are an indirect thing and are put to use in military actions only through assimilation (improving one's power of judgment) by means of normal training applying them. The relationship between the principles of war and doctrines may be shown graphically as follows:

MEANING AND CHARACTERISTICS OF COMBAT POWER

The three factors of combat

Combat is governed by the following three factors:

ENERGY [POWER]—basic factor in striking the enemy

TIME—the natural phenomena of light and darkness, heat and cold, fair and rainy weather, etc., and timeliness

SPACE—character of the terrain and other natural phenomena, the spatial extent, and posture

These three elements are mutually interrelated and either strengthen or weaken energy, which is the essence of combat, and whenever energy is applied, they all are inseparably involved. Even with the present developments in science and technology, the mutual relationship of these three factors continues uncharged; and among these three elements, energy is most easily changed by manpower and is the factors that must be given most attention for combat.

Combat Power

War is a struggle between two parties that have free will; and this struggle is an act of violence employed to cause the opponent to submit, and to realize our will. In other words, among the three factors of combat, energy is the direct instrument for combat, and this fighting energy—energy to fight the enemy in military combat—is combat power. Also, with changes in the times, the importance of combat power is gradually increasing, and the proportional difference in importance between it and the factors of time and space is becoming greater and greater. Combat power is divided into intangible factors and tangible factors.

Intangible factors : The intangible factors are the mental and bodily capabilities of the individuals and groups that comprise the military units (forces), the most important one being the spiritual strength of the units and forces. In other words, these factors include the following:

Quality of command and control : State of discipline (troop morale) and fighting spirit

Quality of training : Esprit de corps and the spirit of teamwork

The characteristics of these intangible factors are as follows:

(1) Their power (action) is not manifested as a definite quantity and, except in actual combat, cannot be demonstrated even experimentally.

(2) They change greatly, depending on people and conditions. In other words, if things go well, multiplied power is brought to bear, but if things go badly, they act as a large minus.

(3) They comprise an indivisible unity with the tangible factors and are basic factors that determine victory.

(4) The capability of the commander exerts enormous influence on the quality of the spiritual factor of his unit.

Tangible factors : The tangible factors are the number of persons (military personnel strength) and the quantity and quality of material. For example, they are the organization and equipment and the performance, power, and quantities of various weapons; and they are used as casualty-producing power, destructive power, tactical mobility, and other physical strengths. Tangible factors, to some extent, can be considered as standards with numerical values, and they are the basis for combat power.

Principles of combat power

Essence of combat power : Combat power is the basic one of the three factors of combat and, over time and space, changes quickly and continuously.

Combat power, essentially, has four properties. These are the four properties of concentration, dispersion, action, and inaction.

"Concentration"—Combat power, when concentrated, is strengthened.

"Dispersion"—Combat power, when dispersed, is weakened.

"Action"—Combat power, when it takes action, is strengthened.

"Inaction"—Combat power, when it remains inactive, is weakened.

In other words, combat power, through application and combination of these four properties, brings its character to bear. No matter how much combat power there is, if it is dispersed or remains inactive, that combat power cannot be fully realized, and only when it is concentrated and takes action is the entire combat power used.

From this, when an attempt is made to strike the enemy, the principles of war of "concentration" x "action" result and, hence, the attack is the best means to secure the initiative and be able to obtain decisive results.

The strength and size of combat power are definitely basic conditions for victory, but understanding the nature of combat power and using it skilfully also are essential conditions for victory. It should be remembered that there is an unbroken list of examples since antiquity of disastrous defeats from mistakes in applying the principles of war while having strong and large combat power.

Characteristics of the application of combat power **:** Items about which caution is necessary in using combat power and in further increasing it, thought out from the three factors of combat and from the nature of combat power, yield the following characteristics:

(1) Multiplication quality : Combat power, multiplied by various factors, is applied and used against the enemy. In other words, combat power, with appropriate selection and combination of its four properties, is further multiplied by the advantages of time (use of weather, seizing tactical opportunities, etc.) and land (use of terrain, favourable posture, etc.), and only then is it applied as counter-enemy power. Aiming for these multiplied results is an art, and combat power is greatly increased by art.

(2) Relativity : In combat, there is always an opponent, and the application of combat power is relative to the enemy, so that there is no basis to be able to show a standard or limit of power that is considered sufficient. Since it is not known whether the enemy will apply power greater than the power we consider optimum, it is necessary conscientiously to muster all factors to the maximum.

(3) Absoluteness : In cases where the various elements related to the use of combat power exert an effect of approximately the same amount in both forces, victory is in direct proportion to the absolute values of tangible combat power.

As already stated, combat power is a multiplication of tangible and intangible factors, but there clearly are limitations to compensating for deficiencies in tangible factors, that is, principally, the physical combat power, by means of intangible factors, that is, principally the spiritual strength of the unit (force). In other words, in cases where there is more than some given limit of difference between physical combat powers, it is clear that physical combat power cannot be compensated for, even by spiritual strength or strategem.

Here is a principle of war concerning the absoluteness of tangible combat power in the application of combat power.

(4) Three-dimensionality : When combat power is applied three-dimensionally in the three dimensions land, sea, and air, it can be largest and most complete.

The three-dimensional nature of combat power makes possible simultaneous neutralization or defence of the entire depth. When land, sea, and air power is applied in a balance that suits the situation, it is strongest, and air superiority strengthens the ground sphere of dominant power and the control of the sea.

Historical example: The historical example of the British forces at Sinzweya in the Akyab Campaign in Burma [1944]

(5) Weakening : A moving force is gradually weakened by attrition and finally comes to a standstill. In a way similar to this principle, combat power also is gradually weakened by movement.

In other words:

(a) Combat power, with a rapid advance, becomes weaker and, on reaching the combat-power change-about point [where the balance shifts to favour the opponent], comes to a standstill.

(b) Confusion produced by the first impact of attack calms down with the passage of time, and the terror effect decreases with the passage of time.

(c) The fighting spirit of the attacker is heightened by the intensity of power, being highest at the time of initial impact, and gradually weakens from enemy resistance.

Hence, it is necessary that combat power advance in a way that maintains increasing speed; and for this purpose, it is necessary to dispose combat power in depth. Historical examples: One of the causes for the failure of the offensive of the German forces on the Western Front at the beginning of World War I.

THE JAPANESE FORCES IN THE IMPHAL CAMPAIGN.

Directionality

(a) Direction of strike by combat power : When power is applied perpendicularly [relative to the enemy], is it strongest physically. In Cases of oblique directions, power becomes divided, dispersed, and weakened. Hence, the direction of orientation of combat power must be perpendicular to the enemy.

(b) Point toward which combat power is directed : If the point toward which combat power is directed is a place where enemy power is superior or equal, success cannot be expected; and it is necessary that direction be toward a point where enemy power is weak, a point that hinders the action of the enemy's (concentration x action), or a place that requires time for (concentration x action).

Hence, as the element to be attacked, the choice is, firstly, the enemy's rear; secondly, the enemy's flank; thirdly, the outer portion of the enemy's wing; and only if unavoidable, it is necessary to select the front.

Creationality : Combat power is created by people. In other words, it is created and improved while functioning in time and space and is applied on the battlefield to determine victory or defeat with the enemy. The commander's creation of combat power is one of the arts. The commander must be a great artist.

Historical example: The concentration of power by the German forces' combining their air force and armoured units at the beginning of World War II.

Timing : In operations, generally, both sides are in action. These actions change from inaction to action, from concentration to dispersion, or the reverse. The occasions that cause these changes of action are weaknesses; and, with the passage of time, these weaknesses usually gradually become strengths.

OGANIZING AND COORDINATING COMBAT POWER

The organizing of combat power is the organizing and coordinating of combat power; strictly speaking, it is coordinating for effective application and is a measure indispensable for applying combat power. In other words, only by effectively organizing and coordinating is it possible to apply integrated and sufficient power. In modern warfare, with the increase in factors comprising combat power and with progress in science and technology, the importance of the effort to organize combat power becomes ever greater. Command in war, in one viewpoint, can be said to be determining the time and direction for use of combat power, organizing and coordinating combat power, advancing combat power, and maintaining combat power. Among these, organizing and coordinating combat power occupy an important segment of the field of command.

Cautionary Items in Organizing Combat Power

Fulfilling conditions for application of integrated combat power : For this purpose, firstly, unity of command is an absolute prerequisite. Since organization is integration in order to achieve effectiveness, if the central point [of command] is absent or multiple, organization itself becomes impossible. In Operation "Overlord," which is said to have greatly shown the influence of organization, this point was what received attention first. Second is unity of the plan or concept. In order to cope with the innumerable changes in battlefield conditions, the initial organizing of combat power estimates changes in the situation and is made with certain assumptions. In this case, when there is disunity in plan and inconsistency in concept, with development of the tactical situation, organization immediately becomes confused, and coordination collapses. Hence, unity of command and of plan or concept is extremely important for integrating combat power and for the attainment of common objectives.

Historical example: Operation "Overlord" of the Allied forces in World War II.

Complete grasp of the characteristics of the combat power inherent in a unit : In organizing units, it is necessary to understand each [characteristic] correctly and to cause the concentration of the individual characteristics in the most effective manner for the objective. Command also can be called the road to grasping and combining the individual factors [time, space, power]. An inherent weakness of organization and coordination is that the interruption or deterioration of the action of one of the factors endangers the application of the entire combat power. Hence, organizing on the basis of inaccurate factors eventuates in no power.

Originality and surprise : In organizing, there are basic rules, but their form is infinitely varied. It is devising these forms that is the art of war, and it is this improved originality that favours victory over the enemy.

Historical examples: Nobunaga's use of muskets in the Battle of Nagashino [1575]

Flexibility : On the battlefield with its innumerable changes, rejection of rigid organization and successive shifts in flexible organization and coordination through flexible thinking, constitute the cardinal principle of command and the basis of success. For this reason, it always is necessary to prepare reserve plans or to formulate supplementary measures, etc., as counterplans to meet changes in the situation.

Coordination must be careful; it is a continuing process, and when a plan is once established, that does not mean that everything is finished.

Historical example: Tactics of Soviet forces at Nomonhan (at first, the Soviet forces rushed tanks to the front, meeting the counterattack of the Japanese forces; thereafter, it used dummy tanks and, after neutralizing exposed positions Japanese forces by means of artillery, applied the combined combat power of infantry combat, achieving success).

Not presenting openings that the enemy can take advantage of : Not leaving openings is not only rational and effective, but also means strength against enemy counterattacks.

For example, the U.S. Navy's circular formation, Germany's Panzerfaust (moving fortress) in World War II, the British-type circular position at Sinzweya in the Second Akyab Campaign, the circular defensive position of the U.S. and Chinese forces in the Hukawng Valley at the northern border of Burma, etc., are good typical examples.

Timeliness in meeting the situation : The accuracy and flexibility of organization increase in direct proportion to the time, and tactical opportunities and coordination are opposites. The elapse of time for organization increases combat power but may miss a valuable tactical opportunity. It is necessary to decide between time (opportunity) and power by proper appraisal of enemy power, of the necessity for organizing our combat power, and of the constraints of time.

For example, in case of an attack, the question arises of whether to coordinate and go with power or to seize the tactical opportunity and go with art. If too much importance is placed on the tactical opportunity and an attack is initiated with insufficient power, the attack will suddenly bog down.

Hence, it is important to grasp this limitation. Ascertaining necessary power and integrating that with the time requirement, results in the organizing of maximum combat power.

Historical examples: Examples of success in organizing combat power:

Normandy Landing Operation

"Cylindrical" defence at Sinzweya [encircled but with aerial supply]

Examples of failure in organizing combat power; Counterattacks of Gallipoli, Guadalcanal, and Saipan.

TACTICAL OPPORTUNITY AND THE SURPRISE ATTACK

Combat power, as already stated, is applied by the multiplication of various factors. Hence, it is self-evident that differences will occur in the power actually applied on the battlefield, irrespective of the intrinsic combat power. Combat is a relative matter, and both sides, respectively, fight with the power that they actually can apply. The power that both sides, respectively, can apply is called the relative combat power.

The outcome of battle receives its verdict of the superior wins and the inferior loses, on the basis of this relative combat power. All the concrete principles of war that are derived from the basic principle of war that the superior wins and the inferior loses, are simply the seeking of the cause-and-effect relationship of how to create and improve relative combat power superior to that of the enemy. Comparison of the power of both sides in the study of tactics is not merely a ratio of firepower or of military-personnel strength; superiority must be evaluated based on this relative combat power.

In combat, for us to have superiority in relative combat power, every effort must be concentrated on utilization of terrain and weather, establishment of a favourable posture, obtaining pertinent intelligence, logistic support, etc.; but the most important tactic is utilization of tactical opportunity and the surprise attack.

Tactical Opportunity

Meaning of tactical opportunity : Tactical opportunity is the chance of victory. In other words, it is an inevitable or chance opportunity in war where we can expect superiority in our relative combat power (our application of combat power sufficient to be able to defeat or destroy the enemy). Also, tactical opportunity is a continually shifting thing. The tactical opportunity normally lasts only a short time, this differing with the size of the unit. Some last only a moment, some continue for some time. Also, there are tactical opportunities that occur not just once bat several times.

How does a favourable combat opportunity arise?

(1) Created by one's own effort :

For example,

(a) Luring the enemy into terrain where one's own combat power can be used but application of enemy combat power is difficult.

(b) Trapping the enemy into a situation where his combat personnel are split.

(c) Acting so that our posture is favourable to us.

In other words, it is causing the enemy to expose his weak points, in judo called "preparatory action and attack" (breaking the opponent's posture, creating a posture where a throw is easily effected, and oneself effecting the throw).

Examples include the following:

(a) Splitting of enemy combat personnel, confusion, carelessness, etc., resulting from the enemy's mistakes.

(b) Deficiency in the enemy's application of combat power because of the effect of terrain and weather.

(c) Seizing the point of termination of an enemy offensive (combat power change-about point).

Use of the tactical opportunity : A tactical opportunity must be grasped and used. For this reason, if the commander gathers timely, appropriate intelligence information, detects a tactical opportunity through discerning foresight and an eye for opportunity, and, at some time, seizes a tactical opportunity, this must be utilized through excellent decisiveness and executive ability.

At that time, within some limit, it is possible to change even numerical inferiority into superior relative combat power through utilization of a tactical opportunity, but for this purpose, it always is necessary to make appropriate preparations in order to be able to seize the tactical opportunity, and particular care must be taken not to jump uselessly at an opportunity, attack without preparation, and be defeated. Also, it is important for commanders of all ranks to stress quick and alert command, the will to seize opportunities, and independent, aggressive action.

Tactic of Mass

a. Meaning of the tactic of mass : The tactic of mass is the concentration of an overwhelmingly large quantity of military manpower and material and the formation of combat power with absolute superiority in quantity over that of the enemy.

   For the Soviet forces, evolving this mass tactic is an essential condition of combat, and in the German-Soviet struggle in World War II, the German forces were crushed by this tactic,

b. Relationship between tactical opportunity and mass : In military history from ancient times on, there are many examples of compensating for inferior mass through utilizing a tactical opportunity and seizing victory, but in cases where there is a great difference in mass, it is difficult for the inferior to obtain a superior position in relative combat power, regardless of his effort to utilize tactical opportunities.

   It is difficult to indicate by figures the difference in mass that can be compensated for, by utilizing a tactical opportunity, but it can be said that the inferior side cannot win against an enemy that has more than some given limit in absolute superiority in mass.

Also, it must be noted that a unit that emphasizes tactical opportunities, once it has missed a tactical opportunity, will experience great impact when a tactical opportunity is seized by the enemy; and on the other hand, a unit that emphasizes the tactic of mass, when mass is lost, also will experience great impact.

Surprise Attack

Meaning of surprise attack : Surprise attack is attempting to gain superiority in relative combat power by taking the enemy unawares and not giving the enemy time to react, Here it must be noted that, even if it is possible to effect a surprise at first, when the enemy, by taking countermeasures, is in a superior position in relative combat power, it is not a surprise attack but merely effecting a surprise. On the other hand, in cases where superiority in relative combat power is retained by a swift and daring sudden strike that does not give the enemy time to take countermeasures, that can be called a surprise attack. In short, not giving the enemy time for counteraction is of primary importance for a surprise attack, and for this reason, power and speed are necessary. The principle of war of surprise attack rests on this.

Note: Increase in power through strategem:

Emphasizing strategem...........surprise attack

Emphasizing power...............assault

From strategem x power.......sudden attack

(The term "surprise attack" in current manuals may be said to be a general term for all three.)

Types of surprise attack : There are various types of measures and methods for achieving a surprise attack, but these may be classified by form, as follows:

(1) Time-type surprise attack

(2) Place-type surprise attack

(3) Mass-type surprise attack

(4) Quality-type surprise attack

(5) Tactics-type surprise attack

All of these are achieved by use of terrain and weather, application of speed, concealment and deception, change of measures and methods, etc.

Effectiveness of the surprise attack : The effectiveness of the surprise attack is, firstly, destruction of the enemy's intangible combat power through spiritual impact, that is, aiming at confusion of command, lowered morale, etc., and secondly, through our swift strike, making difficult the application of the enemy's tangible combat power (personnel, weapons, etc.). In other words, it is an attempt, by combining these two elements, to curtail greatly the application of the enemy's combat power and to gain superiority for our relative combat power.

FRONTAL COMBAT POWER AND COMBAT POWER IN DEPTH

Frontal combat power is each unit's combat power directed toward the front facing the enemy in order to accomplish a battle role. In other words, along with deploying first-line manpower on its own battle front and applying its own combat power, each unit is supported by artillery and aviation firepower and, if necessary, is reinforced with airborne troops and heliborne forces, and it also is directed three-dimensionally, air-defence combat power being directed against the enemy's air power. The question of how much manpower to assign to the first line differs according to mission, terrain, enemy situation, degree of firepower support, etc. Considered in isolation, the greater the manpower density, the greater the combat power; but on the other hand, in cases of density exceeding some definite limit, combat power is decreased. Hence, a manpower density favourable to the application of combat power generally remains within a definite range.

Significance and Necessity of Combat Power in Depth

In order to gain victory, superiority in combat power must be applied continuously and with suitable width and depth not only in the initial period but until achievement of the goal (seizing the objective), and the enemy must be kept under strong pressure throughout. Also, since first-line manpower suffers attrition rapidly with the progress of combat with the enemy, in order to maintain it, continuous and uninterrupted replacement of combat power is necessary. In this way, combat power maintained in depth in order continually to apply maximum frontal combat power and to maintain and improve it, is combat power in depth. On the other hand, maintenance of combat power in depth may generate a doubt as to whether there may not occur the mistake of piecemeal use of combat power, but this will not necessarily occur. This is because the gains achieved by the first-line units are immediately utilized and expanded by units in the rear, so that the initial attack shock effect remains undiminished. In this case, if the opportunity is missed to utilize the gains of the first line, there is slippage into piecemeal use of combat power. Hence, selection of the opportunity and of the appropriate position to introduce combat power in depth and application of tactical mobility are important conditions. At Mikata-ga-hara, Ieyasu Tokugawa was present with a [latent] "inverted wedge" formation as in the sketch map, whereas Shingen Takeda deployed all his units in depth and fought by means of the tactic of "rotating elements in the fighting line." As a result, Ieyasu's force initially was superior, but gradually was overcome by the combat power of Shingen's force deployed in depth; and the fact that, in the end, victory fell to Takeda's force is a good example showing the importance of maintaining combat power in depth. The caution in Sun-tzu, "in communicating-ground [=terrain equally accessible to both forces] do not allow your formations to become separated," also is this principle.

Maintenance of Combat Power in Depth

Maintenance of combat power in depth is dependent on echeloned distribution of combat power and on reserves.

Note: Here, reserves is not only reserve troops but also includes all the combat power of firepower, logistics, etc.

Echeloned distribution of combat power, for example, division into first-and second-line assault units in the assault and into first-and second-line defence units in the defence, has the sole objective of applying combat power in depth.

The mission of reserves is to maintain combat power in depth and to cope with unexpected situations, and they should be used to the maximum in the application of combat power in depth. At that time, concentrated use at critical times and places is important.

The Battle Front and Distribution in Depth

It resembles, for example, the relation between width and

depth in quadrilaterals of the same area. In other words, with a given combat power, if the battle front is increased, distribution in depth is decreased, and if distribution in depth is increased, the battle front is decreased. This correlation is extremely important. The items that should be considered in determining the battle front and distribution in depth, may be listed as follows:

a. Adapting width and depth to the objective to be achieved (objective to be seized)
b. Power in the spearhead exceeding that of the enemy
c. Flank-support relationship
d. The enemy's situation, particularly the front and depth
e. Terrain and weather.

CONTAINMENT AND STRIKE

The 4F Principles in Combat

Combat involves the following four functions:

a. Find (Intelligence function)
b. Fix (Containment action)
c. Fight (Strike action)
d. Finish (Achieving the battle success)

Of these, the main element is the third, strike action, and success in this is an annihilation battle.

Relationship between Containment and Strike

In order to crush (strike) enemy combat power by means of our combat power, the primary condition is the place struck by the enemy's combat power; and for this reason, it is clear that action is necessary that contains enemy combat power to our desired time and place. Thus, containment and the strike have a close and inseparable relationship. Two types of sequences of containment and strike action may be considered, as follows:

(1) The case of first containing the enemy and then effecting the strike

(2) The case of accomplishing the containment and strike simultaneously

Both cases are the same in their relation to the essential nature of containment action, which is "impeding (limiting) the enemy's freedom of action." Containment actions necessary for the strike include the following:

(1) Impeding the movement of combat power

(2) Impeding the organization (reorganization) of combat power

(3) Impeding the change of speed of combat power

(4) Impeding or forcing change of direction of combat power

Examples of applying containment and the strike.

Attack :

(1) Envelopment and turning movement.

"1" Containment of the enemy on his front

"2" Moving to a favourable position and striking

(2) Breakthrough.

"1" Containment (impeding movement) by a secondary attack

"2" Strike by the main attack

Defence.

"1" Blocking of the enemy by positions, interdiction of reinforcement by firepower (containment)

"2" Counterattack by reserves (strike)

Pursuit.

"1" Unit assigned to exert direct pressure.... containment of enemy withdrawal by continuous and unrelenting pressure

"2" Unit assigned to a turning movement.... interdicting the enemy's route of withdrawal and encircling and destroying the enemy (strike)

Defence against amphibious landings: Coastal-defence [large-unit] group (containment) and strike [large-unit] group (strike).

4

Sun Tzu: Art of War Strategy

Technology has evolved and changed the lifestyle but under the surface of all technological advancement lies certain common principles in existence with nature, take for example Newton 3 laws of motion. It has been defined these principles as naturalistic principles, which is a set of principles that are inherent in nature and therefore is applicable timelessly. Newton did not create the law, he mereby observe, test and document it for classical mechanics. Law of nature is also frequently referred to the use of reason to analyze human nature and deduce binding rules of moral behaviour. In a similar context, Sun Tzu focuses on deriving the principles behind strategy with relevance to natural phenomenon.

The Art of War is a Chinese military treatise that was written by Sun Tzu in the 6th century BC, during the spring and autumn period.. It is one of the oldest and most successful books on military strategy. It has had an influence on Eastern military thinking, business tactics, and beyond. Sun Tzu suggested the importance of positioning in strategy and that position is affected both by objective conditions in the physical environment and the subjective opinions of competitive actors in that environment. He thought that strategy was not planning in the sense of working through an established list, but rather that it requires quick and appropriate responses to changing conditions. In modern strategy books, strategy is often written as a process of developing strategy. Planning works in a controlled environment, but in a changing environment, competing plans collide, creating unexpected situations. This is easily digestible as human are more comfortable and familiar with linear thinking. Written in an age of chaos, art of war principles is written in relativity context through the use of strategic principles. Art of War strategies should be situational in nature with consideration of current and possible responses involved.

Strategy is define as a plan of action designed to achieve a particular goal, In game theory, a player's strategy in a game is a complete plan of action for whatever situation might arise; this fully determines the player's behaviour. Traditional management style is hierarchical. Management used planning, budgeting, organization, and problem solving skills. Whilst these skills are essential, it's the new school of leadership which leverage on the vision, strategy, communications of the leaders that will serve the needs of leading organization. Different leaders adopt and embrace different school of thoughts; hence the world is flux of strategies. Art of war touches on the principle underlying the dymanic of interactions between strategies. Strategy is reflexive in nature, hence art of war is principle based applied for formulating situational strategy. In short, sun tzu art of war stresses on strategy that adapt to changes in situations across time according to individual goal.

PRINCIPLES OF WAR

The American acronym KISS (keep it simple, stupid) is of military origin. The advantages of KISS in the stress, uncertainty, and exhaustion of battle are obvious, but if taken above a certain level, the final S may become lapidary. Frederick 'the Great' warned that one should not follow rules 'as a blind man follows a wall', and like all successful military commanders he ignored the accepted principles of war when instinct and experience spoke otherwise. We do tend to read more about those who break the rules and succeed, because those who break them and fail tend to have very brief careers. The first 'principles of war' were probably enunciated by Sun-tzu, in the 4th century BC. He listed five 'factors': moral influence, weather, terrain, command, and doctrine. Other principles which emerge from reading his *Art of War* are deception, speed, know your enemy, and that to win without fighting is the acme of skill.

Clausewitz was acutely aware of the dangers of imposing rules. The genius, he wrote, rises above all rules and laughs at them. But military history has produced no more geniuses than any other sphere of human activity and for the rest he enunciated four principles: employ all available forces with the utmost energy; concentrate where the decisive blow is to be struck; lose no time and surprise the enemy; follow up success with the utmost energy. He also enunciated three general principles for defence, fourteen for offence, eight for troops, and seventeen for use in terrain. Today he is revered, but for much of the 19th century his rival Jomini, a far more superficial and emotional writer, was very much more influential: the triumph of style over substance.

World War I produced a demand for principles which could help prevent a repetition of the disastrous waste of life and resources in that conflict. Beaufre suggested that the one principle of war, based on the writings of Foch, was to reach the decisive point thanks to freedom of action gained by sound economy of force, warning against an over commitment to one course of action until the decisive moment arrives. Fuller wrote of three groups of principles: mental principles—direction, concentration, and distribution; moral principles—determination, surprise, and endurance; and physical principles—mobility, offensive action, and security. These prefigure the modern British army 'components of fighting power'—conceptual, moral, and physical.

The US and British forces have similar principles of war, though expressed slightly differently. What the USA succinctly calls the 'objective', the British call 'selection and maintenance of the aim'; these are followed by maintenance of morale, offensive action, surprise, security, concentration of force, economy of effort, flexibility, co-operation, and administration. The equivalent Soviet principles in the Cold War period were mobility and high tempos of combat operations; concentration of main efforts and creation of the necessary superiority at the decisive place and time (mass, concentration); surprise, combat aggressiveness, and energy (offensive action); preservation of the effectiveness of one's own troops (security); adjust the end to the means (economy of force); and co-operation (unity of command). It will be noted that the Soviet principles are not only nearer to the KISS ideal, but also more Clausewitzian in nature. The primary 'objective' in the Gulf war was the expulsion of Iraqi forces from Kuwait; the second was to degrade Iraq's ability to conduct future regional offensive action. A third, unwritten for political reasons and thus unfulfilled, was to destroy the Republican Guard and deprive Saddam Hussein of the foundations of his repressive regime. Other than that, operations proceeded according to both sets of principles listed above, against an enemy who had ignored most if not all of them.

In the 1990s greater emphasis on peacekeeping and peace enforcement ('operations other than war') begged the question as to whether these operations required different principles. Still, it seemed self-evident that the first principle, 'objective', remained paramount. Thus the NATO attack on the former Yugoslavia in March 1999 fell at the first fence. The stated objective was to protect the Kosovar Albanians, but the operation resulted in an intensification of Yugoslav action against them which, in spite of the promises made by the advocates of air power, NATO proved powerless to stop and for which it had made no provision. Attacks on Yugoslavia's infrastructure were so dramatically counter-productive as regards the stated objective that they gave rise to intense speculation as to what the 'real' objective might be. It should not need saying that the principles of war must be respected by the politicians who start wars as well as by the soldiers who fight them.

PRINCIPLES OF WAR: A HISTORICAL PERSPECTIVE

The principles of war: Objective, Offensive, Mass, Economy of Force, Maneuver, Unity of Command, Security, Surprise, Simplicity. Military officers first learn of these principles as lieutenants and seek to refine their understanding throughout their careers. They hold a place of importance in our doctrine-based force and serve as a "guiding light" to those who would seek success on the battlefield. To facilitate an understanding of these principles, I will briefly address three basic questions. 1) What constitutes a "principle?" 2) Where did they come from? 3) And, what is their significance to the warfighter today?

The principles of war are not expressed in neat algebraic formulas nor do they possess the same characteristics as the laws of nature and science. We teach that these principles should not be adhered to blindly and that each principle may apply directly to one situation and not at all to another. Many even argue that since war is an art and not a science, in the truest sense of the word, principles do not apply to war. But war is both art and science. "Science consists of knowing; art of doing." Regardless, "no art exists without certain fundamental truths, which can be derived from analysis, from logic, and from the successes and failures of those who have plied the art." The bottom line is this: a "principle" of war is, in practice, a guide to action concerning the application of combat power, rather than an unquestioned truth with universal application to every single military operation."

Antonine-Henri Jomini was probably the first individual whose writings led to the concept that a small set of principles could serve as a guide for the commander to succeed on the battlefield. Jomini wrote, "The fundamental principles upon which rest all good combinations of war have always existed, and to them all others should be referred for the purpose of arriving at their respective merits. These principles are unchangeable; they are independent of the arms employed, of times, and of places." Following WWI, the British adopted the first official list of principles of war, due greatly to the influence of J.F.C. Fuller, which included eight items: Maintenance of the Objective, Offensive Action, Surprise, Concentration, Economy of Force, Security, Mobility, and Co-Operation. In 1921, when the U.S. War Department listed principles of war in Training Regulation 10-5, eight of the nine principles listed were identical to those of British origin. However, between the years of 1928 and 1949, not a single definitive list of the principles of war appeared in any official U. S. Army doctrine manual. The list of nine principles that we currently use today did not appear in the U.S. Army Field Service Regulations until 1949.

It is also interesting to note that the principles of war are not the same throughout the major militaries of the world. The

U.S. military currently holds that there are nine principles, the French only three, and the British and Russian military, ten. These principles, even though there is a great degree of similarity in name, are different in definition and application across the board.

This historical perspective highlights several issues. First, the very concept that a certain limited number of "principles", by which warfare should be conducted in all situations and for all times, even exists and can be codified into nine, ten, or eleven principles has always been and still is under debate. Even if a set of "principles of war" do exist, their exact number, content, and definition is a second area of disagreement. Finally, history reveals that even in our own experience as a military, there has not been homogeneous thought about the concept or the content of the principles of war. Russell Glenn provides an excellent summary in his article, "No More Principles of War?" He states, "History reveals that the principles of war have frequently been the subject of long and often inspired debate; their character, number, and definition have changed repeatedly. They took their present form in U.S. Army doctrine only 49 years ago. On the one hand, this span is but a fraction of the years spent in their study. On the other, much has transpired since 1949. One may legitimately ask whether the principles as they stand could meet the needs of U.S. armed forces half a century from now." We, too, should consider the same question, but more specifically, will they meet the needs of the information-based warrior?

Revolution in Military Affairs

Exactly what is a Revolution in Military Affairs? In his article "Calvary to Computer, The Pattern of Military Revolutions", Andrew Krepinevich describes an RMA as "what occurs when the application of new technologies into a significant number of military systems combines with innovative operational concepts and organizational adaptation in a way that fundamentally alters the characteristics and conduct of conflict. It does so by producing a dramatic increase—often an order of magnitude or greater—in the combat potential and military effectiveness of armed forces." The key proponents of the current information-based RMA state that a combination of high-tech sensors, robust information systems, focused intelligence, stealth technologies, advanced C4, and precision weapons will enable the commander to "see and understand everything on a battlefield, and if you see the battlefield, you will win the war." Admiral William A. Owens, former Vice Chairman of the JCS, was one of the early advocates of the information-based RMA. He believed that if the U.S. armed forces could integrate its currently procured subsystems into a higher "systems-of-systems," it would be able to achieve and sustain "information dominance." By communicating this information rapidly throughout the forces they would be able to react with speed, precision, and accuracy that would produce a devastating effect upon the enemy and "propel the U.S. military to a qualitatively new order of military power." In relation to the principles of war, it is critically important to note that it is often the operational innovation, or doctrinal changes, that prove to be more important to the full development of the RMA than is the element of technology itself.

The Principles of War: A New Paradigm

Guiding principles are important to any organization for they form a paradigm that serves as the basis for the way in which its members think and act. In our doctrine-based military, the principles of war serve to form our paradigm concerning the art of war. We must choose our words and definitions carefully, for they convey to our soldiers what we hold to be true about our profession. If the information-based RMA has the potential to deliver on its promises, then we must begin to embrace it by reexamining the underlying elements of our doctrine, the principles of war. The following paragraphs will examine six of the principles which may be most effected by the emergence of information-based warfare.

MASS

The purpose of mass is to concentrate the effects of combat power at the place and time to achieve decisive results. The advent of the information-based RMA may cause us to think of the principle of mass in a significantly different manner.

Most will agree that the tactics used by the 8th Air Force in WWII, in which hundreds of B-17 bombers delivered thousands of tons of bombs on the factories and towns of Germany in the attempt to destroy one single target, is a thing of the past. Today, with the advent of high-tech weapons systems, soldiers no longer talk of massing forces, but of massing effects. It is no longer required to bring forces into the same geographical area to bring their effects to bear on the same target and, in fact, on the modern battlefield it may be dangerous as well.

Consider Colonel Phillip Meilinger's statement that "the result of the trend towards 'airshaft accuracy' in air war is a denigration in the importance of mass." He goes on to say that, in reality, what we have been seeking all along is not mass (any large amount or number) but density (mass per unit volume). It is a waste of resources to "over-destroy" the target, but neither do we want to have to come back again to finish the job another day. What we ultimately desire to achieve is the right effect on the right target at the right time. Mass has nothing to do with one F-117 Stealth Fighter delivering a precision-guided weapon down the airshaft of a telecommunications building with the resulting effect of destroying the main critical node contained in that building. That particular attack involved one airplane delivering one weapon, but had the same effect as hundreds of B-17s.

We should reconsider the concept of mass as used by Napoleon and WW II air campaign planners and refine our understanding of this principle for three reasons. First, precision guided weapons are expensive, and in the climate of reduced budgets we must be somewhat judicious in the employment of these weapons. In an attempt to destroy a peer competitor's information infrastructure, we may soon realize that the number of targets required to be hit could place a strain on the number of available weapons. That is not to mention the possibility of fighting a second major regional conflict within a short period of time, as our current military strategy requires. Second, if we are required to resort to physical destruction of information-based targets, they are likely to be located (or co-located) in urban areas that have a highly concentrated civilian population.

In this instance we will probably not be able to employ a large amount of non-precision firepower (traditional mass) because the American people will require that we avoid civilian casualties. Third, a significant factor of the information-based RMA will be speed with which wars are won or lost. If our objective is to bring strategic paralysis to our enemy before he has the chance to do the same to us, we must deliver the right weapon to the right target the first time. Logistical constraints will demand that we not bring more than we need, which may leave some targets uncovered, and we may not be given a second chance if peer competitor is equally successful at attacking us. We should begin to think in terms of "density," rather than "mass," as this word more fully exemplifies the concept of rapid precision strike that the US military will need to embrace as this information-based RMA unfolds.

Objective

The purpose of the objective is to direct every military operation toward a clearly defined, decisive, and attainable objective. Field Manual 100-5, Operations, published by the U.S. Army, states as its first sentence in the explanation of the principle of objective, "The ultimate military purpose of war is the destruction of the enemy's armed forces and will to fight." However, the information-based RMA, with its promise of the capability to render the enemy "strategically paralyzed" in a relatively short period of time focuses less on the enemy's armed forces and more on his leadership, C2, and infrastructure. In addition, the continuing improvements in sensors, the "sensor-to-shooter" information systems, and the accuracy of precision weapons means that in the future more of the enemy's forces will be seen and more of what is seen can be destroyed. John Orme states, "Once the (information-based) RMA power has demonstrated the ability to kill nearly all of what it sees, simply communicating to the enemy that 'we know where you are' may be enough to persuade them to surrender or withdraw." So, even though the principle of the objective will retain its importance, the information-based RMA may serve to refocus it away from the long standing concept of the destruction of the enemy's armed forces.

Another aspect to consider is time, that is, when in the course of a conflict should one consider the principle applicable? Traditionally, commanders have thought of the objective in predominantly physical terms, such as a ridgeline, an enemy force, or as a condition to be achieved, such as air superiority. This paradigm tells us the "objective" is achieved primarily by "force-on-force" and does not apply until hostilities are eminent. However, with the advent of the information-based RMA, the early struggle for information dominance may begin by simply inserting a computer virus into the enemy's C4I networks. This could occur days, weeks, or even months before the onset of forces being employed. Thus, commanders may now wish to consider their "objectives" much sooner than in the past, as well as thinking of this principle as much in "intangible", as well as tangible, ways.

Offensive

The purpose of an offensive action is to seize, retain, and exploit the initiative. Throughout the history of warfare theorists have sought to determine the stronger position in war, the offensive or the defensive. Traditionally, most have agreed with Clausewitz, "we must say that the defensive form of warfare is intrinsically stronger than the offensive." However, the information-based RMA will reinforce the principle of the offensive and possibly reverse this long-held axiom. It has always been clear to military commanders that you do not achieve victory in most conflicts without some offensive action. The offensive also allows the commander to maintain the initiative, forcing the enemy to react rather than act as he wishes, and denying him the opportunity to pursue his own objectives.

Maintaining and exploiting the initiative is all about attaining information dominance. The "fog of war," which serves to paralyze the commander and leads to inaction, is due primarily to a lack of information concerning his opponent. He is reluctant to act for fear of failure, but knows that he must do something or forfeit the initiative. The information-based RMA, by establishing information dominance, will serve to lift the "fog" for the commander relative to his opponent and make him more eager to act. Major Aresenio T. Gumahad states, "These future warriors will quickly outflank and outmaneuver an enemy with knowledge of its position and combat situation. With information age weapons at their disposal they will engage an enemy precisely and decisively." This confidence in the individual commander's ability to seize and maintain the initiative will provide a synergistic effect on the battlefield and serve to propel the "order of magnitude" effects this RMA will produce.

Also, the age old requirement for the offense to concentrate forces in order to break through the defence is greatly reduced under the information-based RMA. John Orme predicts, "With continued improvements in the range and accuracy of weaponry and the effectiveness of command and coordination, it will become increasingly possible for the offense to concentrate fire but not forces before the enemy, which may shift the eternal contest between offense and defence decisively in favour of the attacker." Another aspect which will favour the offensive is the speed in which an information-based RMA force will be able to act. Wars may no longer last months or even years. The requirement to establish information dominance early in a conflict may require a massive preemptive attack on the enemy's information infrastructure as well as his capability to retaliate in kind. One who waits too long may find himself unable to launch credible resistance very soon after hostilities breakout. These issues considered, the information-based RMA should cause us to examine the traditional balance between the offensive and the defensive roles of warfare.

Economy of Force

The purpose of the economy of force is to allocate minimum essential combat power to secondary objectives. At the heart of the current concept of economy of force is the need to preserve combat power for sustained and follow-on operations. This principle focuses one to think of a campaign primarily in a sequential nature in which several enabling objectives are achieved prior to ultimately arriving at the final goal. Lt Col

Frederick Strain, USAF, in his article "The New Joint Warfare" describes it this way, "Each phase establishes the requisite environment or conditions for the next operation. Developing campaign plans designed to "peel the onion" layer by layer to get to the centre of gravity is old thinking." The Gulf War demonstrated the capability to attack the enemy at all levels-strategic, operational, and tactical-simultaneously, in a brief period of time, and effectively "locked out" many of Saddam's options very early in the conflict. As the information-based RMA unfolds, warfare will become less sequential and more simultaneous, promoting the concept of parallel attack in future campaign operations.

The information-based RMA may require us to think differently about the concept of reserve forces also. The following comments by General Dennis Reimer, Chief of Staff of the US Army help to illustrate this point, "We talk now about situational awareness...if we can do that (achieve it) we can change the way we operate. If you go to Ft. Leavenworth they teach in terms of operations when there is uncertainty and risk you keep a large reserve. Generally, most of the Army students will tell you it's two (units) up and one (unit) back. That's the way it has been for a long time. But if you can take that risk out of there, you can get more of your combat systems in the fight." The primary reason to keep forces in reserve is to preserve combat power to be able to counter the unpredictable nature of the enemy. If information dominance renders the enemy significantly more predictable, the logic for a reserve force becomes less valid. The result is that the information-based RMA will allow JFCs to employ forces in a more simultaneous than sequential manner, as well as employing more of the force from the onset of hostilities.

Unity of Command

The purpose of unity of command is to ensure unity of effort under one responsible commander for every objective. Military units have traditionally been hierarchical organizations with the commander at the top and many successive layers to the bottom. In a hierarchy there are strictly defined lines of communication, known as "the chain of command," in which data and information go up and commands come back down. New data is routed to commanders, who assess its impact and then direct an organizational response. However, members of a hierarchy routinely act on incomplete information because they receive only the command and not the information underlying it. Therefore, subsequent decisions on the lower levels are likely to be made on incomplete or late data resulting in uninformed action.

Another characteristic of a hierarchy is that each successive level upward in the chain of command is likely to have a "bigger picture" of the battlefield than the last, thus rendering the commander the most capable individual in the unit to make decisions. However, consider the effect the information-based RMA will have on this hierarchical structure. What if the individual at the lower level was able to acquire the same "big picture" as the individual at the top? Before, the individual acted without question because all he received was a command without the underlying information, now this may no longer be true. Imagine, as well, the situation described by Major James K. Morningstar, "It is easy to envision brigade commanders having to fight the urge to bypass less experienced battalion and company commanders to guide platoon leaders at objectives via direct digital links." The information-based RMA will force our "chain of command" to function more like a network (in a pure network, all individuals are equal and autonomous, all possible lines of communication can be used, there is no leader, any individual can interact directly with any other individual, and all decisions are reached by consensus) resulting in a more flattened and responsive command structure. In this sense, the information-based RMA may challenge our current "hierarchical" concept of unity of command.

Surprise

The purpose of surprise is to strike the enemy at a time or place or in a manner for which it is unprepared. The principle of surprise will be defined in two entirely different ways depending on whether or not we are fighting a peer-competitor.

If we are engaging an adversary who has not mastered the information-based RMA, the principle of surprise could be an important aspect of the way we will employ force. Throughout the history of warfare the element of surprise has been the exception rather than the rule. Forces were seldom surprised because of their ability to understand the enemy and to plan for his most likely courses of action. However, by achieving information dominance early on in the conflict, we will be able to "see" and "engage" the enemy's forces, while denying him that same capability. This ability to "surprise at will" may cause the enemy to withdraw or surrender simply by communicating to him that "we know where you are." In this instance surprise may become the norm, rather than the exception, for an information-based RMA power.

Conversely, with the capability of a peer-competitor to employ surveillance technologies and rapidly communicate information to his forces, the ability to "surprise at will" will probably not be a realistic option. In this type of conflict the principle of surprise will be defined by two key elements: stealth and speed. "Stealth strengthens the attacker by restoring the prospects for surprise, perhaps close to the levels prevailing before the invention of radar, while accuracy radically diminishes the number of aircraft and tonnage of bombs needed to destroy a given set of targets." For example, in Operation DESERT STORM F-117 Stealth Fighters flew more than 1,250 sorties, attacking valuable strategic targets in downtown Baghdad, without losing a single aircraft. Additionally, the speed at which information-based RMA forces will be able to act will allow them to continually operate inside the enemy's decision cycle always leaving our opponent a step behind.

THE 10TH PRINCIPLE OF WAR: LEGITIMACY

Not only will the information-based RMA alter our understanding of the current nine principles of war, entirely new principles may become applicable, such as the "Principle of Legitimacy." The American people are a large part of the American way of war, but the current principles give no consideration to this important fact. Long ago, Clausewitz wrote that war was not only the business of the military and the government, but of the people, as well. More recently, the so-called Weinberger and Powell Doctrines urged that the U.S. military should not be employed unless they enjoyed the support of the American people. Several articles have been written over the years that proposed the principle of morale should be added to the current list of principles. The morale of the troops is a very important factor, but the principle of legitimacy is much more encompassing than the morale of the military alone. Legitimacy encompasses the morale of the nation, and perhaps that of the entire world. This information age we are currently experiencing is forever changing the way in which Americans view national and world events. Consider the impact of millions of people viewing the battlefield in real time from their living rooms every evening. According to Major A. J. Echevarria, "Images of war and peace—either real or contrived— (will be able to) decisively influence national will or public opinion before authorities confirm or repudiate their authenticity." CNN is now able to cover any conflict from the first deployment to the last shot fired, virtually as it unfolds. This trend will increase, as we are not far from the day when the war reporter will have the capability to transmit real-time video and audio feed directly from the battlefield.

Another aspect of the principle of legitimacy is the fact that the U.S. has shown reluctance to act unilaterally in recent years, not for lack of military capability, but for the political realities of favourable world opinion. Americans, historically isolationists, have always sought the "moral high ground" when it comes to using force. Precisely because we are now the world's only superpower, the U.S. will continue to seek coalition partners in order to avoid being labeled the "bully" of the free world.

We should have learned to heed the principle of legitimacy as a result of the Vietnam War. Our inability to properly address this important issue cost us dearly in that conflict. Military theory, historical perspective, and future realities make it clear that commanders should consider the impact of legitimacy just as importantly upon their future military operations as they considered mass, maneuver, and security in the past.

The information-based RMA, characterized by its ability to collect, digest, and distribute vast amounts of information, all at incredible speeds, promises to lift the "fog of war" and increase our military capability "orders of magnitude" above our peers. However, we should not forget that it is often the operational innovation, or doctrinal changes, that prove to be more important to the development of the RMA than is the technological element itself. In order to fully realize the potential of the information-based RMA we must challenge the paradigms we have formed concerning the "enduring bedrock" of our military doctrine, the nine principles of war. Commanders of tomorrow must think differently about the ways in which these principles govern and guide the employment of our "information warriors" of the future. We must constantly examine these principles and allow them to evolve along with the "advances in technology, adaptations by adversaries and potential adversaries, better understanding of military theory, and revisions in national strategy." The revolution of the information-based RMA has shown us the times have changed, so must the paradigm we hold of the principles of war.

THE TEXT OF THE ART OF WAR

LAYING PLANS

Sun-tzu said:

The art of war is of vital importance to the state. It is a matter df life and death, a road either to safety or to ruin. Hence under no circumstances can it be neglected.

The art of war is governed by five constant factors, all of which need to be taken into account. They are: the Moral Law; Heaven; Earth; the Commander; Method and discipline,

The Moral Law causes the people to be in complete accord with their ruler, so that they will follow him regardless of their lives, undismayed by any danger.

Heaven signifies night and day, coid and heat, times and seasons.

Earth comprises distances, great and small; danger and security: open ground and narrow passes; the chances of life and death.

The Commander stands for the virtues of wisdom, sincerity, benevolence, courage, and strictness.

By *Method and discipline* are to be understood the marshaling of the army in its proper subdivisions, tkte gradations of rank among the officers, the maintenance of roads by which supplies may reach the army, and the control of military expenditure.

These five factors should be familiar to every general. He who knows them will be victorious; he who knows them not will fail.

Therefore, when seeking to determine your military conditions, make ybur decisions on the basis of a comparison in this wise:

Which of the two sovereigns is imbued with the Moral Law?

Which of the two generals has the most ability?

With whom lie the advantages derived from Heaven and earth?

On which side is discipline most rigorously enforced?!

Which army is the stronger?

On which side are officers and men more highly trained?

In which army is there the most absolute certainty that merit will be properly rewarded and misdeeds summarily punished?

By means of these seven considerations I can forecast victory or defeat.... But remember: While heeding the profit of my counsel, avail yourself also of any helpful circumstances over and beyond the ordinary rules and modify your plans accordingly.

All warfare is based on deception. Hence, when able to attack, we must seem unable; when using our' forces, we must seem inactive; when we are near, we must make the enemy helieve we are far away; when far away, we must make him believe we are near. Hold out baits to entice the enemy. Feign disorder, and crush him. If he is secure at all points, be prepared for him. If he is in superior strength, evade him. If your opponent is of choleric temper, seek to irritate him. Pretend to be weak. that he may grow arrogant.

lf he is taking his ease, give him no rest. If his forces are united, separate them. Attack him where he is unprepared, appear where you are not expected.

ON WAGING WAR

When you engage in actual fighting, if victory is long in coming, the men's weapons will grow dull and their ardor will be dampened. If you lay siege to a town, you will exhaust your strength, and if the campaign is protracted, there sources of the state will not be equal to the strain. Never forget: -When your weapons are dulled, your ardor dampened, your strength exhausted, and your treasure spent, other chieftains will spring up to take advantage of your extremity. Then no man, however wise, will be able to avert the consequences that must ensue. Thus, though we have heard of stupid haste in war, cleverness has never been seen associated with long delays. In all history, there is no instance of a country having benefited from prolonged warfare. Only one who knows the disastrous effects of a long war can realize the supreme. importance of rapidity in bringing it to a close. It is only one who is thoroughly acquainted with the evils of war who can thoroughly understand the profitable way of carrying it on.

The skilful general does not raise a second levy, neither are his supply wagons loaded more than twice. Once war is declared, he will not waste precious time in waiting for reinforcements, nor will he turn his army back for fresh supplies, but crosses the enemy's frontier without delay. The value of time-that is, being a little ahead of your opponent-has counted for more than either numerical superiority or the nicest calculations with regard to commissariat.

In war, then, let your great object be victory, not lengthy campaigns. Thus it may be known that the leader of armies is the arbiter of the people's fate the man on whom it depends whether the nation shall be in peace or in peril.

THE SHEATHED SWORD

To fight and conquer in all your battles is not supreme excellence; supreme excellence consists in breaking the enemy's resistance without fighting. In the practical art of war, the best thing of all is to take the enemy's country whole and intact; to shatter and destroy it is not so good. So, too, it is better to capture an army entire than to destroy it, to capture a regiment, a detachment, or a company entire than to destroy them.

Thus the highest form of generalship is to balk the enemy's plans; the next best is to prevent the junction of the enemy's forces; the next in order is to attack the enemy's army in the field, and the worst policy of all is to besiege walled cities because preparation of mantlets, movable shelters and various implements of war will take up three whole months and the piling up of mounds over against the walls will take three months more. The general, unable to control his irritation, will launch his men to the assault like swarming ants, with the result that one third of his men are slain, while the town still remains untaken. Such are the disastrous effects of a siege.

The skilful leader subdues the enemy's troops without any fighting; he captures their cities without laying siege to them; he overthrows their kingdom without lengthy operations in the field. With his forces intact he disputes the mastery of the empire, and thus, without losing a man, his triumph is complete.

This is the method of attacking by stratagem of using the sheathed sword. It is the rule in war: If our forces are ten to the enemy's one, to surround him; if five to one, to attack him; if twice as numerous, to divide our army into two, one to meet the enemy in front, and one to fall upon his rear; if he replies to the frontal attack he may be crushed from behind; if to the reaward attack, he may be crushed in front.

If equally matched we can offer battle; if slightly inferior in numbers, we can avoid the enemy; if quite unequal in every way, we can flee from him. Though an obstinate fight may be made by a small force, in the end it must be captured by the larger force.

The general is the bulwark of the state: if the hulwark is strong at all points, the state will be strong. There are three ways in which a sovereign can bring misfortune upon his army: By commanding the army to advance or to retreat, being ignorant of the fact that it cannot obey. This is called hobbling the army. By attempting to govern an army in the same way as he administers a kingdom, being ignorant of the conditions that obtain in an army. This causes restlessness in the soldiers' minds. Humanity and justice are the principles on which to govern a state, but not an army; opportunism and flexibility, on the other hand, are militray rather than civic virtues.

He will win who knows when to fight and hen not to fight. He will win who knows how to handle both superior and inferior forces. He will win whose army is animated by the same spirit throughout all its ranks. He will win who, prepared himself, waits to take the enemy unprepared. He will win who has military capacity and is not interfered with by the sovereign. If you know the enemy and know yourself, you need not fear the result of a hundred battles. If you know yourself but not the enemy, for every victory gained you will also suffer a defeat. If you know neither the enemy nor yourself, you will succumb in every battle.

TACTICS

The good fighters of old first put themselves beyond the possibility of defeat, and then waited for an opportunity of defeating the enemy. To secure ourselves against defeat lies in our own hands, but the opportunity of defeating the enemy is provided by the enemy himself. Hence the saying: One may know how to conquer without being able to do it. Security against defeat implies defensive tactics; ability to defeat the enemy means taking the offensive. Standing on the defensive indicates insufficient strength; attacking, a superabundance of strength.

The general who is skilled in defence hides in the most secret recesses of the earth: he who is skilled in attack flashes forth from the topmost heights of heaven. Thus, on the one hand we have ability to protect ourselves; on the other to gain a victory that is complete To see victory only when it is within the ken of the common herd is not the acme of excellence. Nor is it the acme of excellence if you fight and conquer and the whole empire says, "Well done!" True excellence is to plan secretly, to move surreptitiously, to foil the enemy's intentions and balk his schemes, so that at last the day may be won without shedding a drop of blood......

What the ancients called a clever fighter is one who not only wins, but excels in winning with ease. But his victories bring him neither reputation for wisdom nor credit for courage. For inasmuch as they are gained over circumstances that have not come to light, the world at large knows nothing of them, and he therefore wins no reputation for wisdom; and inasmuch as the hostile state submits before there has been any bloodshed, he receives no credit for courage. He wins his battles by making no mistakes. Making no mistakes is what establishes the certainty of victory, for it means conquering an enemy that is already defeated.

Hence the skilful fighter puts himself into a position that makes defeat impossible and does not miss the moment for defeating the enemy. Thus it is that in war the victorious strategist only seeks battle after the victory has been won, whereas he who is destined to defeat first fights and afterward looks for victory. A victorious army opposed to a routed one is as a pound's weight placed in the scale against a single grain. The onrush of a conquering force is like the bursting of pent-up waters into a chasm a thousand fathoms deep. The consummate leader cultivates the Moral Law and strictly adheres to method and discipline; thus it is in his power to control success.

5

Application of the Principles in Time of War

The principles of the art of war are in themselves extremely simple and quite within the reach of sound common sense. Even though they require more special knowledge in tactics than in strategy, this knowledge is of such small scope, that it does not compare with any other subject in extent and variety. Extensive knowledge and deep learning are by no means necessary, nor are extraordinary intellectual faculties. If, in addition to experienced judgment, a special mental quality IS required, it would be, after all that has been said cunning or shrewdness. For a long time the contrary has been maintained, either because of false veneration for the subject or because of the vanity of the authors who have written about it. Unprejudiced reflection should convince us of this, and experience only makes this conviction stronger. As recently as the Revolutionary War we find many men who proved themselves able military leaders, yes, even military leaders of the first order, without having had any military education. In the case of Condé, Wallenstein, Suvorov, and a multitude of others it is very doubtful whether or not they had the advantage of such education.

The conduct of war itself is without doubt very difficult. But the difficulty is not that erudition and great genius are necessary to understand the basic principles of warfare. These principles are within the reach of any wellorganized mind, which is unprejudiced and not entirely unfamiliar with the subject. Even the application of these principles on maps or on paper presents no difficulty, and to have devised a good plan of operations is no great masterpiece. The great difficulty is this:

To Remain Faithful Throughout To The Principles We Have Laid Down For Ourselves.

To call attention to this difficulty is the purpose of these closing remarks, and to give Your Royal Highness a clear idea of it I consider the most important object of this essay. The conduct of war resembles the workings of an intricate machine with tremendous friction, so that combinations which are easily planned on paper can be executed only with great effort.

The free will and the mind of the military commander, therefore, find themselves constantly hampered, and one needs a remarkable strength of mind and soul to overcome this resistance. Many good ideas have perished because of this friction, and we must carry out more simply and moderately what under a more complicated form would have given greater results. It may be impossible to enumerate exhaustively the causes of this friction; but the main ones are as follows:

1. Generally we are not nearly as well acquainted with the position and measures of the enemy as we assume in our plan of operations. The minute we begin carrying out our decision, a thousand doubts arise about the dangers which might develop if we have been seriously mistaken in our plan. A feeling of uneasiness, which often takes hold of a person about to perform something great, will take possession of us, and from this uneasiness to indecision, and from there to half measures are small, scarcely discernible steps.
2. Not only are we uncertain about the strength of the enemy, but in addition rumor (i.e., all the news which we obtain from outposts, through spies, or by accident) exaggerates his size. The majority of people are timid by nature, and that is why they constantly exaggerate danger. All influences on the military leader, therefore, combine to give him a false impression of his opponent's strength, and from this arises a new source of indecision.

We cannot take this uncertainty too seriously, and it is important to be prepared for it from the beginning.

After we have thought out everything carefully in advance and have sought and found without prejudice the most plausible plan, we must not be ready to abandon it at the slightest provocation. On the contrary, we must be prepared to submit the reports which reach us to careful criticism, we must compare them with each other, and send out for more. In this way false reports are very often disproved immediately, and the first reports confirmed. In both cases we gain certainty and can make our decision accordingly. Should this certainty be lacking, we must tell ourselves that nothing is accomplished in warfare without daring; that the nature of war certainly does not let us see at all times where we are going; that what is probable will always be probable though at the moment it may not seem so; and finally, that we cannot be readily ruined by a single error, if we have made reasonable preparations.

3. Our uncertainty about the situation at a given moment is not limited to the conditions of the enemy only but of our own army as well. The latter can rarely be kept together to the extent that we are able to survey all its parts at any moment, and if we are inclined to uneasiness, new doubts will arise. We shall want to wait, and a delay of our whole plan will be the inevitable result.

   We must, therefore, be confident that the general measures we have adopted will produce the results we expect. Most important in this connection is the trust which we must have in our lieutenants. Consequently, it is important to choose men on whom we can rely and to put aside all other considerations. If we have made appropriate preparations, taking into account all possible misfortunes, so that we shall not be lost immediately if they occur, we must boldly advance into the shadows of uncertainty.

4. If we wage war with all our strength, our subordinate

commanders and even our troops (especially if they are not used to warfare) will frequently encounter difficulties which they declare insurmountable. They find the march too long, the fatigue too great, the provisions impossible. If we lend our ear to all these DIFFICULTIES, as Frederick II called them, we shall soon succumb completely, and instead of acting with force and determination, we shall be reduced to weakness and inactivity.

To resist all this we must have faith in our own insight and convictions. At the time this often has the appearance of stubbornness but in reality it is that strength of mind and character which is called firmness.

5. The results on which we count in warfare are never as precise as is imagined by someone who has not carefully observed a war and become used to it.

   Very often we miscalculate the march of a column by several hours, without being able to tell the cause of the delay. Often we encounter obstacles which were impossible to foresee. Often we intend to reach a certain place with our army and fall short of it by several hours. Often a small outpost which we have set up achieves much less than we expected, while an enemy outpost achieves much more. Often the resources of a region do not amount to as much as we expected, etc.

   We can triumph over such obstacles only with very great exertion, and to accomplish this the leader must show a severity bordering on cruelty. Only when he knows that everything possible is always being done, can he be sure that these small difficulties will not have a great influence on his operations. Only then can he be sure that he will not fall too far short of the aim which he could have reached.

6. We may be sure that an army will never be in the condition supposed by someone following its operations from an armchair. If he is sympathetic to the army he will imagine it from a third to a half stronger and better than it really is. It is quite natural that the military

commander will make the same mistake in planning his first operations. Consequently, he will see his army melt away as he never thought it would, and his cavalry and artillery become useless. What appeared possible and easy to the observer and to the commander at the opening of a campaign is often difficult and even impossible to carry out. If the military leader is filled with high ambition and if he pursues his aims with audacity and strength of will, he will reach them in spite of all obstacles; while an ordinary person would have found in the condition of his army a sufficient excuse for giving in.

Masséna proved at Genoa and in Portugal the influence of a strongwilled leader over his troops. At Genoa, the limitless exertion to which his strength of will, not to say his harshness, forced people, was crowned with success. In Portugal he at least retreated later than anyone else would have.

Most of the time the enemy army is in the same position. For example, Wallenstein and Gustavus Adolphus at Nuremberg, and Napoleon and Bennigsen after the battle of Eylau. But while we do not see the condition of the enemy, our own is right before our eyes. The latter, therefore, makes a greater impression on ordinary people than the first, since sensuous impressions are stronger for such people than the language of reason.

7. The provisioning of troops, no matter how it is done, whether through storehouses or requisitions, always presents such difficulty that it must have a decisive influence on the choice of operations. It is often contrary to the most effective combination, and forces us to search for provisions when we would like to pursue victory and brilliant success. This is the main cause for the unwieldiness of the whole war machine which keeps the results so far beneath the flight of our great plans.

A general, who with tyrannical authority demands of his troops the most extreme exertions and the greatest privations, and an army which in the course of long wars has become hardened to such sacrifices will have a tremendous advantage over their adversaries and will reach their aim much faster in spite of all obstacles. With equally good plans, what a difference of result!

8. We cannot stress the following too much: Visual impressions gained during actual combat are more vivid than those gained beforehand by mature reflection. But they give us only the outward appearance of things, which, as we know, rarely corresponds to their essence. We therefore run the risk of sacrificing mature reflection for first impression.

The natural timidity of humans, which sees only one side to everything, makes this first impression incline toward fear and exaggerated caution. Therefore we must fortify ourselves against this impression and have blind faith in the results of our own earlier reflections, in order to strengthen ourselves against the weakening impressions of the moment.

These difficulties, therefore, demand confidence and firmness of conviction. That is why the study of military history is so important, for it makes us see things as they are and as they function. The principles which we can learn from theoretical instruction are only suited to facilitate this study and to call our attention to the most important elements in the history of war. Your Royal Highness, therefore, must become acquainted with these principles in order to check them against the history of war, to see whether they are in agreement with it and to discover where they are corrected or even contradicted by the course of events. In addition, only the study of military history is capable of giving those who have no experience of their own a clear impression of what I have just called the friction of the whole machine.

Of course, we must not be satisfied with its main conclusions, and still less with the reasoning of historians, but we must penetrate as deeply as possible into the details. For the aim of historians rarely is to present the absolute truth. Usually they wish to embellish the deeds of their army or to demonstrate the concordance of events with their imaginary rules. They invent history instead of writing it. We need not study much history for the purpose we propose. The detailed knowledge of a few individual engagements is more useful than the general knowledge of a great many campaigns. It is therefore more useful to read detailed accounts and diaries than regular works of history. An example of such an account, which cannot be surpassed, is the description of the defence of Menin in 1794, in the memoirs of General von Scharnhorst. This narrative, especially the part which tells of the sortie and break through the enemy lines, gives Your Royal Highness an example of how to write military history. No battle in history has convinced me as much as this one that we must not despair of success in war until the last moment. It proves that the influence of good principles, which never manifests itself as often as we expect, can suddenly reappear, even under the most unfortunate circumstances, and when we have already given up hope of their influence.

A powerful emotion must stimulate the great ability of a military leader, whether it be ambition as in Caesar, hatred of the enemy as in Hannibal, or the pride in a glorious defeat, as in Frederick the Great. Open your heart to such emotion. Be audacious and cunning in your plans, firm and persevering in their execution, determined to find a glorious end, and fate will crown your youthful brow with a shining glory, which is the ornament of princes, and engrave your image in the hearts of your last descendants.

Principles Governing the Use of Troops

If we cannot dispense with firearms (and if we could, why should we bring them along?), we must use them to open combat. Cavalry must not be used before the enemy has suffered considerably from our infantry and artillery. From this it follows: That we must place the cavalry behind the infantry. That we must not be easily led to use it in opening combat. Only when the enemy's disorder or his rapid retreat offer the hope of success, should we use our cavalry for an audacious attack. Artillery fire is much more effective than that of infantry. A battery of eight sixpounders takes up less than onethird of the front taken up by an infantry battalion; it has less than oneeighth the men of a battalion, and yet its fire is two to three times as effective. On the other hand, artillery has the disadvantage of being less mobile than infantry. This is true, on the whole, even of the lightest horseartillery, for it cannot, like infantry, be used in any kind of terrain. It is necessary, therefore, to direct the artillery from the start against the most important points, since it cannot, like infantry, concentrate against these points as the battle progresses. A large battery of 20 to 30 pieces usually decides the battle for that section where it is placed. From these and other apparent characteristics the following rules can be drawn for the use of the different arms:

(a) We should begin combat with the larger part of our artillery. Only when we have large masses of troops at our disposal should we keep horse and footartillery in reserve. We should use artillery in great batteries massed against one point. Twenty to thirty pieces combined into one battery defend the chief part of our line, or shell that part of the enemy position which we plan to attack.

(b) After this we use light infantry either marksmen, riflemen, or fusileers being careful not to put too many forces into play at the beginning. We try first to discover what lies ahead of us (for we can seldom see that clearly in advance), and which way the battle is turning, etc.

If this firing line is sufficient to counteract the enemy's troops, and if there is no need to hurry, we should do wrong to hasten the use of our remaining forces. We must try to exhaust the enemy as much as possible with this preliminary skirmish.

(c) If the enemy should lead so many troops into combat that our firing line is about to fall back, or if for some other reason we should no longer hesitate, we must draw up a full line of infantry. This will deploy between 100 and 200 paces from the enemy and will fire or charge, as matters may be.

(d) This is the main purpose of the infantry. If, at the same time, the battle array is deep enough, leaving us another line of infantry (arranged in columns) as reserve, we shall be sufficiently master of the situation at this sector.

This second line of infantry should, if possible, be used only in columns to bring about a decision.

(e) The cavalry should be as close behind the fighting troops during battle as is possible without great loss; that is, it should be out of the enemy's grapeshot or musket fire. On the other hand, it should be close enough to take quick advantage of any favourable turn of battle.

In obeying these rules more or less closely, we should never lose sight of the following principle, which I cannot stress enough: Never bring all our forces into play haphazardly and at one time, thereby losing all means of directing the battle; but fatigue the opponent, if possible, with few forces and conserve a decisive mass for the critical moment. Once this decisive mass has been thrown in, it must be used with the greatest audacity.

We should establish one battleorder (the arrangement of troops before and during combat) for the whole campaign or the whole war. This order will serve in all cases when there is no time for a special disposition of troops. It should, therefore, be calculated primarily for the defensive.

This battle array will introduce a certain uniformity into the fightingmethod of the army, which will be useful and advantageous. For it is inevitable that a large part of the lower generals and other officers at the head of small contingents have no special knowledge of tactics and perhaps no outstanding aptitude for the conduct of war.

The army consists of several such independent corps, which have their own general and staff. They are drawn up in line and behind each other, as described in the general rules for combat. It should be observed at this point that, unless we are very weak in cavalry, we should create a special cavalry reserve, which, of course, is kept in the rear. Its purpose is as follows:

(a) To fall upon the enemy when he is retreating from the field of battle and to attack the cavalry which he uses to cover up his retreat. Should we defeat the enemy's cavalry at this moment, great successes are inevitable, unless the enemy's infantry would perform miracles of bravery. Small detachments of cavalry would not accomplish this purpose.

(b) To pursue the enemy more rapidly, if he should be retreating unbeaten or if he should continue to retreat the day after a lost battle. Cavalry moves faster than infantry and has a more demoralizing effect on the retreating troops. Next to victory, the act of pursuit is most important in war.

(c) To execute a great (strategic) turning move, should we need, because of the detour, a branch of the army which moves more rapidly than the infantry.

In order to make this corps more independent, we should attach a considerable mass of horse artillery; for a combination of several types of arms can only give greater strength. The battleorder of troops described thus far was intended for combat; it was the formation of troops for battle. The order of march is essentially as follows: Each independent corps (whether brigade or division) has its own advancedand rearguard and forms its own column. That, however, does not prevent several corps from marching one behind the other on the same road, and thus, as it were, forming a single column. The corps march according to their position in the general formation of battle. They march beside or behind each other, just as they would stand on the battlefield. In the corps themselves the following order is invariably observed: the light infantry, with the addition of one regiment of cavalry, forming the advanced and rearguard, then the infantry, the artillery, and last the remaining cavalry.

This order stands, whether we are moving against the enemyin which case it is the natural order or parallel with him. In the latter case we should assume that those troops which in the battle formation were behind each other should march side by side. But when we have to draw up the troops for battle, there will always be sufficient time to move the cavalry and the second line of infantry either to the right or left.

Principles for the Use of Terrain

The terrain (the ground or country) offers two advantages in warfare. The first is that it presents obstacles to the enemy's approach. These either make his advance impossible at a given point, or force him to march more slowly and to maintain his formation in columns, etc. The second advantage is that obstacles in the terrain enable us to place our troops under cover.

Although both advantages are very important, I think the second more important than the first. In any event, it is certain that we profit from it more frequently, since in most cases even the simplest terrain permits us to place ourselves more or less under cover. Formerly only the first of these advantages was known and the second was rarely used. But today the greater mobility of all armies has led us to use the former less frequently, and therefore the latter more frequently. The first of these two advantages is useful for defence alone, the second for both offense and defence. The terrain as an obstacle to approach serves chiefly to support our flank, and to strengthen our front. To support our flank it must be absolutely impassable, such as a large river, a lake, an impenetrable morass. These obstacles, however, are very rare, and a complete protection of our flank is, therefore, hard to find. It is rarer today than ever before, since we do not stay in one position very long, but move about a great deal. Consequently we need more positions in the theatre of war. An obstacle to approach which is not wholly impassable is really no point d'appui for our flank, but only a reinforcement. In that case troops must be drawn up behind it, and for them in turn it becomes an obstacle to approach.

All kinds of terrain, which cannot be passed by troops marching in line, all villages, all enclosures surrounded by hedges or ditches, marshy meadows, finally all mountains which are crossed only with difficulty, constitute obstacles of this kind. We can pass them, but only slowly and with effort. They increase, therefore, the power of resistance of troops drawn up behind them. Forests are to be included only if they are thickly wooded and marshy. An ordinary timberforest can be passed as easily as a plain. But we must not overlook the fact that a forest may hide the enemy. If we conceal ourselves in it, this disadvantage affects both sides. But it is very dangerous, and thus a grave mistake, to leave forests on our front or flank unoccupied, unless the forest can be traversed only by a few paths. Barricades built as obstacles are of little help, since they can easily be removed.

From all this it follows that we should use such obstacles on one flank to put up a relatively strong resistance with few troops, while executing our planned offensive on the other flank. It is very advantageous to combine the use of entrenchments with such natural obstacles, because then, if the enemy should pass the obstacle, the fire from these entrenchments will protect our weak troops against too great superiority and sudden rout.

When we are defending ourselves, any obstacle on our front is of great value. Mountains are occupied only for this reason. For an elevated position seldom has any important influence, often none at all, on the effectiveness of arms. But if we stand on a height, the enemy, in order to approach us, must climb laboriously. He will advance but slowly, become separated, and arrive with his forces exhausted. Given equal bravery and strength, these advantages may be decisive. On no account should we overlook the moral effect of a rapid, running assault. It hardens the advancing soldier against danger, while the stationary soldier loses his presence of mind. It is, therefore, always very advantageous to put our first line of infantry and artillery upon a mountain.

Often the grade of the mountain is so steep, or its slope so undulating and uneven, that it cannot be effectively swept by gunfire. In that case we should not place our first line, but at the most only our sharpshooters, at the edge of the mountain. Our full line we should place in such a way that the enemy is subject to its most effective fire the moment he reaches the top and reassembles his forces. All other obstacles to approach, such as small rivers, brooks, ravines, etc., serve to break the enemy's front. He will have to reform his lines after passing them and thus will be delayed. These obstacles must, therefore, be placed under our most effective fire, which is grapeshot (400 to 600 paces), if we have a great deal of artillery or musketshot (150 to 200 paces), if we have little artillery at this point.

It is, therefore, a basic law to place all obstacles to approach, which are to strengthen our front, under our most effective fire.

But it is important to notice that we must never completely limit our resistance to this fire but must hold ready for a bayonetcharge an important part of our troops (1/3 to 1/2) organized into columns. Should we be very weak, therefore, we must place only our firingline, composed of riflemen and artillery, close enough to keep the obstacle under fire. The rest of our troops, organized into columns, we should keep 600 to 800 paces back, if possible under cover. Another method of using these obstacles to protect our front is to leave them a short distance ahead. They are thus within the effective range of our cannon (1000 to 2000 paces) and we can attack the enemy's columns from all sides, as they emerge. (Something like this was done by Duke Ferdinand at Minden. In this way the obstacle contributes to our plan of active defence, and this active defence, of which we spoke earlier, will be executed on our front.

Thus far we have considered the obstacles of the ground and country primarily as connected lines related to extended positions. It is still necessary to say something about isolated points. On the whole we can defend single, isolated points only by entrenchments or strong obstacles of terrain. We shall not discuss the first here. The only obstacles of terrain which can be held by themselves are:

(a) *Isolated, steep heights:* Here entrenchments are likewise indispensable; for the enemy can always move against the defender with a more or less extended front. And the latter will always end up by being taken from the rear, since one is rarely strong enough to make front towards all sides.

(b) *Defiles:* By this term we mean any narrow path, through which the enemy can advance only against one point. Bridges, dams, and steep ravines belong here.

We should observe that these obstacles fall into two categories: either the aggressor can in no way avoid them, as for example bridges across large rivers, in which case the defender can boldly draw up his whole force so as to fire upon the point of crossing as effectively as possible. Or we are not absolutely sure that the enemy can not turn the obstacle, as with bridges across small streams and most mountain defiles. In that case it is necessary to reserve a considerable part of our troops 1/3 to 1/2 for an attack in close order.

(c) *Localities, villages, small towns, etc. :* With very brave troops, who fight enthusiastically, houses offer a unique defence for few against many. But, if we are not sure of the individual soldier, it is preferable to occupy the houses, gardens, etc., only with sharpshooters and the entrances to the village with cannons. The greater part of our troops (1/2 to 3/4) we should keep in close columns and hidden in the locality or behind it, so as to fall upon the enemy while he is invading.

These isolated posts serve in large operations partly as outposts, in which case they serve not as absolute defence but only as a delay to the enemy, and partly to hold points which are important for the combinations we have planned for our army. Also it is often necessary to hold on to a remote point in order to gain time for the development of active measures of defence which we may have planned. But, if a point is remote, it is ipso facto isolated. Two more observations about isolated obstacles are necessary. The first is that we must keep troops ready behind them to receive detachments that have been thrown back. The second is that whoever includes such isolated obstacles in his defensive combinations should never count on them too much, no matter how strong the obstacle may be. On the other hand, the military leader to whom the defence of the obstacle has been entrusted must always try to hold out, even under the most adverse circumstances. For this there is needed a spirit of determination and selfsacrifice, which finds its source only in ambition and enthusiasm. We must, therefore, choose men for this mission who are not lacking in these noble qualities.

Using terrain to cover the disposition and advance of troops needs no detailed exposition. We should not occupy the crest of the mountain which we intend to defend (as has been done so frequently in the past) but draw up behind it. We should not take our position in front of a forest, but inside or behind it; the latter only if we are able to survey the forest or thicket. We should keep our troops in columns, so as to find cover more easily. We must make use of villages, small thickets, and rolling terrain to hide our troops. For our advance we should choose the most intersected country, etc. In cultivated country, which can be reconnoitered so easily, there is almost no region that can not hide a large part of the defender's troops if they have made clever use of obstacles. To cover the aggressor's advance is more difficult, since he must follow the roads.

It goes without saying that in using the terrain to hide our troops, we must never lose sight of the goal and combinations we have set for ourselves. Above all things we should not break up our battleorder completely, even though we may deviate slightly from it.

If we recapitulate what has been said about terrain, the following appears most important for the defender, i.e., for the choice of positions:

(a) Support of one or both flanks.

(b) Open view on front and flanks.

(c) Obstacles to approach on the front.

(d) Masked disposition of troops. And finally

(e) Intersected country in the rear, to render pursuit more difficult in case of defeat. But no defiles too near (as at Friedland), since they cause delay and confusion.

It would be pedantic to believe that all these advantages could be found in any position we may take up during a war. Not all positions are of equal importance: the most important are those in which we most likely may be attacked. It is here that we should try to have all these advantages, while in others we only need part. The two main points which the aggressor should consider in regard to the choice of terrain are not to select too difficult a terrain for the attack, but on the other hand to advance, if possible, through a terrain in which the enemy can least survey our force. I close these observations with a principle which is of highest significance, and which must be considered the keystone of the whole defensive theory:

Never to depend completely on the strength of the terrain and consequently never to be enticed into passive defence by a strong terrain.

For if the terrain is really so strong that the aggressor cannot possibly expel us, he will turn it, which is always possible, and thus render the strongest terrain useless. We shall be forced into battle under very different circumstances, and in a completely different terrain, and we might as well not have included the first terrain in our plans. But if the terrain is not so strong, and if an attack within its confines is still possible, its advantages can never make up for the disadvantages of passive defence. All obstacles are useful, therefore, only for partial defence, in order that we may put up a relatively strong resistance with few troops and gain time for the offensive, through which we try to win a real victory elsewhere.

STRATEGY

This term means the combination of individual engagements to attain the goal of the campaign or war. If we know how to fight and how to win, little more knowledge is needed. For it is easy to combine fortunate results. It is merely a matter of experienced judgment and does not depend on special knowledge, as does the direction of battle. The few principles, therefore, which come up in this connection, and which depend primarily on the condition of the respective states and armies, can in their essential parts be very briefly summarized:

General Principles

Warfare has three main objects:

(a) To conquer and destroy the armed power of the enemy;

(b) To take possession of his material and other sources of strength, and

(c) To gain public opinion.

To accomplish the first purpose, we should always direct our principal operation against the main body of the enemy army or at least against an important portion of his forces. For only after defeating these can we pursue the other two objects successfully. In order to seize the enemy's material forces we should direct our operations against the places where most of these resources are concentrated: principal cities, storehouses, and large fortresses. On the way to these objectives we shall encounter the enemy's main force or at least a considerable part of it. Public opinion is won through great victories and the occupation of the enemy's capital. The first and most important rule to observe in order to accomplish these purposes, is to use our entire forces with the utmost energy. Any moderation shown would leave us short of our aim. Even with everything in our favour, we should be unwise not to make the greatest effort in order to make the result perfectly certain. For such effort can never produce negative results. Suppose the country suffers greatly from this, no lasting disadvantage will arise; for the greater the effort, the sooner the suffering will cease.

The moral impression created by these actions is of infinite importance. They make everyone confident of success, which is the best means for suddenly raising the nation's morale. The second rule is to concentrate our power as much as possible against that section where the chief blows are to be delivered and to incur disadvantages elsewhere, so that our chances of success may increase at the decisive point. This will compensate for all other disadvantages. The third rule is never to waste time. Unless important advantages are to be gained from hesitation, it is necessary to set to work at once. By this speed a hundred enemy measures are nipped in the bud, and public opinion is won most rapidly.

Surprise plays a much greater role in strategy than in tactics. It is the most important element of victory. Napoleon, Frederick II, Gustavus Adolphus, Caesar, Hannibal, and Alexander owe the brightest rays of their fame to their swiftness. Finally, the fourth rule is to follow up our successes with the utmost energy. Only pursuit of the beaten enemy gives the fruits of victory. The first of these rules serves as a basis for the other three. If we have observed it, we can be as daring as possible with the last three, and yet not risk our all. For it provides us with the means of constantly creating new forces in our rear, and with fresh forces any misfortune can be remedied. Therein lies the caution which deserves to be called wise, and not in taking each step forward with timidity. Small states cannot wage wars of conquest in our times. But in defensive warfare even the means of small states are infinitely great. I am, therefore, firmly convinced that if we spare no effort to reappear again and again with new masses of troops, if we use all possible means of preparation and keep our forces concentrated at the main point, and if we, thus prepared, pursue a great aim with determination and energy, we have done all that can be done on a large scale for the strategic direction of the war. And unless we are very unfortunate in battle we are bound to be victorious to the same extent that our opponent lags behind in effort and energy.

In observing these principles little depends on the form in which the operations are carried out. I shall try, nevertheless, to make clear in a few words the most important aspects of this question. In tactics we always seek to envelop that part of the enemy against which we direct our main attack. We do this partly because our forces are more effective in a concentric than in a parallel attack, and further because we can only thus cut off the enemy from his line of retreat.

But if we apply this to the whole theatre of war (and consequently to the enemy's lines of communication), the individual columns and armies, which are to envelop the enemy, are in most cases too far away from each other to participate in one and the same engagement. The opponent will find himself in the middle and will be able to turn against the corps one by one and defeat them all with a single army. Frederick II's campaigns may serve as examples, especially those of 1757 and 1758. The individual engagement, therefore, remains the principal decisive event. Consequently, if we attack concentrically without having decisive superiority, we shall lose in battle all the advantages, which we expected from our enveloping attack on the enemy. For an attack on the lines of communication takes effect only very slowly, while victory on the field of battle bears fruit immediately.

In strategy, therefore, the side that is surrounded by the enemy is better off than the side which surrounds its opponent, especially with equal or even weaker forces. Colonel Jomini was right in this, and if Mr. von Bülow has demonstrated the opposite with so much semblance of truth, it is only because he attributed too great an importance to the interruption of provisions and carelessly and completely denied the inevitable success of battle.

To cut the enemy's line of retreat, however, strategic envelopment or a turning movement is very effective. But we can achieve this, if necessary, through tactical envelopment. A strategic move is, therefore, advisable only if we are so superior (physically and morally) that we shall be strong enough at the principal point to dispense with the detached corps. The Emperor Napoleon never engaged in strategic envelopment, although he was often, indeed almost always, both physically and morally superior.

Frederick II used it only once, in 1757, in his invasion of Bohemia. To be sure, the result was that the Austrians could not give battle until Prague, and what good was the conquest of Bohemia as far as Prague without a decisive victory? The battle of Kolin forced him to give up all this territory again, which proves that battles decide everything. At the same time he was obviously in danger at Prague of being attacked by the whole Austrian force, before Schwerin arrived. He would not have run this risk had he passed through Saxony with all his forces. In that case the first battle would have been fought perhaps near Budin, on the Eger, and it would have been as decisive as that of Prague. The dislocation of the Prussian army during the winter in Silesia and Saxony undoubtedly caused this concentric maneuver. It is important to notice that circumstances of this kind are generally more influential than the advantages to be gained by the form of attack. For facility of operations increases their speed, and the friction inherent in the tremendous warmachine of an armed power is so great in itself that it should not be increased unnecessarily.

Moreover, the principle of concentrating our forces as much as possible on the main point diverts us from the idea of strategic envelopment and the deployment of our forces follows automatically. I was right, therefore, in saying that the form of this deployment is of little consequence. There is, however, one case in which a strategic move against the enemy's flank will lead to great successes similar to those of a battle: if in a poor country the enemy has accumulated with great effort stores of supplies, on whose preservation his operations absolutely depend. In this case it may be advisable not to march our main forces against those of the enemy, but to attack his base of supply. For this, however, two conditions are essential:

(a) The enemy must be so far from his base that our threat will force him into a considerable retreat, and

(b) We must be able to obstruct his advance in the direction followed by his principal force with only a few troops (thanks to natural and artificial obstacles), so that he cannot make conquests somewhere else which will compensate for the loss of his base.

The provisioning of troops is a necessary condition of warfare and thus has great influence on the operations, especially since it permits only a limited concentration of troops and since it helps to determine the theatre of war through the choice of a line of operations.

The provisioning of troops is carried on, if a region possibly permits it, through requisitions at the expense of the region. In the modern method of war armies take up considerably more territory than before. The creation of distinct, independent corps has made this possible, without putting ourselves at a disadvantage before an adversary who follows the old method of concentration at a single point (with from 70,000 to 100,000 men). For an independent corps, organized as they now are, can withstand for some time an enemy two or three times its superior. Then the others will arrive and, even if the first corps has already been beaten, it has not fought in vain, as we have had occasion to remark.

Today, therefore, the divisions and corps move into battle independently, marching side by side or behind each other and only close enough to take part in the same battle, if they belong to the same army.

This makes possible immediate provisioning without storehouses. The very organization of the corps with their General Staff and their Commissariat facilitates this. If there are no MORE decisive motives (as for example the location of the enemy's main army), we choose the most fertile provinces for our operations; for facility of provisioning increases the speed of our actions. Only the situation of the enemy's main force which we are seeking out, only the location of his capital and the place of arms which we wish to conquer are more important than provisioning. All other considerations, such as the advantageous disposition of our forces, of which we have already spoken, are as a rule much less important. In spite of these new methods of provisioning, it is quite impossible to do without any depots whatever. Therefore, even when the resources of the region are quite sufficient, a wise military leader does not fail to establish depots in his rear for unexpected emergencies and in order to be able to concentrate his forces at certain points. This precaution is of the sort which are not taken at the expense of the final goal.

Defensive

Politically speaking defensive war is a war which we wage for our independence. Strategically it is the kind of campaign in which we limit ourselves to fighting the enemy in a theatre of war which we have prepared for this purpose. Whether the battles which we wage in this theatre of war are offensive or defensive, makes no difference. We adopt a strategic defensive mainly when the enemy is superior. Fortresses and entrenched camps, which constitute the chief preparations for a theatre of war, afford, of course, great advantages, to which may be added the knowledge of the terrain and the possession of good maps. A smaller army, or an army which is based on a smaller state and more limited resources, will be better able to withstand the enemy WITH these advantages than without them.

In addition there are the following two reasons which can lead us to choose a defensive war.

First, when the regions surrounding the theatre of war render operations extremely difficult because of lack of provisions. In this case we avoid a disadvantage which the enemy is forced to undergo. This is the case now (1812) with the Russian army. Second, when the enemy is superior in warfare. In a theatre of war which we have prepared, which we know, and in which all minor conditions are in our favour, war is easier to conduct, and we commit fewer mistakes. When lack of trust in our troops and generals forces us to wage defensive war, we often like to combine tactical with strategic defensive. In that case we fight battles in prepared positions because we are thus again exposed to fewer mistakes. In defensive just as in offensive warfare, it is necessary to pursue a great aim: the destruction of the enemy army, either by battle or by rendering its subsistence extremely difficult. Thus we shall disorganize it and force it into a retreat, during which it will necessarily suffer great losses. Wellington's campaign in 1810 and 1811 is a good example.

Defensive warfare, therefore, does not consist of waiting idly for things to happen. We must wait only if it brings us visible and decisive advantages. That calm before the storm, when the aggressor is gathering new forces for a great blow, is most dangerous for the defender.

If the Austrians after the battle of Aspern had increased their forces threefold, as they might have and as the Emperor Napoleon did, then and only then would they have made good use of the lull which lasted until the battle of Wagram. This they did not do, and consequently the time was lost. It would have been wiser to profit from Napoleon's disadvantageous position, and to gather the fruits of the battle of Aspern. The purpose of fortifications is to keep a considerable part of the enemy's army occupied as siege troops, to give us an opportunity to defeat the rest of his army. Consequently, it is best to fight our battles behind our fortifications and not in front of them. But we must not stand by idly, while they are being conquered, as Bennigsen did during the siege of Danzig.

Large rivers, across which it is difficult to throw a bridge (such as the Danube below Vienna and the Lower Rhine), offer a natural line of defence. But we should not distribute our forces evenly along the river bank in order to prevent any crossing whatsoever. That would be most dangerous. On the contrary, we should watch the river and fall upon the enemy from all sides the minute he crosses, while he has not yet reassembled his forces and is still restricted to a narrow space on the river bank. The battle of Aspern offers a good illustration. At Wagram the Austrians had yielded to the French too much territory without the slightest necessity, so that the disadvantages inherent in a river crossing had disappeared.

Mountains are the second obstacle which offers a good line of defence. There are two ways of using them. The first is to leave them in front of us, occupying them only with light troops and considering them, so to speak, a river which the enemy will have to cross. As soon as his separated columns emerge from the passes, we fall upon one of them with all our force. The second is to occupy the mountains ourselves. In that case we must defend each pass with just a small corps and keep an important part of the army (1/31/2) in reserve, in order to attack with superior forces one of the enemy columns that succeed in breaking through. We must not divide up this large reserve to prevent completely the penetration of any enemy columns, but must plan from the outset to fall only upon those columns which we suppose to be the strongest. If we thus defeat an important part of the attacking army, any other columns which have succeeded in breaking through will withdraw of their own accord.

In the midst of most mountain formations we find more or less elevated plains (plateaus) whose slopes are cut by ravines serving as means of access. Mountains, therefore, offer the defender a region in which he can move rapidly to the right or left, while the columns of the aggressor remain separated by steep, inaccessible ridges. Only mountains of this kind are well adapted for defensive warfare. If, on the other hand, their whole interior is rough and inaccessible, leaving the defender dispersed and divided, their defence by the bulk of the army is a dangerous undertaking. For under these circumstances all advantages are on the side of the aggressor, who can attack certain points with great superiority, and no pass, no isolated point is so strong that it cannot be taken within a day by superior forces. In regard to mountain warfare in general, we should observe that everything depends on the skill of our subordinate officers and still more on the morale of our soldiers. Here it is not a question of skilful manoeuvring, but of warlike spirit and wholehearted devotion to the cause; for each man is left more or less to act independently. That is why national militias are especially suited for mountain warfare. While they lack the ability to maneuver, they possess the other qualities to the highest degree.

Finally, it should be observed that the strategic defensive, though it is stronger than the offensive, should serve only to win the first important successes. If these are won and peace does not follow immediately, we can gain further successes only through the offensive. For if we remain continually on the defensive, we run the great risk of always waging war at our own expense. This no state can endure indefinitely. If it submits to the blows of its adversary without ever striking back, it will very likely become exhausted and succumb. We must begin, therefore, using the defensive, so as to end more successfully by the offensive.

Offensive

The strategic offensive pursues the aim of the war directly, aiming straight at the destruction of the enemy's forces, while the strategic defensive seeks to reach this purpose indirectly. The principles of the offensive are therefore already contained in the "General Principles" of strategy. Only two points need be mentioned more fully. The first is constant replacement of troops and arms. This is easier for the defender, because of the proximity of his sources of supply. The aggressor, although he controls in most cases a larger state, must usually gather his forces from a distance and therefore with great difficulty. Lest he find himself short of effectives, he must organize the recruiting of troops and the transport of arms a long time before they are needed. The roads of our lines of operation must be covered constantly with transports of soldiers and supplies. We must establish military stations along these roads to hasten this rapid transport.

Even under the most favourable circumstances and with greatest moral and physical superiority, the aggressor should foresee a possibility of great disaster. He therefore must organize on his lines of operation strong points to which he can retreat with a defeated army. Such are fortresses with fortified camps or simply fortified camps. Large rivers offer the best means of halting the pursuing enemy for a while. We must therefore secure our crossing by means of bridgeheads, surrounded by a number of strong redoubts. We must leave behind us a number of troops for the occupation of these strong points as well as the occupation of the most important cities and fortresses. Their number depends on how much we have to be afraid of invasions or of the attitude of the inhabitants. These troops, together with reinforcements, form new corps, which, in case of success, follow the advancing army, but in case of misfortune, occupy the fortified points in order to secure our retreat.

Napoleon always took great care with these measures for the protection of the rear of his army, and therefore, in his most audacious operations, risked less than was usually apparent.

6

Napoleon's Strategy and Tactics of War

"Read over and over again the campaigns of Alexander, Hannibal, Caesar, Gustavus, Turenne, and Frederic the Great. This is the only way to become a great general... "-*Napoleon Bonaparte*

Napoleon, "this once despotic sovereign of the battlefield, in whose presence but few generals ventured to maneuver, striving only to ward off his blows... "-*Mikhailovskii-Danilevskii*

INTRODUCTION.

"Why,in this age of nuclear weapons and guided missiles should the student of military affairs be concerned with the campaigns of Napoleon?"-*Col.John Elting,US Army*

Napoleon's greatness as a commander and leader was evident virtually from the start of his remarkable career. Victory followed upon victory for over a decade. Success in the field, and in supporting the right political faction at the right moment, brought him a generalship at 24 and command of the Army of Italy at 26.

Of the French Republic's 13 field armies, the Army in Italy was the most neglected. It was in horrible condition when Bonaparte arrived. Bonaparte's army lacked sufficient cavalry and artillery and his infantry was weakened by detachments sent to guard the coast against British and Sardinian navies. The French soldiers were chronically unpaid and short of everything: uniforms, shoes, greatcoats, bayonets, ammunition etc. etc. They kept themselves alive by plundering the countryside. In Italy the outlook for France seemed desperate. With Bonaparte's arrival everything changed. General Sir Archibald P. Wavell writes, "If you discover how... [Bonaparte] inspired a ragged, mutinous, half-starved army and made it fight as it did, how he dominated and controlled generals older and more experienced than himself, then you will have learnt something."

Young Bonaparte's campaign in Italy was a masterpiece. "In a fortnight he was ready for the field and made his first move. Five days later he had already 4 times defeated the Austrians. Then he turned upon the Sardinians, who in another 5 days were in helpless retreat on Turin."------Wilkinson, Spenser-"The French army before Napoleon; *lectures delivered before the University of Oxford" p 9-10*

From 1796, when he assumed his first independent military command, until 1809, Napoleon displayed an astonishing near-invincibility in battle and an equally astounding ability to use that battlefield success to compel his enemies to grant him his political objectives. A dazzled Clausewitz (famous military historian and military theorist) had good reason to call Napoleon the "god of war."

Yet if Napoleon's genius was obvious, his method was not. Nor was he particularly helpful in the matter. Napoleon committed to paper neither the principles that guided his conduct of operations nor the techniques that he employed to implement those principles. "As a result, even before his ambitions led him to ultimate destiny, military commentators undertook the difficult task of explaining his ways of war." (-*Albert Nofi*)

Although Napoleon played a major role in the history and development of the military art he was no great innovator as a soldier. In developing his art of war, he modified and applied the ideas he found in the writings of 18th-century military theorists and commanders.

"He distrusted novel ideas, disbanding the balloon companies inherited from the armies of the Revolution and rejecting Roger Fulton's offer of submarines (ext. link) and naval mines. His genius was essentially practical, and his military concepts evolved from the close study of earlier commanders, particularly Frederick the Great. He made the fullest use of the ideas of his predecessors and breathed life into them." (*David Chandler-"Dictionary of the Napoleonic wars" p 18*)

According to English military historian, L Petre, Napoleon's genius was not that of a creator. Indeed, he made few practical reforms or innovations in the military art. His talents lay elsewhere, in the strategic and administrative areas of war. Napoleon had the ability to visualize with great clarity the military situation confronting him and to determine the most profitable course of action. He could conceive the most remarkably bold undertakings, and then execute them, making full use of the considerable abilities of the reformed French army. He developed an aggressive strategic style based largely on de Bourcet's proposals. And he used the Republic as a model in his ability to tap the ultimate resources of France, frequently stamping whole new armies out of the ground in the face if disaster. Thus Napoleon's genius lay in the fact that he saw the ways in which all of the innovations of the late 18th century could be orchestrated into a virtually invincible military system.

Napoleon is credited with being great tactician and a military genius. His campaigns formed the basic of military education throughout the western world. (By "western world" I mean western and central Europe, Australia, and northern America). A lot of the military thinking is still influenced by the great Frenchman. In military academies around the World, including the famous West Point, USA, students were taught French language so that they might be able to read books on Napoleon's strategy and tactics. Majority of European and American Civil War generals copied the methods of Napoleon with various success. Even in the years of defeat Napoleon proved a resorceful, imaginative, and unpredictable commander. "His enemies could not match his skills nor those of his armies. Their victories were due more to overwhelming numbers than to the talents of their generals." (*-Loraine Petre*)

For example:

- in 1813 at Leipzig, 250,000-350,000 Allies troops (Russians, Austrians, Prussians and Swedes) commanded by Schwarzenberg, Barclay de Tolly, Bennigsen, Bernadotte and Blucher, defeated Napoleon with 175,000-200,000 troops.
- in 1814 at La Rothiere, 50,000-55,000 Allies troops (Russians, Austrians, and Germans) under Blucher and Barclay de Tolly defeated Napoleon with 40,000-45,000 troops.
- in 1815 at Waterloo, 100,000-120,000 Allies troops (68,000 Wellington's British, German, and Netherland troops and 32,000-52,000 Blucher's Prussians) defeated Napoleon with 70,000-75,000 men.
- Few, if any, commanders, before or since, fought more wars and battles under more varied conditions of weather, terrain, and climate, and against a greater variety of enemies than the French Emperor.
- campaign in the snow covered, vast plains of Russia (summer, fall, and winter)
- campaigns in central and western Europe (Germany, France, Poland)
- campaigns in the desert-like Egypt and Syria
- campaigns in mountainous Italy and Spain

Enemies:

- Austrians (regulars and landwehr)
- Prussians (regulars and landwehr)
- Piedmontese and Sardinians (regulars)
- Swedes and Brits (land forces and navies)
- Spaniards and Portuguese (regulars and guerillas)
- Russians (regulars and Cossacks, Bashkirs, Kalmuks)
- French royalists

Napoleon's understanding of mass warfare and his success in raising, organizing, and equipping mass armies revolutionized the conduct of war and marked the origin of modern warfare.

John Elting, however, ask why in this age of nuclear weapons and guided missiles, should the student of military affairs be concerned with the campaigns of Napoleon ?

"A simple answer would be: for historical or professional background. But there are more compelling reasons.... Gigantic operations of huge forces, such as were undertaken on World War II, are no longer feasible. Dispersion of forces and logistical facilities is essential to avoid appalling casualties and massive destruction.... Over-all success in military ground operations will be dependent upon the aggregate of the individual tactical successes and failures of basic units, operating virtually independently. Such basic units must be of moderate size, highly mobile, compact and powerful armed, self-sustaining, and bravely led-precisely the attributes that characterized a typical Napoleonic force....

It matters not whether tactical nuclear weapons would or would not be used; the mere threat posed by their existence dictates a corresponding reorganization of forces and modification of tactics. There is no assurance that Napoleon's advice would not be taken literally; "It is principle of war that when thunderbolts are available, they should be used in place of cannon."... The conduct of war is an art based on ageless fundamental concepts that have remained valid irrespective of the prevailling means and methods of warfare....

The Emperor did not imply that one must seek to memorize all the details of the campaigns of great captains of past wars. No two battles or campaigns have ever been exactly the same. Many fluctuating factors exert their influences; weather and terrain conditions tactics, weapons, transportation facilities, training, morale, and leadership. The specific nature of all these factors is pertinent in a military study, but the subject of paramount importance is the skill with which the leader wielded the means available and exploited the victory, or, conversely, how through ineptitude, poor judgement, or other deficiencies he lost opportunities or suffered defeat."

In the 16th and 17th century and for much of 18th as well the conduct of war was rather formal and stylized. Limited war for limited objectives was the rule. It was the sport of the kings, carefully calculated undertaking designed to secure relatively modest gains at minimal cost. Armies acquired lengthy and clumsy logistical trains.

The art of fortifications rose to remarkable level, resulting in the proliferation of fortified places for defence and for the protection of the vulnerable lines of supply, and in the necessity of dragging heavy siege guns about. Armies themselves became more skilled, necessitating long years of meticulous and expensive training and maintenance. The net result was the tempo at which was conducted slowed. Bold strategic strokes were unusual. Sieges became the norm. "Washington, Marlborough, Prince Eugene, Prussia's Frederick the Great, and Marshal Saxe all knew how to fight a battle when necessary. But even these unusually able commanders did so relatively rarely." (*-Loraine Petre*)

The age that immediately followed Frederick the Great chose to imitate his caution rather than his aim.Military theory was characterized by ideas of victory without battle, manoeuvring for position, a system of lines and angles of operation. Cunning tricks and artifices replaced the aim to destroy enemies. Great emphasis was put on terrain and the occupation of key geographic points. During the French Revolution armies grew rapidly in size. This necessitated dividing the army first into divisions and later into corps. Although the French corps varied in size, they all shared one thing: each was a balanced, all-arm force of infantry, cavalry, artillery, engineers and staff. It was in fact a self-reliant miniature army able to take on much stronger enemy for a limited time.

The rigid line formations of well-trained but few troops firing volleys gave way to infantry fighting in fast moving battalion columns and skirmish lines. Napoleon took advantage of these developments to pursue a "strategy of annihilation" that cared little for the mathematical perfection of the geometric strategy. He invariably sought to achieve decision in battle, with the sole aim of utterly destroying his opponent. Napoleon used as little force as possible against non-critical objectives. "There are in Europe many good generals," he declared in 1797, "but they see too many things at once. I see only one thing, namely the enemy's main body. I try to crush it, confident that secondary matters will then settle themselves." According to David Chandler here lies the central theme, of Napoleon's concept of warfare.

In order to concentrate superior combat strength in one place, economy of force must be exercised in other places. Economy of force requires the acceptance of prudent risks in selected areas to achieve superiority at the point of decision. One account has it that Napoleon allowed a subordinate to draw up a plan for the disposition of his troops. Not knowing what the Emperor wanted, the subordinate distributed the forces equally in neat little groups along the border. On seeing it Napolean remarked "Very pretty, but what do you expect them to do? Collect customs duties?". :-)

Napoleon's staff.

The staff provided the administrative and logistical support, that he found necessary to make his army operate over long distances and in little known parts of Europe. His army was able to operate across the continent with great easy and speed. A Ministry of War handled the "civil" functions of the army, such as conscription, pay, and record keeping. Napoleon himself headed *Grand-Quartier-General*, which actually supervised the army. Under him was his personal staff, *La Maison*, which included an operational headquarters, a traveling cabinet of France, and the Bureau Topographique, his intelligence and planning staff. The two principal subordinate agencies of *G-Q-G* were the General Commissariat of Army Stores, which supervised all types of supply, and General Headquarters of the Army, under Marshal Berthier.

Berthier directed the "General Staff", which had several distinct sections and departments, each dealing with a well defined area of responsibility, such as troop movements and intelligence, personnel and records, and legal affairs, plus special staffs for each arm of service.

The staff of Napoleon's army provided the administrative, logistical and communications support that Napoleon found necessary to make his army operate over long distances and in little known territories. Napoleon's army was able to operate across Europe with great easy and speed. For example in 1796 Napoleon's army dropped out of the clouds of Switzerland, passed through terrain thought impassable for an army, to strike and destroy the enemy in Italy. In 1805 Napoleon's army flew across northern France at speeds unimaginable to the rest of Europe's army commanders. In 1814 Napoleon's found enemy scattered armies along the road to Paris, with none of them being within supporting distance of any other. This led Napoleon's four stunning victories at Champaubert, Montmirail, Chatteu Thierry and Vauchamps.

The staff consisted of several "divisions":

1st-handled troop movements, orders of the day, correspondence, etc.

2nd-supply, police, hospitals and headquarters administration

3rd-recruiting, prisoners of war, deserters, and military justice

4th-supervising the army's lengthening line of communications

5th-reconnaissance, correspondence with fortress commanders etc.

In 1812 the chief of staff had 9 aides, a General Staff with 5 generals, 11 adjutants and 50 supporting officers. There were also geographical engineers and cartographers, 19 officers of military administration, war commissioners, inspectors of reviews, and artillery staff.

The professionalism of Napoleon's staff shortly before the battle of Austerlitz contrasted sharply with the confusion prevailing in the Russian and Austrian staffs. Napoleon had produced a plan of battle well in advance and his staff had issued written orders the evening before, in the Russian and Austrian headquarters the plan had not been completed until the night of DEcember 1st and "the column commanders had only learned of the details after midnight. "Under such circumstances, confusion was inevitable." (*Goetz-"1805: Austerlitz" pp 120-121*)

Napoleon's staff organization was quite efficient, but had certain limitations, the principal ones being Napoleon and Berthier themselves. Having worked so long together, the two became incapable of working efficiently with anyone else. Napoleon had but utter a few words for Berthier to comprehend his meaning and frame pages of clear, accurate orders. No one could do that.

In effect, Napoleon's staff organization was a personal staff, rather than a genuine general staff. A further problem was that Napoleon's staff tended to grow, for he was not merely running his army, but all the other armies of France and the government as well. Nevertheless, the French example was far superior to any other in Europe and began to be adopted rather widely, by many other countries. In Prussia certain refinements were introduced, increasing specialization and laying the foundations fore the evolution of modern military staff.

"Like Frederick the Great, Napoleon was sovereign, commander-in-chief, and chief-of-staff; his subordinates viewed strategy as the emperor's domain. Pride and jealousy among the corps commanders also hindered the coordination of French forces, particularly in Iberia and Russia. Although hundreds or even thousands of miles from the area of operations, the emperor had to issue detailed orders and instructions to his subordinates. Napoleon's inability to grasp the concept of a competent General Staff system contributed to the eventual breakdown of the French command structure. This defficency became acute when the number of forces and theaters of war multiplied between 1808 and 1813." (*Leggiere-"Napoleon and Berlin" p 12*)

"Napoleon was, as both Emperor and Commander in Chief, responsible to no one, called no councils of war and was able, on the basis of a general plan of operations, to direct campaigns as well as issue orders for specific engagements. His headquarters was, therefore, geared entirely to Napoleon personally-not to the commander, regardless of who that might be." (*Riley-"Napoleon as a general" p 25*)

Five principles guiding the development of his plans. Before every campaign Napoleon considered all possible options. The Emperor wrote, "There is no man more pusillanimous than I when I am planning a campaign. I purposely exaggerate all the dangers and all the calamities that the circumstances make possible. I am in a thoroughly painful state of agitation. This does not keep me from looking quite serene in front of my entourage; I am like an unmarried girl laboring with child."

In the months and weeks before operations actually commenced he would begin to collect information. In addition to reading an enormous number and variety of books bearing on the enemy and the theatre of war, he studied the copious volumes of intelligence reports forwarded by the agents that he had scattered throughout Europe. He would pursue works of polirical history, accounts of the state of roads and bridges, reportss on the politicians and generals, and even studied local patterns of food stockpiling and distribution.

Napoleon's 5 principles to guide the development of his plans designed to hasten the attainment of victory :

The primary objective is the destruction of the enemy's armies or the main army. That done, any remaining problems could be easily solved.

If the enemy did not want to risk a battle, they might be forced to do so by a threat to their capital city.

All forces must concentrate on the task of attaining the objective.

Operations must be designed to surprise and confuse the enemy.

Always, he sought to seize and keep the initiative, to impose his will on the enemy.

Every effort must be made to render the enemy helpless through the severance of his lines of supply, communications, and retreat. His favourite movement was to envelop one of the enemy's army's flanks and threaten its rear and communications, forcing it either to retire hurriedly or to turn and fight at a disadvantage.

The security of French forces must be guarded to prevent surprise.

Rapidity of movements.

"Travelling light."

Napoleon's army was know for fast marching.

George Nafziger writes, "In the 17th and 18th centuries the military had evolved a supply system based on the amassing of supplies in magazines and fortifications augmented by purchases from civilian contractors who followed in the wake of every army. These supply systems were rudimentary at best, and it was not possible for any army to sustain itself at any distance from its magazines. This restriction led to a system of military operations that were carefully planned, long in advance, and supported by the accumulation of military supplies for months prior to the actual inception of the campaign.... The wars of this period were like the jousting of turtles and seldom penetrated far into the country of either nation involved. These wars were primarily wars of maneuver where one army attempted to establish itself in the enemy's territory in a strong position.... These wars resulted in a continual squabbling over border provinces that exchanged hands every few years.

When the French Revolution erupted, the French military establishment found itself undergoing a major revolution itself. The logistical administration and its supply system rapidly decayed, proving incapable of providing the logistical support required by the newly raised French armies. As a result, the French armies were frequently on the verge of starvation.... By necessity they found themselves forced to fend for themselves, as their government had proven incapable of providing for them. What began initially as the simple pillaging of the countryside by starving soldiers rapidly evolved into a systematic requisitioning and amassing of supplies in a given area....

The French quickly became expert at estimating the ability of an area to support an army and developed skills in locating supplies in areas where other armies would have quickly starved if forced to live off the land. These skills had permitted the

French to execute the massive maneuvers that gave them smashing victories in 1800, 1805, 1806, and 1809.

It also led to the mystique that the French army could outmarch every other army in Europe. The ablity to maneuver strategically had been seriously handicapped for years by the necessity to provide a wagon train for supplies.... The French, lacking this military train and having the ability to live off the land they were traversing, were able to march as fast as their soldiers' legs could carry them, instead of at the pace of the oxen pulling the wagons." (*Nafziger-"Napoleon's Invasion of Russia." pp 83-85, 1998*)

The system of living off the land worked well, but it had its limitations.

It could only work efficiently where the local resources were extensive.

In prosperous countries large armies could be supported.

But in inpoverished regions, a large army would starve. When foraging using Napoleon's methods, an army of 100,000 men with 250 guns and

40,000 horses could be sustained in an area of about:

-65 miles across in France, Germany, Netherlands, (northern) Italy

-105 miles in Spain and Poland

-102 miles in Russia

The French troops were unable to live off the land in 1812 in Russia.

Russia was described by many westerners as a "wasteland" with poor roads, few cities, and long distances. Napoleon was forced to reorganize and expand his military train and supply system. Supplies were stockpiled all along the Vistula and Odra rivers. The munitions Napoleon gathered together for his 1812 campaign compare favorably with the efforts of the heavily industralized nations during the First World War.

Napoleon used to say, "Strategy is the art of making use of time and space.

I am less concerned about the later than the former. Space we can recover, lost time never."

March or die was the napoleonic formula-and it did not appeal to the young soldiers. No one was allowed to lag behind and in 1813 special NCO detachments knew how to make the "lame" walk. Most often Napoleon pushed on with the attack, maintaining a constant element of surprise. He used to say: "I have destroyed the enemy merely by marches."

The fast marching army gave Napoleon the advantage of selecting one or another part of enemy line and forcing the enemy to time consuming regrouping and sometimes causing temporary disorder in his ranks. He believed always in the attack, speed, maneuver and surprise.

Napoleons troops travelled light.

They marched 15-50 km a day without any cumbersome baggage trains as they lived off the land. Napoleon writes, "The strength of an army, like the power in mechanics, is estimated by multiplying the mass by the rapidity; a rapid march augments the morale of an army, and increases its means of victory, Press on !"

Napoleon wrote to Murat "The best marchers should be able to do 25-30 miles a day." (In 1812 Roguet's division had covered a distance of 465 miles by wagon and over 700 on foot !)

Paul Britten Austin described how the French marched during the invasion of Russia, "Each division sets out after the one ahead of it at 2-day intervals. With a distance of 100 paces (70 m) between battalions, its regiments march "in two files sharing the road whose crown they leave free.' Halting for '5 minutes in every hour and at three-quarters of the day's march for half an hour' and with a day's rest every fifth, they tramp on northwards at an everage speed of 25 miles a day. Every second day they pick up rations, provided along the route by Count Daru's administration." (*Austin-"1812: The March on Moscow" pp 27-28*)

The old-fashioned attitudes of Allies' officers also contributed to the slowness with which their armies moved. "In the middle of the century the aristocratic officer had always maintained a lifestyle in the field that was consonant with his social position. This meant transporting large amounts of gear such as tents, and even porcelain, accompanied by the necessary servants to look after them.

The Duke of Cumberland, for example, travelled around with 145 tons of baggage.

This was not looked on as showing off, but rather as necessary for a man of high position, and to do otherwise would have brought contempt rather than admiration. While everybody else did the same thing, it had little effect on the army's performance, but once the enemy started to do things differently, it had grave consequences, as an Austrian noted: *Almost every day our army loses half a march to the French. Their soldiers carry the same load as our men, but what an effort it takes us to get under way ! The French officer accompanies his troops on foot, and if necessary he carries his pack himself. In our army on the other hand, every company had a whole tail of carts just to transport the officers' baggage. If possible, these gentlemen would like to bring along warm stoves and arm-chairs as well.*

The slowness with which the army moved was probably also a consequence of slow decision-making on the part of the commanders... Bonaparte himself provides an illustration of their bewilderment with an anecdote concerning the early part of his 1796 campaign. It is taken from his memoirs, which were written in the third person:

Napoleon, in his nightly rounds, encountered a bivouac of prisoners, where there was a garrulous old Hungarian officer, whom he asked how matters went on with them. The old captain could not deny that they went on very badly. 'But' he added, 'there is no understanding it at all. We have to do with a young general who is in this moment before us, then again behind us, then again on our flanks-one does not know where to place oneself. This manner of making war is insufferable and violates all usage and custom'.

This was rather like the cry of a gentleman who had gone to fight a duel in the proper ritualised fashion, and found an opponent who insisted on firing before he was told to, and his behind trees to make a more difficult target. Unfortunately, in this case there was no umpire." (*Boycott-Brown-"The Road to Rivoli"*) In 1805, one Austrian general informed Marshal Murat, Napoleon's cavalry commander, that his troops desperately needed a rest, and therefore requested him not to advance on Vienna too rapidly. :-)

With the exception of the Light Division (in 1812 they covered 62 miles in 26 hours), the British army was also considered as one of the slow armies in Europe. John Mills of British Regiment of Coldstream Guards wrote: "Their (French) movements compared with ours are as mail coaches to dung carts. In all weathers and at all times the French are accustomed to march, when our men would fall sick by hundreds..."

In the very end of the battle of Waterloo, Wellington and Blucher decided together that the Prussians alone would continue the pursuit. This decision is usually explained by citing the exhausted condition of Wellington's infantry, but Blucher's were surely no less tired. More likely the choice reflected the plodding management and slowness of movement that characterized British troops.

In the beginning of the 1815-Campaign the Prussians got 3/4 of their men to the right place at the right time, Wellington only miserable 1/3 of his total forces. Prussian officer Müffling asked Wellington why the British advance so slowly and Wellington explained: "Do not press me on this, for I tell you, it cannot be done. If you knew the composition of the British Army and its habits better, then you would not talk to me about that. I cannot leave my tents and supplies behind. I have to keep my men together in their camp and supply them well to keep order and discipline." [-*Peter Hofscshroer*]

The Spaniards reproached the British for the tardiness of their marches. French General Thiebault writes that the scattered state of the French army in Spain rendered its situation desperate, and that the slowness of Sir Arthur Wellesley saved it several times. The French troops were known for their skills of extracting provisions locally-much to the annoyance of local population.

Gates writes: "In contrast, the Allies, particularly the British, seem to have been peculiarly inept at surviving without plenty of supplies. Even in times of minor food shortages, indiscipline erupted on a vast scale. The British divisions went to pieces in the lean days after Talavera for example-and as late as the Waterloo campaign of 1815, we find Wellington commenting to his Prussian friends that 'I cannot separate from my tents and supplies. My troops must be well kept and well supplied in camp..."

Wellington: "It is certainly astonishing that the enemy [French] have been able to remain in this country so long; and it is extraordinary instance of what a French army can do.... With all our money and having in our favour the good inclinations of the country, I assure you that I could not maintain one division in the district in which they have maintained not less than 60,000 men and 20,000 animals for more than two months."

Certainly, seeing the French army on the march seems to have been an unique experience. In 1805 (Ulm-Austerlitz Campaign) a French officer with the Bavarian corps attached to the French army, described its progress:

Ulm taken and negligently occupied, the army of Bonaparte, the victorious army, was disbanded, and appeared to me no longer anything but an army in rout; but in rout in advance instead of retreat. This torrent took the direction of Vienna, and henceforth there was nothing but an 'arrive qui peut' by roads full and encumbered. Our German corps alone marched like regular troops.

This impression of organised chaos is confirmed by the recollections of a pastor who saw in Germany advancing to attack in 1796. Compared to the Austrian army, he said: *One did not see so many wagons or so much baggage, such elegant cavalry, or any infantry officers or horseback below the rank of major. Everything about these Frenchmen was supple and light-movements, clothing, arms, and baggage.*

The lack of conventional discipline and order, indeed the army's general scruffiness and air of destitution, seems to have led its enemies (especially the Prussians and Austrians) seriously to underestimate its fighting potential.

Napoleon concentrated his troops before battle as no other general before and after him.

He wrote, "Gustavus Adolphus, Turenne, and Frederick, as well as Alexander, Hannibal, and Caesar, have all acted upon the same principles. These have been-to keep their forces united..." It was Napoleon's method that when several corps begin an aggressive action they should concentrate at a place away from the enemy to prevent the opposing army from destroying the approaching armies piecemeal. Speed of maneuver and speed of concentration were crucial components of victory.

Napoleon's favourite strategies:

- strategy of the central position
- strategy of indirect approach

"To make the utmost use of the superior mobility and inspiration of his armies, he developed two major strategic systems. When facing a foe superior in numbers, the strategy of the central position was employed to split the enemy into separate parts, each of which could then be eliminated in turn by adroit manoeuvring to gain the French a local superiority of force in successive actions by bringing the reserve into action at the critical time and place....

Conversely, when the enemy was inferior to the French, Napoleon would often employ a maneuver of envelopment-pinning the foe's attention with a detachment while the bulk of the army swept against the hostile lines of communications to sever the enemy's links with his bases.... On occasion, Napoleon would merge features of these two classic strategies." (*Chandler-"Dictionary of the Napoleonic Wars" p 19*)

Napoleon had two favorites strategies: strategy of indirect approach and strategy of the central position. He often used the two strategies interchangeably. In 1805, for example, he used the indirect approach to place himself in the central position between the Austrian and Russian armies.

In 1806 he did it again. In 1813 he took advantage of his central position in Germany to undertake a series of indirect approaches, though his victories at Lutzen and Bautzen were by no means as decisive as he had hoped. To be truly decisive, a victory had to result not merely in the defeat of the enemy, but also in pusruing him *a outrance* to total destruction. This desirable goal was but rarely achieved operationally.

In Italy in March and April of 1797 he managed to chase the Austrians almost all the way back to Vienna, and in 1806, in the 23 days following his victory at Jena, the French army totally overran Prussia against triffling resistance. A few weeks more and the French were knocking at the gates of Warsaw !

Allied strategy in the long wars pales beside that of Napoleon. The bulk of his adversaries were able, but unspectacular. Wellington of Britain and Archduke Charles of Austria were the exceptions. The best strategy most of Napoleon's enemies could come up was to shove armies in his direction. Indeed, given endless manpower, this strategy of the concentric advance-advancing armies from all directions-ultimately led to Napoleon's defeat in 1813 and again in 1814. His enemies grew wary. The more often he defeated them, the more they learned how to avoid these defeats. The Allies had confidence in the concentric advance, for Napoleon might win some battles, but he could not be everywhere at once, and they would surely win the last battle.

STRATEGY OF INDIRECT APPROACH

It was used when he had plenty of manpower and manoeuvring room. It was more sophisticated and more dangerous than Strategy of the Central Position. Essentially it entailed a vast turning movement in the face of the enemy. One of two army corps would be detached to pin the attention of the enemy to his front. Meanwhile, Napoleon would take the bulk of his army on a swift, wide march around one of the enemy's strategic flanks, behind a thick screen of cavalry, optimally with some sunstantial geographic feature providing a "curtain of maneuver." As he advanced toward the enemy's rear, he would trust a corps or two and some cavalry forward to prevent reinforcements from coming up, and then fall upon the enemy from the rear, having severed his lines of communication and retreat. It was this strategy which brought about the smashing victories of Ulm in 1805, Jena in 1806, and Friedland in 1807. There was a great risk in this strategy. Only bold execution, swift movement, and aggressive use of the pinning forces and the cavalry could make it work. If the enemy gained any notion of what was afoot, as in 1807 when the Russians intercepted an order revealing Napoleon's intentions before Eylau, he might slip away, or even attack the relatively vulnerable and separated marching columns.

Strategy of the Central Position

It was used in situations where his armies were weaker than its enemy, but the latter was dispersed in two widely separated concentrations, such as during the opening phases of the campaign of 1809 in Austria and in 1815 in Belgium, and with remarkable brilliance in the face of overwhelming odds in 1814, culminating in the tripple victories of Champaubert, Montmirail, and Vauchamps. This strategy necessitated bold leadership, careful timing, and aggressive movement, for it required the army to get between the enemey concentrations, thereby preventing them from uniting. By movong swiftly into the central position, Napoleon could concentrate the bulk of his forces against the more threatening enemy contingent and seek a decisive battle, while a corps or two undertook to hold off the other enemy contingent as long as possible. Things could go wrong, of course. The enemy could discern his intentions and withdrew, as occured in April 1809 in the war with Austria, or the pursuit after battle might be poorly handled (for example after the Battle of Ligny 1815), allowing a defeated contingent to march to support of its comrades, both of which occured in 1815.

The Napoleonic campaigns were a series of wars involving France and changing sets of European allies and opposing coalitions that ran from 1790s to 1815. Some of the campaigns were truly brilliant. Our favorites are the Austerlitz and the Jena campaigns.

The Italian Campaign 1796

"As he himself once said, it was not genius that suggested what he should do, but reflection. His skill at thinking through the scenarios... "*-Martin Boycott-Brown*

"Italy was a secondary theatre, locked in a defensive strategy at the time Napoleon assumed command. His-strategy clearly was to divide the Piedmontese Army from their Austrian senior partners. Initially, his campaign against the Piedmontese was unsuccessful and wasteful. His frontal assaults at Ceva were futile. This is not the Napoleon of legend; the aggressiveness is there, but not the tactical finesse. Italy was Napoleon's "on-the-job training." He did not spring, fully developed, into the great military mind that history holds him. But the seeds of military genius are present in this campaign. He was eventually able to neutralize the Piedmont Army by a threatened movement against Turin. His subsequent campaigns against the Austrian Army in Italy further honed his strategic and tactical skills." (*-David Gibson*)

By maintenance of the initiative, rapidity of maneuver and concentration of superior forces at the right moment and the right place, he defeated in Italy every army thrown at him. According to British historian Liddell Hart "For a century the first (Napoleon's) campaign in Italy has been described-I am almost tempted to say, sung-as a triumphant epic of offensive movements, according to which Bonaparte conquered Italy so easily because he followed up attack with attack, with a boldness that was equal to his good luck."

According to American historians Vincent Esposito and John Elting, Bonaparte's Italian campaign revolutionized the prevaling deliberate, chessboard concepts of the art of war. Luck not favored Bonaparte, the weather had clogged his operations, and the carelessness of his generals and poor supplies invited disaster. Bonaparte's instinct for war had met every challenge !" At the end of the campaign, Bonaparte's first year of independent command (!), he stood less than 100 miles from Vienna, the Austrian capital. He forced the Austrians to a truce and then a peace, captured 160,000 prisoners of war,

170 flags and more than 2,000 guns, and extorted untold millions of francs in contributions. Within next months Bonaparte had defeated 7 armies. It was astounding success.

"By any measure, his achievements during that year (1796) had been absolutely extraordinary. At its beginning, the French had been easily perched on the edge of the Liguarian mountains, and their previous commander had been talking of a retreat into Provence. Now they were masters of the whole of northern Italy, having defeated Piedmont in the space of a few days, driven and harried the Austrians for several hundred miles, and turned back four attempts to relieve Mantua.

Every hostile power in Italy, including Naples and the Papal States, had been reduced to grudging, sometimes humuliating acquiesnence.

How had Bonaparte done it ?

It was a question that a writer, Antoine Arnault, asked Bonaparte himself when he met him in Italy: *With few exceptions, he said, it is the most numerous troops that victory is assured. The art of war therefore consists in finding oneself with superior numbers at the point where one wishes to fight. Is your army less numerous than that of the enemy ? Do not leave the enemy time to unite his forces: surprise him in his movements, and moving rapidly on the various corps which you have had the art to isolate, arrange your movements in such a way that you can oppose your whole army to army divisions in every encounter. It is in this way that with an army half the strength of that of the enemy you will always be stronger than he on the foeld of battle. It is in this way that I successively annihilated the armies of Beaulieu, Wurmser, Alvinczy and Prince Charles.*

It sounds simple, but of course if it had been simple, everyone would have done it. Bonaparte's remarkable achievemnt was to put the theories he had learned from books into practice. The factors that made this possible were many. His incontestable superiority as a strategist was partly based on a profound knowledge of the georgraphy and military history of the campaign area. Using this knowledge, he was able to analyse a military situation, calculate speeds and timings of marches, and exploit his formidable power to envisage and assess all the possible scenarios he might be faced with. As he himself once said, it was not genius that suggested what he should do, but reflection. His skill at thinking through the scenarios..."

In the two centuries since it took place, the 1796-7 campaign has been largelrly overshadowed by the later triumphs of Austerlitz and Jena, not to mention the glitter of the Napoleonic Empire. In part, this may be because there were by then many people who were conscious that Napoleon was moulding the history of Europe, and were keen to record their involvement in the process, giving us an abundance of familiar accounts....

But were Austrelitz and Jena really greater achievements than Montenotte, the crossing of the Po, or Rivoli ? This must be a matter of opinion, of course, but it is worth pointing out that in 1805 and 1806 Napoleon had various advantages that he did not have in 1796-7. For one thing, he controlled French policy and diplomacy and could call on the resources of the whole country. Moreover, he was more experienced commander, and had an army that was much better prepared." (*Boycott-Brown-"The Road to Rivoli"*)

THE ULM-AUSTERLITZ CAMPAIGN 1805

Napoleon's decision to hurl upon the enemy his army was taken at once. It was executed with unparalleled rapidity and exactness.

In 1805, Great Britain, Austria, Sweden, and Russia formed the Third Coalition to overthrow the French. When Bavaria sided with France, the Austrians, 80,000 strong under General Mack, prematurely invaded while the Russians under Kutuzov were still marching through Poland. Bavarian force, 21,500 men under General Deroi, barely escaped. Napoleon's decision to hurl upon the enemy his army was taken at once. It was executed with unparalleled rapidity and exactness and in no time Napoleon had 180,000 men facing the Austrians. Five French cavalry divisions under Murat, crossed the Black Forest to deceive the Austrians and to screen the enveloping movements made by the French army.

On October 7, the Austrian commander, General Mack, learned that Napoleon planned to march round the right flank of the Austrian army so as to threathen their supply lines and cut him off from the Russian army under Kutuzov.

French troops began to cross the Rhine River on a front of 260 km (160 miles). The French cavalry under Murat screened the advance of the army and made demonstrations across the Black Forest Mountains. The main French forces followed Murat and then swung towards the southeast, a move that was supposed to isolate Mack and interrupt the Austrian lines of supplies. The Austrian commander changed front, placing his left at Ulm and his right at Rain, but the French went on and crossed the Danube at Neuburg.

Through feverish marching, Napoleon conducted a large wheeling maneuver that captured the enemy army. On the 20th October the unhappy General Mack was surrounded in Ulm. He soon capitulated with 30,000 men, all that remained under his command of the 80,000-90,000 with whom he had invaded Bavaria few weeks before.

The Russians withdrew to await reinforcements and to link up with surviving Austrian troops. Napoleon followed, but soon found himself in a difficult situation: Prussian intentions were unknown, and the Russian and Austrian armies now converged. Napoleon realized that the only way to capitalize on the success at Ulm was to force the the Russians and Austrians to battle and defeat them. Meanwhile the Austrian troops in Italy under Archduke Charles, were compelled to retreat in the hope of covering Vienna, now threatened by Napoleon's advance. Negotiations for armistice failed. Napoleon had entered Vienna. On the anniversary of his coronation Napoleon inflicted on the Austrians and Russians the decisive defeat at Austerlitz. Austria agreed to the terms of the treaty of Pressburg.

The campaign is generally regarded as a strategic masterpiece. The rapidity of movememnts of the French army was impressive. Tsar Alexander of Russia wrote, "... the rapidity of Napoleon's manoeuvres [in 1805] never allowed time to succour any of the points which he successively attacked: his troops everywhere were twice as numerous as we were." Austrian General Stutterheim praised the French too, "... the French generals manoeuvered their troops with that ability which is the result of the military eye, and of experience..."

THE AUERSTADT-JENA CAMPAIGN 1806

Napoleon's strategic plan of this campaign, was simple and beautiful. For a perfect campaign, we need look no further than that of 1806 against Prussia. Supremely confident of victory, the Prussians bragged that clubs would be all they needed to thrash Napoleon's French 'cobblers.' Berliners cheered wildly when Queen Louise, wearing a crimson and blue colonel's uniform, paraded before the regiment of dragoons that bore her name.

Napoleon's plan of this campaign was beautiful. To base himself on the Rhine River and upper Danube and simply advance north-eastwards on Berlin would, perhaps, be the easiest for Napoleon, but it would offer no strategical advantages; for if he met and defeated the Prussians on this west-east line, he would simply drive them backwards on their supports, and then on Russians, whose advance from Poland was expected.

To turn the Thuringian Forest Mountains by an advance from his right, was a less safe movement; but, it offered great advantages:

- Napoleon would threaten the Prussian supply lines, line of retreat, and line of communications with Berlin.
- Napoleon would separate the Prussians and the Russians.

The danger with this maneuver was this that the Prussians by a rapid advance through the Thuringian Forest Mountains against his communication line, might sever him from France!

Of particular interest in this campaign is Napoleon's use of the *bataillon carre* advancing behind a cavalry screen to execute nearly perfect *manoeuvre sur les derries,* in order to bring the enemy to battle under circumstances particularly favourable to himself. The French cavalry rode ahead and located the enemy, then reported back to Napoleon the positions of enemy's troops. As soon as the Emperor plotted them on the map, he would order one or both of his wing commanders to engage the nearest enemy force. The reserve was made of heavy cavalry and the Imperial Guard. All troops marched within supporting distance of one another. The wings consisted of one or two army corps each.

In the end of September the Prussian army was spread over a front of 190 miles. Their allies, the Saxons, had not yet completed their mobilisation. Within few days the Prussians shortened their front to 85 miles in a direct line. (At the same time Napoleon had huge army assembled on a front of 38 miles!)

Napoleon arrived at Bamberg on October 6. The following day he received the Prussian ultimatum. Prussian advance guards were sent in the direction of the Thuringian Forest. The Prussians also detached small corps from Ruchel's force against Napoleon's supply lines. But by doing this they weakened their own main army. Meanwhile the French army launched their 19th-century-style blitzkrieg. The army marched in three columns. Bernadotte's I Corps was at the head of the centre column, followed by Davout's III Corps, and the reserves (Murat's Cavalry Reserve and the Imperial Guard). The right column was made up of Soult's IV Corps, Ney's VI Corps and Bavarian corps. The left column was made up of Lannes' V Corps, followed a day's march behind by Augereau's VII Corps.

The French light cavalry encountered the Prussian advance posts at Schleiz and drove them back. Lannes' troops ran into Hohenlohe's advance guard under Prince Ludwig Ferdinand at Saalfeld and also drove them back. The commander-in-chief of the Prussianarmy realized the French were about to outflank him. He began to concentrate his troops and shift them to the east to meet the advancing enemy. Rüchel was ordered to join the army. Hohenlohe was to remain at Jena to cover the left flank.

Napoleon issued orders to wheel the whole army to the left, onto the line of the Saale River. Heavy fighting began when elements of Napoleon's main force encountered Prussian troops near Jena. The Battle of Jena cost Napoleon approx. 5,000 men, but the Prussians had a staggering 25,000 casualties. At Auerstadt Marshal Davout's also crushed the enemy. Napoleon initially did not believe that Davout's single corps had defeated the Prussian main body unaided, and responded to the first report by saying "Tell your Marshal he is seeing double". As matters became clearer, however, the Emperor was unstinting in his praise. Over the next few days the remaining forces were unable to mount any serious resistance to Murat's ruthless cavalry pursuit. Davout led his troops into Berlin on 25 October.

The French army secured the total annihilation of the Prussian army and state in one month. It was a remarkable demonstration of what the French military system could accomplish under Napoleon's guidance. Prussia was broken by the war, her army was ruined, she had no money and had lost half of her former territory. Napoleon's brilliance as a strategist only served to bring the enemy to the battlefield. "Battle was always the ultimate object of all of Napoleon's planning and thought. Indeed, he conducted more battles than most great commanders before or since and managed to win most of them." (*Petre-"Napoleon at War" p 165*)

Once enemy contact was established, the advance guard seized the most favourable position available, striving to fix the enemy. While the advance guard spent itself, these fresh units went into action on its flanks. The light infantry probed in, developing weak spots and tying down the enemy. Behind the light infantry the light artillery moved aggressively forward and the real fighting began. Once the enemy was engaged Napoleon had but one purpose: destruction.

The Emperor preferred to fight offensively under all circumstances, even when on the defensive. At Austerlitz he did actually stand on the defensive, lured his enemies into a trap, and then attacked.

Normally he struck at one wing of a hostile army, preferably the one nearer its communications. The flanking movement forced the enemy to turn, to make quick adjustments in the midst of fighting, either through a retreat or reinforcing the threatened flank and weakening other flank, centre or reserves.

Napoleon recommended a maneuver upon the flank of enemy and assured that in such situation "The victory is in your hands". (When Napoleon's own flank was attacked at Leipzig, La Rothiere and at Waterloo, and in the three battles he was defeated.)

The Emperor had two basic battle plans:

Battle of maneuver (66 % of his battles)

It required some superiority in numbers.

The main force held the enemy ' s attention to his front, while another force fell upon one of his flanks, and then rolling up the rest of the line.

The cavalry was sent in pursuit. The advantage of this tactic was that it inflicted a major defeat on the enemy at minimal cost.

But things could go wrong. A movement of reserves in the enemy's rear could thicken up the threatened flank. Enemy deployed with a ridge or wood on his flank would be immune to this method.

Austerlitz, Jena, and Eylau, were all essentially battles of maneuver. Battle of attrition (33 %)

It was a frontal match in which firepower was poured into the enemy in enormous amounts until he appeared to be weakening, and then great masses of men would be thrown in to smash their way through his lines. Such a battle was costly affair,but there were times when no other course was possible.

Some were incredible costly victories like Wagram and Borodino, and several battles were defeats, such as La Rothiere and Waterloo. There was much that could go wrong in such a battle. For example the enemy might prove more numerous, or receive support from another army, or built strong fieldworks.

Napoleon's greatest victories in 1805-15:

1. Austerlitz 1805

2. Jena 1806
3. Friedland 1807
4. Ulm 1805
5. Dresden 1813.

Napoleon possessed the common human habit of embellishing his best exploits and blaming others for his reverses. For example he developed the account of his mediocre Marengo Campaign into a first-class epic romance.

According to Colonel John Elting, "Napoleon's close followers, because of hero worship or personal considerations, also suppressed and invented. On the other hand, his enemies strove to portray him as a monster, and to present his best victories as lucky accidents."

•Napoleon made several military and political mistakes : fighting on several fronts at once. His invasion of Russia resulted in the loss of half-million of his best troops and 1,000 cannons. After that disaster he never regained his greatness. (Napoleon believed that after a few quick battles, he would bring Tzar Alexander to his knees. Then Napoleon also decided that if he took Moscow the Russians would ask for peace.

However, when he eventually occupied Moscow, the Tsar still did not surrender. He could not surrender because if he did, he would be assassinated by the nobles.) the severity of Napoleon's terms to Prussia undermined the security of the peace his policy towards England contemplated nothing short of her total ruin his aggression raised Tirol, Calabria, Portugal and Spain as fresh enemies.

As a commander, Napoleon was becoming predictable, and his enemies were beginning to appreciate the counter-measures and use them against him. Increasingly he refused to face up to reality and suppressed all traces of criticism.

"Nevertheless, when all was said and done, he remained a giant surrounded by pygmies; his reputation survived his fall, for his basic greatness was inviolable." (*David Chandler- "Waterloo-the hundred days" p 41*)

Napoleon's defeats: 1796 combat at Caldiero is significant as being Bonaparte's first undisputable defeat in open field, and although most of the Napoleonic authors passed quickly over this episode to describe and analyze the following battle of Arcole in much more detail, the fact remains that by the standards of the Italian Campaign Caldiero is a significant engagement. Napoleon was much depressed by his defeat, and on next day he wrote a letter to the Directory that he would oppose the Austrians once again but that he had no hope of stopping their drive to Mantua and would probably retreat to the line of the river Ada.

Austrian commander: Alvinczi

Armies: 12,500 French vs 12,000 Austrians.

1809 Aspern-Essling

Although he would later claim a victory, the Emperor had sufferred his first major defeat. He lost out to the determined Austrians under Archduke Charles.

After Essling, Napoleon's position was one of extreme anxiety. The news of the reverse spread like wildfire throughout Europe offering every encouragement to his enemies.

Allied commanders: Archduke Charles

Armies: 65,000 French vs 90,000 Austrians

1812 Beresina Crossings

Napoleon lost 25,000 killed, wounded, and prisoners. The Russians lost 20,000. Additionally at least 10,000 Frenchmen were masacred by Cossacks,while another 20,000 died in the freezing river or were crushed to death in the panic to cross-the bridges. Only few thousands managed to escape. In this situation the Russians became the undisputed masters of the battlefield. (Some pro-French authors consider Beresina as French victory.)

1813 Leipzig [2]

Napoleon withstood Allies assaults and then counterattacked.

Meanwhile another army (under Bennigsen) attacked his flank. It forced Napoleon to abandon his strongpoints and withdraw his army closer to Leipzig. Then he was surrounded & crushed.

In terms of casualties and political & strategical results it was probably Napoleon's greatest defeat. Allied commanders were: Allies' commanders: Schwarzenberg (Austrians), Tolly (Russians) Bernadotte (Swedes) and Blucher/Gneisenau (Prussians). Armies: 200,000 French, Poles, and Germans vs 300,000 Allies

1814 La Rothiere

While he exchanged blows with the Russians to his front, the

Austrians, Bavarians and Wirtembergians attacked his flanks.

Napoleon retreated, it was his first defeat on French soil.

The allied commanders (with the exception of Gneisenau) were entirely carried away by their enthusiasm and, instead of organising a vigorous pursuit, wasted the day following the battle in feasting and mutual congratulations.

1814 Laon

Allies' stand had prevented Napoleon from driving them north.

The Allies were still in a position to advance on Paris, which they did at the end of March.

Armies: 35,000 French vs 60,000 Russians and Prussians

Allies commanders: Blucher/Gneisenau

1815 Waterloo

While Napoleon attacked the British-Netherland army (under Wellington), part of the Prussian army (under Blucher) attacked his flank. Napoleon was crushed. In strategy as in tactics the flank attack is one of the most powerful.

Armies: 75,000 French vs 122,250 Allies

Allies commanders: Wellington (British, German, Netherland) and Blucher's/Gneisenau's (Prussians)

The defeat at Aspern-Essling is explained by Loraine Petre. "For the defeat of Essling the Emperor had himself to blame. He had certainly been careless in his preparations for the crossing [of the Danube River], once more a result of his unbounded pride and his contempt for his enemy. He had been amply warned of the dangers of a sudden rise of the Danube, the fate of the Austrian bridge at Mauthausen should have warned him of the dangers to a bridge of boats from barges and other masses floated down the rapid stream. Yet he trusted his army to a single bridge of boats without any protection by stockades, or by boats cruising about to arrest such floating masses above the bridge. His information regarding Charles' position seems to have been bad and to have led him not to expect serious resistance immediately after the passage. Even on the morning of Essling, his cavalry had failed to detect the advance of the whole Austrian army. Essling was the first great success of an Austrian army against Napoleon in person.... There is no clearer proof that Napoleon realised his own rashness in the first crossing than the infinite care which he bestowed on his preparations for the second, and the perfection with which they were carried out." (*Petre-"Napoleon at War" pp 261-2, publ. 1984*)

"In the autumn of 1813, the Allies adopted a strategy of not letting any one of their three armies face Napoleon alone. Should the master place himself at the head of his troops, then the Allied army facing him was to withdraw, while the other advanced. While Napoleon was chasing air, the opportunity was taken to bring certain of his marshals to battle and defeat them individually." (*-Peter Hofschroer*)

It worked wonders. In August Marshal Oudinot's corps was trashed at Gross Beeren, Marshal MacDonald was defeated at Katzbach, and General Vandamme at Kulm. In September Marshal Ney was routed at Dennewitz. On the strategic level Napoleon was succesful until 1812.

The invasion of Russia broke his backbone ("sealed his fate").

1800 Marengo Campaign-Napoleon won

1805 Austerlitz Campaign-Napoleon won

1806 Jena Campaign-napoleon won

1807 Friedland Campaign-Napoleon won

1809 Wagram Campaign-Napoleon won

1812 Invasion of Russia-it cost him around half a million of his men (!)

It also badly tarnished Napoleon's reputation. (The Emperor barely escaped with his life.)

1813 Saxon Campaign-Napoleon's defeat

1814 Campaign of France-Napoleon's defeat

1815 Waterloo Campaign-Napoleon's defeat

Although serious military thinkers today are more likely to refer to Clausewitz, in the Napoleonic age itself, Antoine de Jomini was more likely to have that distinction. "It is probably fair to say that in general Clausewitz addressed the political and strategic levels of war and Jomini addressed the operational level. The two were born only a year apart. They held similar staff-officer positions in the Napoleonic wars, albeit in different armies.

Jomini was by far the more celebrated thinker in his own lifetime.... It is important to remember what Jomini is and what Jomini is not. Almost all of his work answers one question: how does one deploy units successfully in the main battle? For officers who must answer this question, Jomini's ideas, the Principles of War, are extremely useful and extremely important. For officers trying to answer any other questions, Jomini is not so useful.... There is almost no treatment of politics, no strategy, no technological change, no strategic resource base, no psychology, no people's war, no adversary, and indeed no unexpected adversity in Jomini's work." (*-U.S. ARMY Command and General Staff College C600-8*)

"To Jomini Napoleon was the compeer of Caesar, of Hannibal, and of Alexander. To Clausewitz he was 'the very god of war.' Each of them prepared himself for his theory by writing the history of campaigns both of Napoleon and of his predecessors. But their ways of regarding their subject were different. Jomini's object was to find out by comparison between Napoleon's campaigns and those of Frederick the principles of action which were common to them both and might therefore be of universal validity. He analysed their operations and classified them according to their geometrical form. The base of operations, the direction of an army's advance and that of its front can each be represented as a line.... Jomini's analysis and classification of operations in spite of its artificial terminology, was correct and useful. It was the first scientific exposition of strategy as a system of principles, and it has been used by all the subsequent strategical thinkers. Willisen in Germany and Hamley in England are Jomini's disciples...

If Jomini sought for the common element in the generalship of Napoleon and his predecessors, Clausewitz dwelt on the difference between them. Jomini sought for principles as precepts for guidance in action. Clausewitz thought general principles in the shape of precepts or rules of little avail in the presence of the infinite variety of the situations of war.

The question which Clausewitz put to himself was how it came about that Napoleon's wars were so-fundamentally different from most of those which had proceeded them. His answer was that the energy with which a war is carried on is a product of two factors, the strength of the motive which actuates the belligerents and the degree to which that motive appeals to the population of the States concerned. The French Revolution had called a nation to arms. France therefore acted with the utmost energy. On the other hand, the cause for which the Governments of the Coalition were fighting was by no means vital to them and scarcely interested their people.

The success of France was therefore predetermined. When the French forces came under the control of Napoleon the overthrow of the old monarchies was inevitable. But the pressure of the French Empire upon the populations then aroused such bitter resentment that the nations one after another rushed to arms, and thus the overthrow of Napoleon was as much predetermined as had been his unprecedented conquests.

This portion of the theory of Clausewitz is, however, not derived from the generalship of Napoleon. Its root idea comes from an essay in which Scharnhorst in 1797 reviewed the revolutionary war of 1792-5, in which Napoleon had not yet had a command. Scharnhorst attributed the success of the French to the energy of unity of the French nation, and the failure of the Allies to their discord and their inadequate efforts.

The subsequent exertions of Prussia in and after 1813 confirmed Clasewitz in his view of the importance of the distinction between national and dynastic war." (*Wilkinson, Spenser-"The French army before Napoleon; lectures delivered before the University of Oxford..." pp 14-16*)

NAPOLEON ON CIVIL WAR TACTICS AND STRATEGY

At the onset of the American Civil war both North and South scrambled to establish powerful armies to support their causes. The military leaders on both sides, however, all shared the same basic military training as well as the basic concept of how an army should be built and how a war should be fought. The military training as well as tactics of the civil war was geared towards emulating the grand armies created by Napoleon.

The campaigns of Napoleon formed the bases of formal military education through out the western world. At the start of the civil war European observers were anxious to see to what extent the American campaigns would conform to the accepted doctrines of Napoleonic warfare. All of the military thinking of the day was influenced by Napoleon. These lessons learned from the "Great Corsican" were relayed through the writings of Antoine Henri Jominie. Through his writings an emphasis was put on the Napoleonic strategy. Keenly aware of the dominance of French military arms many civil war leaders looked back to the Napoleonic method of wagging war for enlightenment. Through 23 years of war the French army became the world's model of a fighting machine.

Through the study of the tactics, training, and even mistakes of Napoleon it was hoped that a copy of the "Grande Armee" could be recreated in America. In West point the writings of Jomini were used as a textbook through Henry W. Halleck's "Elements of Military Art and Science", which was essentially a translation of Jomini.

As the curriculum at West Point leaned in the direction of engineering, mathematics, fortifications and administration most cadets absorbed this text, as it was the only resource on military strategy. Today many of these tactics seem to be common sense, their application was so universal. These tactics were such concepts as, concentrate a mass of your own fore against a fraction of our enemy, menace the enemy's communications while protecting your own, attack the enemy's weak point with your own strength. These rules seem to echo the strategy and execution of Sherman's great march for "Salt water."

One of the lessons learned from Napoleon was his concept of concentration, as well as the rules of concentration. It was Napoleons strategy that when 2-3 armies begin a camping to conquer a territory they should converge at a place away from the enemy to prevent the opposing army from destroying the approaching armies piecemeal. This tactic was seen so often in the civil war that a compilation of examples would seem endless here. Among the many other maxims of Napoleon that found their way onto the American battle fields were the call for Skirmishers. When his army was on the move he would deploy advanced guards and flanking parties. This tactic became the standard operating procedure for armies on the move in the civil war, and even today. When not on the move encamped armies established picket lines, the same technique only stationary. Entrenching was also a Napoleonic device for the encamped armies to maximize its strength in order to hold off a superior force. This Maxim offered the Confederates their last bit of hope when Grant converged on Richmond. Had Lee himself not studied the many rules of Napoleonic warfare then perhaps the siege on Richmond would have simply been a battle.

Many of the General officers on both sides of the war had received their military training at West Pont. At West Point all cadets studied tactics under Mahan, the professor of engineering and the art of war from 1830-1871. Having studied the art of war in France Mahan was greatly influenced by Napoleon and would pass his fascination with Napoleonic Warfare on to his cadets.

One of the texts used by Mahan's student was "Traite des Grandes Operations Miltaire" by Jomini, a Swiss aid of Napoleons. Jomini was intrigued by Napoleons strategies and sought to systematize his methods. Jomini emphasized the necessity of good internal lines of operations. Another concept, previously mentioned, was concentrating a superior force against an inferior one. This is easily said, but Jomini laid out Napoleons blue print for achieving this. This action could be carried out through effective establishment and exploitation of strong interior lines. Unfortunately the lesson was not long enough and found to be too short to adequately translate the Corsicans methods. To better impart the Great tacticians knowledge upon his students Mahan established the "Napoleon Club."

Through this club cadets could study the campaigns and histories of the Great Corsican. Once war finally broke out this study did not cease. Sherman required that all of his officers study up on Napoleon through the works of Jomini.(5) One of the troubles with this mode of independent study was that, at the time, all copies available were in French.

At the academy, West Point, students were taught French so that they might be able to read the treatise and reports on the Napoleonic wars. The view was held, at West Point that since the time of the ancient Greeks wars had been getting bigger and better. Students were taught to see the battle field through the eyes of Napoleon, a chessboard where opposing armies faced off in complex deployments. Union General George B McClellan was another student of Napoleon, often referred to as "the young Napoleon".

McClellan saw through his study of Napoleon that freedom of movement was essential. McClellan not only implemented these ideas in his marches but also in the design of his uniforms. He took the ideas from the French Napoleonic armies and rebuilt the motley Federal army. Under McClellan's Napoleon plan the Federal army became a model of a fighting force. Discipline and uniforms were not his only contribution. The "McClellan Saddle" found its way into the cavalry, based on those used by the French, and the Shelter Half has been standard issue ever since.

Now soldiers could simply carry their shelter with them enabling quick set up and even faster evacuation of an encampment One of Napoleons greatest contribution to the American military, through McClellan, was the Bayonet Manuel, which McClellan translated from French into English. On the other side of the war was one of the countries greatest tacticians, Robert E. Lee. At West Pont the first book Lee ever checked out was a study of Napoleons campaigns, one which he became very familiar with while at the academy. Latter Lee became a master at using Napoleonic tactics of concentrating his armies against a weaker portion of the North's.

Napoleon emphasized the importance of turning movements. The ancient Spartan frontal assault featuring two armies pounding away at each other until one side would give way was gone. Napoleon developed the turning movement to effectively attack an enemy flank. The effect was that the enemy being turned would be forced to adjust, either through a retreat or reinforce the flank, exposing another area of its defence. What this tactic essentially did is forced an attacking or defending army to scrap its battle orders and attempt to make quick adjustments in the midst of battle. In the Civil war this was the goal of all Generals, to effectively execute turning movements against their enemies. McClellan's Peninsula campaign had this Maxim at the heart of his strategy.

Examples set by Napoleon did not only appear on the battle field. A larger unit of army organization was introduced, the division. The division was a part of an army commanded by a General officer and was strong enough to engage an enemy successfully until other divisions arrived. No longer would one see large armies forming massive single line formations. This also enabled American Generals the flexibility to move rapidly across the battle field and take full advantage of the terrain. Rapid deployment of the large American armies was made possible due to this new organization of the army into divisions. In marching each division constituted a column. In separating on the march they cold move more rapidly while covering a wider area and never loose their unity.

The commanding General could now ride out in advance and with great ease place his army accordingly. Now armies were extremely flexible and easier to command. Through this innovation alone battles would constantly turn from one side of victory to another. This new technique also enabled armies to remain engaged for days before finally being forced from the field.

In the South the Napoleonic concept of exploiting interior lines was greatly applied to all battle orders. Generals were reluctant to stretch their lines of communication to far. This influenced greatly Lee's strategy of drawing out the enemy. These interior lines were now more effective than even Napoleon could have imagined. The use of rail roads and the telegraph made possible the rapid communication of battle orders and troop movement reports.

The era of Napoleon produced armies with great maneuverability. Now capable of rapid deployment from March to battle formation and subdivided into corps and division's armies grew extremely flexible and more resistant to attacks and flanking movements. General P.G.T. Beauregard tirelessly preached the need to use the railroad and the telegraph to apply the Napoleonic strategy of an offensive concentration at the enemy's weak point. In the West, Beauregard's theatre of operations, President Davis was aware that the confederate army could not meet the enemy with an equal force. He adhered to Beauregard's interpretations of warfare and ordered Johnston to coordinate Pemberton's Mississippi department with Brags and Kirby Smith to "Operate in Napoleons manner" and unite forces in Mississippi and Tennessee utilizing these interior lines. One can quite often see that when baffled by logistical dilemmas the Civil War tacticians simply copied the examples of Napoleon.

One of the wars greatest examples of Napoleonic influence can be found in P.G.T. Beauregard. Being fluent in French Beauregard was able to study the works of Jomini and other French histories of Napoleons campaigns. While Beauregard was always ready with elaborate Napoleonic battle orders, his green army was not quite up to the ask.

At Blackburns Ford Beauregard proposed an effective, in theory, strategy of tacking the offensive against the Federal invaders. He proposed that the valley army of Johnston move in two columns. One army was to come by rail to Manassas, exploiting thier interior lines, while the other would cross the mountains to the North and in effect come in to the Federals rear. This was truly a Napoleonic battle order, but it had only one major flaw, Johnston's army was to "green" and small to undertake such an expedition.

The Creoles ingenious interpretation of Napoleonic warfare was scraped. Beauregard devised his own strategy as well as his own interpretations of the rules of war based on his intensive study, almost obsession, of Napoleon. He would latter greatly criticize those who would deviate from these rules set by Napoleon. Early in the war, at Corinth, the Confederates were planning a defensive-offensive strategy hoping to cut Grants line of communications. When drawing up battle orders for the coming battle Beauregard was using a copy of Napoleons order for the battle of waterloo. The examples of Napoleon, even his greatest defeat, were so revered that even the Napoleonic bureaucracy found its way into civil war camps. An inexperienced class of Generals now faced off. They could not help but to rely, almost verbatim, on the lessons taught by Napoleon. There was a consensus among some of the Generals, Longstreet, Johnston, and Beauregard, that in order to crush the Union army in the west they must use European tactics, as established by the Great Corsican. The belief was that the tactics became the basic rules of war and conflict.

One of the best known campaigns of the Civil War was Sherman's march to the sea. Venturing deep into enemy territory it was impossible for him to maintain lines of communication.

Sherman, rather than waist resources trying to do the impossible, also followed the example of Napoleon. Faced with a similar dilemma Napoleon, as did Sherman, supplied his army off the land. This not only eliminated the need to maintain long lines of communication but carried out a plan of exhaustion devastating the moral of the Southern people. Sherman's army swarmed across the country like a horde of locusts.

McClellan's Peninsula campaign, early in the war, was another great example of Napoleonic innovations. His entire campaign was based on a massive waterborne turning movement. He believed that by forcing the Confederates to attack in order to preserve their interior lines he could take Richmond and essentially end the war. McClellan's campaign would have succeeded had the commander of the Confederate forces, General Johnston, not been inured. Johnston was replaced by another West Pointer and avid student of Napoleonic warfare, Robert E. Lee.

Unfortunately not all of the implemented tactics of Napoleon had practical application on the Civil War battlefield. Due to the inaccuracy of the earlier muskets close order formation was essential for maximizing firepower. With the advent of the new rifled musket accuracy, and their for lethality, was now greatly improved. While weaponry, artillery also benefited from riffling, advanced tactics on the battlefield did not. While many of the Napoleonic tactics helped Generals, on both sides, to victory this one out of date tactic imposed a high cost on victory. This tactic is the main cause for the ranking of the Civil war causalities as the highest in the history of American conflict.

Napoleon warned not to allow gaps to develop in battle formation; this is one lesson that was better off left on the book shelves. Napoleon spoke of the inaccuracy of muskets. He preached that linear formations should only be two rows deep as the first line would be in danger of being struck by the third line. Though this tactic was essential to battlefield success prior to the Civil War it was now disastrous. The fact that the Civil War soldier could now hit what he aimed at made all the soldiers on the field in formation "sitting Ducks".

A good comparison to the effectiveness of the weaponry of the two eras can be seen in the following journal entries from soldiers of that time.

First from an American in the Revolutionary war followed by a Confederate soldier account. "One of the soldiers, thinking he could do a bit of mischief by killing some of us...kept firing at us as we passed along the bank. Several of his shots passed between our files, but we took little notice of him..." The weaponry advancement can be compared in the following exert of a similar scenario. "I had taken a rest for my gun by the side of a sapling... Finally wee saw him sort o' peep round the tree... and bang! We saw the Yankee tumble out like a squirrel." Two different wars, similar circumstance and different effects based on modern weaponry.

The reason for the great slaughter that the Civil-war became is based on the error of studying the use of linear formations. Though the original concept of the tactic was sound it was the creation of the.58 caliber rifle brought together with the Minnie ball that made it obsolete.

Though many military thinkers were aware of the new improvements in weaponry they had no idea of how this would change tactical relations on the battle field. Since the foundation of virtually all military thought had deep roots in Napoleonic thinking it is no wonder that no one questioned this, soon to be proven, suicidal technique. It is with great ease that we now look back and condemn the use of Napoleons linear formations, but we must remember that to the Antebellum and Civil War mind there existed no imaginable alternative.

The innovations of Napoleon were revolutionary in his time. In an era where technology was quickly approaching 20th century standards there was no manual instructing how to harness the power of these new advancements. Military trainers and tacticians could only look to the European wars of Napoleon for guidance. Through formal education as well as independent study the works of Jomini were encouraged reading material for all aspiring military officers. The Civil war has been called the first modern war, it began with the suicidal linear tactics of European warfare and ended with the nightmarish trench warfare, soon to be spread to Europe. Though many, if not all, Napoleonic maxims seems common sense today they were on the cutting edge of military thinking in Antebellum and civil war times and many of them have become a part of our modern military culture.

STRATEGY (CIVIL WAR)

In this military art, troops are maneuvered outside the battlefield to achieve success in a large geographic area. That geographic expanse can be a "front" (in the Civil War, part or all of one state) or a "theatre" (several contiguous states possessing geographical, geopolitical, or military unity). When the expanse encompasses an entire country, the corresponding waging of war on the largest scale to secure national objectives is called "grand strategy."

"Offensive strategy" carries war to the enemy, either directly by challenging his strength or indirectly by penetrating his weakness." Defensive strategy" protects against enemy strategic offensives. And "defensive-offensive strategy" (which Confederates often practiced) uses offensive maneuvers for defensive strategic results (e.g., Gen. R. E. Lee and Maj. Gen. Thomas J. "Stonewall" Jackson took the offensive May-June 1862 to defend Richmond and Virginia).

Strategic objectives include defeating, destroying, or forcing enemy armies to retreat; seizing enemy strategic sites (supply lines, depots, arsenals, communications centres, and industry) crucial to his military effort; capturing the enemy capital; disrupting his economy; and demoralizing his will to wage war. While seeking such goals, the strategist must correspondingly protect his own army, strategic sites, capital, economy, and populace. He must strike proper balance between securing his rear and campaigning in his front. Supply lines and homelands must be guarded; especially in war between 2 republics, which the Civil War really was, the compelling necessity of protecting the political base cannot be ignored. Yet if too many troops are left in the rear, too few remain to attack or even defend against enemy armies at the front.

Of these objectives, European experience, from which Civil War strategic doctrine derived, emphasized 3 strategies: destroying the enemy's army in 1 battle, seizing strategic sites, and capturing the enemy's capital. In the Civil War, attacking and defending Richmond and Washington consumed much effort, but their actual strategic importance, though great, was more symbolic than substantial, since neither was its country's nerve centre, as European capitals were. Also illusory were quests for victory through seizing strategic sites and cutting "lines of communication" (supply lines); only a few Civil War campaigns, such as Holly Springs and Second Bull Run, were decided or even significantly affected by such captures. Most chimerical of all were hopes of annihilating the enemy's army in 1 great Napoleonic victory.

Rather, Civil War strategists used a series of battles--each of them indecisive but cumulatively effective--to cripple the enemy, drive him back, and overrun or protect territory. Some strategies aimed directly at such battles. Other strategies sought first to maneuver so as to gain advantage of ground or numbers and only then to give battle under such favourable conditions. Whatever the overall numbers in the theatre, strategy strove to assure numerical superiority on the battlefield; this principle was called "concentrating masses against fractions." Both sides practiced it, but it was especially important to the overall weaker Secessionists, as when Jackson performed it so effectively in the Shenandoah Valley.

Again, each side, particularly the Confederates, used "interior lines" to move forces from quiet fronts through the interior to threatened fronts more quickly than the enemy could move around the military border. But, in practice, Southern supply lines were so primitive and Federal supply lines were so good that, despite longer distance, Northerners often moved in shorter time due to their "superior lateral communications." Even more effective against Confederate reliance on interior lines was Ulysses S. Grants grand strategy of concerting the armed might of the Union for simultaneous advances to pin and defeat Confederate troops on all major fronts.

Besides these approaches, Civil War strategists, especially Union commanders such as William T. Sherman and Philip H. Sheridan, usually reluctantly but increasingly came to make the enemies economy and populace suffer. For the first time since the Thirty Years War, those 2 targets regained legitimacy. While free from the brutality of 1618-48, Federal strategy eventually crippled Southern capability and will to wage war though, to be effective, such strategy could only complement Northern success in maneuver and battle. Long-range strategic cavalry raids--in brigade to corps strength--played some role in such crippling, but those raids rarely had much military effect before collapse became imminent in 1865. Instead, the principal unit of strategic maneuver was the infantry corps, and the basic element of strategic control was the army. And in theaters where I side had several armies, those armies themselves became maneuver units, and control resided at military division headquarters or with the general-in-chief himself.

Whatever the elements and whatever the means, the fundamental goal of strategy remains the same: the overall use of force to accomplish broad military and political objectives.

THE STRATEGY OF THE CIVIL WAR LEADERS

But strategy, unfortunately, is a very unpopular science, even among soldiers, requiring both in practice and in demonstration constant and careful study of the map, the closest computation of time and space, a grasp of many factors, and the strictest attention to the various steps in the problems it presents. At the same time, it is a science which repays the student, although he may have no direct concern with military affairs; for not only will a comprehension of its immutable principles add a new interest to the records of stirring times and great achievements, but will make him a more useful citizen.-"Stonewall Jackson and the Civil War," by Lieutenant-Colonel G. F : R. Henderson, C. B.

The student has great advantage over the actor in war, particularly when he makes his study after a lapse of fifty years. His point of view is illuminated by the stories as told by both contestants, by the disputes and explanations of many participants. He also pursues his investigations without any of the distracting influençes of war itself. It may not, therefore, be entirely fair to take each man's act before the bar of history and to require him to justify himself to the critics of a later day. In a larger sense, though, it is right, because past experience gives the best lessons and guides for the future. Until we have another war, we shall continue to study the great conflict of 1861-5, and to read the secrets of our future in its tale of failure or success.

"Strategy" is a comparatively recent addition to our language. It is derived from the Greek meaning generalship, and has several valuable derivatives, as "strategic" and "strategist," which make it a more useful word than generalship. It means the art of the general and indicates the time, place, and way to fight battles.

The War of the States was viewed at first with indifference by foreign military men. For many years past, however, it has claimed their close attention, because they have come to realize that new conditions were tested then, and that new influences, which changed the art of the general even from the respected models of Napoleon fifty years before, were at work. Ironclads, entrenchments, railroads, the breech-loader, a new kind of cavalry were the fresh factors in the problem.

Although hostilities at first began over an area half as large as Europe, the region of decisive operations was, on account of lack of communication, narrowed to the country between the Atlantic and the Mississippi, about seven, hundred miles in an air-line. The line was unequally divided by the towering barrier of the Allegheny Mountains, about two hundred miles wide, over which communication was difficult. The eastern section of the country beyond the range was about one hundred miles wide and the western section was about four hundred miles wide. In Maryland, northwestern Virginia, Kentucky, and Missouri sentiment was divided between the Union and the Confederacy. The Mississippi River separated three of the seceding States from the remaining eight.

The immense amount of supplies needed for a great army caused military operations on a large scale to be confined to rail and water lines. Of the former, both the North and South had several routes running east and west for lateral communication, and the South had several running north and south in each section, which could be used for lines of military operations.

In respect to water routes, the North soon demonstrated its complete control of the sea and was thus able to choose its points of attack, while interior water routes were available by the Mississippi, Tennessee, Cumberland, and James rivers. The advantage of the water route over that by rail was at once utilized by the Northern generals. It was not so vulnerable to attack as the railroad. All navigable rivers within the area of operations were used for this purpose, and McClellan, Burnside, and Grant used the Chesapeake Bay and its tributaries to carry their base of supplies close to Richmond. The operations of the Confederates, on the other hand, were greatly restricted by being confined to railroad lines.

Several natural features which were certain to influence events to a great extent are to be noticed. In Virginia, numerous rivers, running parallel to the direct line of advance, form good lines for defence and also obstacles to an advance. Several mountain valleys leading north at the eastern ranges of the Alleghanies gave opportunities for leading large forces safely into Pennsylvania from Virginia, or vice versa. Within the mountain district, a railroad from Lynchburg, Virginia, to Chattanooga, in Tennessee, about four hundred miles long, gave an opportunity for transferring troops from one section to the other, while the corresponding distance at the North was three times as great. In the western section, the Tennessee and Cumberland rivers are separated at one place by a narrow neck about two miles wide, thus somewhat simplifying the problem of controlling these two important streams. The strategic chess-board, then, gave great opportunities to skilful generalship.

The Virginia rivers gave strength to long defensive lines, screened marches from east to west, and forced the Northern generals to seek the flank rather than the front attack. The

Shenandoah valley afforded a safe approach to Washington from the rear. This was availed of by Lee, Jackson, and Early to keep many thousand men of the army of the North in idleness. In the West, the long line defended by scattered troops was weak at every point and was quite easily broken by Grant, particularly when the South was slow in grasping the situation there. The advantage of the Richmond-Chattanooga railroad was not used by the Confederates until too late for success.

The strategy, on account of political and other influences, was not always chosen according to the best military principles. Such influences always exist, and it is the duty of the soldier to conform and to make his plan to suit as best he can. Under the head of policy. would come Lee's several invasions of the North, undertaken with insufficient forces and too far from his base of supplies.

Numerous causes have been given for these campaigns, the most plausible of which were of a political and not of a strategic nature. It was thought that a victory won on Northern soil might lead to intervention on the part of foreign nations, or that it would increase the disaffected element in the North to such an extent that the South could dictate a peace.

The policy of making military operations conform to the desire to help Northern sympathizers in eastern Tennessee had a powerful influence on the entire war. In the spring of 1862, it would have taken Buell into eastern Tennessee, instead of to the assistance of Grant and would have changed the course of events in the Mississippi valley. Three months later, it was one of the potent influences that led to the breaking up of Halleck's army at Corinth. It finally caused Buell's relief from command because of his disapproval. It caused Burnside's army to be absent from the battle of Chickamauga.

In 1864, the campaigns of Price in Missouri and Hood in Tennessee are said to have been intended to affect the presidential election at the North by giving encouragement to the party which was claiming that the war was a Federal failure. If that was not the case might not Hood have done better by marching in the track of Longstreet through Knoxville, Tennessee, and Lynchburg, Virginia, to join Lee, while Sherman was marching to the sea, entirely out of reach?

An unreasonable importance, from a military point of view, was given to the capital of each government. The capital of the United States had been captured in two wars without producing more than local effect, but every plan in Virginia was contingent upon the safety of Washington, thus causing the diversion of many thousand soldiers for that single duty. On the Southern side the correct military decision would have been to abandon Richmond as soon as Petersburg was invested, but the Government delayed, for political reasons, until it was too late, and the defending army surrendered as a consequence.

In the distribution of troops the Federal authorities were hampered by the rival claims of the border States, which thought they required protection. Hence, Ohio sent an army into West Virginia; Pennsylvania, into the Shenandoah valley; the national Government concentrated troops for the protection of its capital; the Western States gathered along the Ohio River and in Missouri. This great dispersion existed on both sides and continued more or less till the end of the war. The advantage it gave was in the protection of the friendly portion of the population and in the good recruiting ground thus secured. The great difficulty of holding troops in service, whose home country had been overrun, was appreciated by both sides and exercised a strong influence on the plans of the generals. These conditions dictated much of the strategy which is subject to criticism, and should not be forgotten.

The policy of furloughing great numbers of soldiers during the war, as an inducement to reenlist, was probably unavoidable, but it helped to cause inactivity during many months and in the case of Sherman's Atlanta campaign it caused the absence of two of his divisions. Absenteeism is one of the inevitable consequences of a long war, with troops untrained in time of peace by modern methods. Lincoln complained of it and the generals seemed powerless to limit or prevent it. Probably the latter are entitled to most of the blame. It was not uncommon for a general to call for reenforcements at a time when large numbers of his troops were absent. The armies were indeed long in getting over the characteristics of raw troops, but the generals in their early movements do not appear much better than the troops. Every man who had been graduated from West Point was regarded as a " trained soldier," which was a mistake, because West Point was a preparatory school, and such men as had studied the art of high command had done so by themselves. The trade of the general was new to all, and had to be learned in the hard school of experience.

In four of the early campaigns in which the Federal troops were practically unopposed, they marched on an average of less than seven miles per day, while, in case of opposition by a greatly inferior force, the average was down to a mile a day, as in the Peninsula campaign and the advance on Corinth.

The plans for the early battles were complicated in the extreme, perhaps due to the study of Napoleon and his perfect army opposed by poor generals. Bull Run, Wilson's Greek, Seven Pines, Glendale, Malvern Hill, Shiloh, Gaines' Mill were of this kind, and failed. Even at Gettysburg, July 2, 1863, Lee's failure to execute his echelon attacks showed that his army 'was not yet ready to perform such a delicate refinement of war.

As an example of improvement, however, take Jackson's march of fourteen miles on a country road and the battle fought on May 2, 1863, all between daylight and dark of one day. In battles, also, we notice the fine play of early campaigns replaced by a savage directness and simplicity at a later period, in the Wilderness by Lee and at Spotsylvania by Grant. Thus it was that both leaders had ceased to count on the inefficiency of the enemy. At the beginning of the movement on Richmond both Lee and Grant seemed reckless in the risks they took. It was not so earlier.

The earliest form of strategy was the practice of ruse, stratagem, and surprise, but they have long been considered as clumsy expedients which are no longer effective against the best troops and commanders. Among instances which are often classed in this category are Shiloh, Chancellorsville, and the Wilderness.

Some forms of strategy have not changed in several thousand years. Sherman, for instance, crossed the Chattahoochee, which was held by Johnston, in 1864, in the same way that Alexander crossed the Hydaspes in the year 326 B. C., by feinting at one flank and crossing at the other.

The Vicksburg campaign gave great fame to General Grant and is really one of the most complete and decisive examples in history. In this campaign, he deliberately crossed the river north of Vicksburg, marched south and crossed again below Vicksburg. Then, relying on the country for supplies, he moved to Jackson, forty-five miles east of Vicksburg, where he interposed between the fractions of the Confederate army under Pemberton and Johnston. He then turned back again toward the Mississippi, drove Pemberton into Vicksburg, established a base of supplies at the North and invested the city. In this case, it is noticeable that the tendency to rate localities at too high a value is shown in Pemberton's retreating to Vicksburg, which was quite certain to be surrendered, instead of joining forces with Johnston to oppose Grant in the interior.

The same point is illustrated by the siege of Petersburg. As soon as Grant's army crossed the James and began this siege the fate of Richmond was sealed, for Grant had a great army and numerous means of extending his fortified lines until they crossed every avenue of approach to Richmond.

Moltke remarked that strategy was nothing more than common sense, but he acknowledged that it was often difficult to decide what was common sense and what was not. He might easily have had our Civil War in his mind. In 1861, the art of war had been greatly complicated by pedantic study, principally by officers of the French school, in attempting to reduce it to an exact science. The true lesson of Napoleon's campaigns had either been lost or the effect of new conditions had not been appreciated. It seems rather commonplace to say at this time that the first thing to do in war is to decide on your objective; but in the Civil War an incalculable amount of time was wasted, much treasure expended, and many lives were lost in a blind search for an objective. By objective is meant, of course, a point upon which to concentrate the greatest effort, the gaining of which will mean the success or failure of the cause.

In 1862, when the hostile armies opposed each other in front of Washington, McClellan insisted on attacking Richmond instead of Johnston's army. His plan resulted in the transfer of his army to the Peninsula and carried him to within six miles of Richmond with insignificant loss.

For this, great credit has been claimed and unfavorable comment made on later campaigns. But McClellan found the undefeated Confederate army at Richmond, and he was weakened by a vast army which had been kept back to guard Washington. Without entering into this great controversy, we may simply say that to fight the foe as far from Richmond as possible would now be considered the correct solution of that problem.

It is well known that Lincoln disapproved of McClellan's plan, whether by the counsel of wise military advisers or by his own common sense we know not. Again, in 1862, when Halleck with much trouble and skill had collected a great army of one hundred thousand men at Corinth, the army was dispersed, contrary to his desire, it appears, and the true objective was lost. The Confederate leader repaired his losses and soon recovered from his serious defeats. At that time the army could have gone anywhere, whether to Vicksburg to open the Mississippi, or to Chattanooga and even to Richmond: This is the opinion of those best qualified to know. Burnside, also, in the fall of 1862, marched away from Lee's army when he went to Fredericksburg.

So deep-rooted is the idea of choosing locality as the objective of a campaign instead of a hostile army, that Rosecrans' campaign, in the summer of 1863, has gone into history as the " Campaign for Chattanooga," and it has been claimed by his admirers that the possession of that place was worth what it cost--a heavy defeat at Chickamauga. In 1864, Grant had authority to lay down a choice of objective, which he had already announced in 1862. For himself it was clearly Lee's army, and it was intended to be the same with other commands as well. General Sherman, however, was not so clear in his manner of execution as was his chief. His strategy creates a suspicion that it was designed to force Johnston to retreat and to relinquish territory.

There was an idea that Johnston would not give up Dalton, which he had strongly fortified, but Sherman's heavy turning movement against his rear forced him to retreat without a battle. The same strategy continued until Atlanta was reached, and still Johnston's army was undefeated, while Sherman had weakened his army by guarding a long line of communication. Judging from this, we are disposed to suspect that Atlanta, rather than Johnston's army, was Sherman's main objective.

Later, the historic " March to the Sea " introduces a novel element into the question, for Sherman abandoned Hood's army as a first objective, and chose Lee's army instead. It will be remembered that Sherman had difficulty in getting consent from Grant, who wanted him to ruin Hood's army first. As it turned out, Sherman marched one thousand miles and was several hundred miles from Lee at the end of the campaign. If Lee's army had been his real objective there were other ways of reaching it: first, by sending his army by sea north from Savannah, as was suggested by Grant, which would have taken two months, say until the end of February, 1865; second, by sending the troops by rail, as Schofield was moved with fifteen thousand men and as Hooker was moved with twenty-three thousand men, and, third, by marching on Lynchburg by the Knoxville road, which would have been about one-third to one-half the distance actually marched.

Looking upon the war with all the advantage of today, it is not difficult to assume that the hopes of both sides rested on two great armies, one in the East and one in the West, and the destruction of either meant the destruction of the other. This clear estimate seems to have come quite naturally and easily to only one man during the war, and that man was Grant. Such a conception clears away a mass of secondary objectives, such as so-called " strategic points " along the coast and west of the Mississippi, which consumed hundreds of thousands of troops and had only a minor effect on the final issue.

It must be admitted that Grant used some seventy-five thousand men on secondary objectives which were not successful, in 1864, when these men would have had a great effect either with the armies of Sherman or himself. He probably thought that an army of one hundred and twenty thousand men was large enough for his purposes, but he found it was a mistake.

Equally fallacious with the importance given to " strategic points " was that ascribed to the occupation of territory. The control of Kentucky and Tennessee was given by Grant's Fort Donelson campaign, but the injury inflicted on the Confederate army by the large capture of men at Donelson and Island Number 10 was the real and vital result. The control of territory that was not accompanied by the defeat of the foe often had many disadvantages. Such was the experience of Grant and Sherman, the former in his first advance on Vicksburg, and the latter in the Atlanta campaign.

For the South it was an easier task to decide upon an objective because it was the weaker side and its acts were determined by those of the stronger. The main idea of the strategy of the Southern generals was to divert attention to side issues, to induce the opposing general to weaken his forces at decisive points. Numerous examples of diversions are afforded by campaign, in 1862, which kept many thousand men away from McClellan; Early's march on Washington, and many cavalry raids. The result of a study of objectives shows that, with good troops, and safe, but not brilliant, generals on both sides, the only way to overthrow the opponent is to attack and defeat his main army. The long periods of inactivity in the several armies of the North seem to have been largely, but not always, due to the frequent change of commanders. The other causes. would take long to analyze. Lee made six campaigns in fourteen months, from May, 1862, to July, 1863, a performance unequaled in history. But McClellan's army was inactive for ten months after Bull Run; Rosecrans' army for five months after Murfreesboro, and Grant's army for four months after Vicksburg, while Grant's army was almost in the same class during its ten months before Petersburg.

The concentration of scattered forces at decisive points, which is technically called in the text-book the use of interior lines, and in more homely phrase, " getting there first with the most men," was often skillfully performed on both a large and small scale. Thus, Johnston joined Beauregard at Bull Run in time to win the battle; Jackson alternately attacked the divided forces of his opponents and neutralized their greatly superior forces, and finally joined Lee for another campaign; Longstreet joined Bragg to win Chickamauga; Ewell joined Breckinridge to defeat Sigel. Many opportunities were lost, even in the very campaigns mentioned, as we see them today.

The conduct of pursuits confirms the idea that it is the most difficult operation presented to a general. Johnston after Bull Run, McClellan after Antietam, Meade after Gettysburg, Bragg after Chickamauga, Grant after Chattanooga, and Lee after Fredericksburg practically allowed the defeated enemy to escape without further injury.

Lee's pursuit of McClellan in the Seven Days' Battles on the Peninsula and of Meade in the operations of October,1863, had only partial success. Near the end of the war Thomas' pursuit of Hood, after Nashville, showed a much higher efficiency than had yet been reached, and the Appomattox campaign gives the only entirely successful instance in about one hundred years of military history.

The campaigns of Lee and Jackson were models of their kind. Napoleon has said that the general who makes no mistakes never goes to war. The critic of Lee finds it hard to detect mistakes. No general since Hannibal, and perhaps Napoleon, in the last two years of his campaigns, has made war under greater disadvantages and accomplished so much with an inferior force. While all great generals before him inherited a ready-made army, Lee, like Washington, made his own army.

He fought soldiers of the same race and generals of the same school as himself. His genius was shown in many ways, but nowhere more than in his ability to calculate chances, even when he was violating the so-called rules of war. He used converging columns which met upon the field of battle; he detached inferior forces against the Federals' rear; he divided his army in the presence of the foe; he uncovered his lines of retreat and fought battles in that position; he did not hesitate to throw his last reserve into the fight.

On two occasions he withdrew his army across the Potomac River, in good order and without loss, in the presence of a powerful hostile army. His use of the ground to compensate for inferior numbers and to hide his movements from the Federals shows how clearly he saw the secrets of Napoleon's generalship, while his battles in the woods were entirely original and his use of entrenchments was effective. The power of the modern fire-arm in the hands of his opponents forced him to accept less decisive results than great soldiers who preceded him. As with other great soldiers, his best success was due to the inefficiency of his opponents in the early days. He was probably the last of the race of generals who, like Napoleon, dominated the field of war by genius alone. He will be replaced by the safe leader who is never brilliant, but makes no mistakes and at the same time commands the heaviest battalions. The absence of a broad and comprehensive plan of operations was particularly noticeable on both sides. It never seemed to have been developed in the North until Grant issued his orders for a general advance, in 1864. In the South, Longstreet seems to have prepared a strategic plan for the movement of all Confederate armies after Chancellorsville, but this was not approved. The immense area occupied by the opposing forces, greater than had ever before been occupied in a single war, may be the excuse for this.

Great fame has come to the various generals who each made some well-planned maneuver, which forced the foe to relinquish territory and retreat to a rear position. McClellan before Manassas, Rosecrans before Shelbyville, and Sherman before Dalton did all this, but it is a debatable question whether the final issue was hastened or delayed.

Sherman gained Atlanta with a loss of thirty-two thousand men, and Rosecrans gained Chattanooga with a loss of eighteen thousand men, but the foe was not defeated. On the other hand, Grant, in his year from the Rapidan to Appomattox accomplished the desired result, but with severe losses, it is true. After all is said, the subject may be narrowed down to the statement that Lee, Jackson, and perhaps Johnston handled inferior forces with as great skill as any commanders since Hannibal and Napoleon. On the other side it was also an American soldier, even before Sedan and Mukden, who formulated the modern idea of strategy which has been so closely followed in recent wars-to seek out the foe, get close to him, and fight it out by short arm jolts.

TACTICS

Tactics is the military art of manoeuvring troops on the field of battle to achieve victory in combat. 'Offensive tactics" seek success through attacking; "defensive tactics" aim at defeating enemy attacks.

In Civil War tactics, the principal combat arm was infantry. Its most common deployment was a long "line of battle," 2 ranks deep. More massed was the "column," varying from 1 to 10 or more companies wide and from 8 to 20 or more ranks deep. Less compact than column or line was "open-order" deployment: a strung-out, irregular single line. Battle lines delivered the most firepower defensively and offensively. Offensive firepower alone would not ensure success. Attackers had to charge, and massed columns, with their greater depth, were often preferable to battle lines for making frontal assaults. Better yet were flank attacks, to "roll up" thin battle lines lengthwise. Offensive tacticians sought opportunity for such effective flank attacks; defensive tacticians countered by "refusing" these flanks on impassable barriers. In either posture, tacticians attempted to coordinate all their troops to deliver maximum force and firepower and to avoid being beaten "in detail" (piecemeal). Throughout, they relied on open-order deployment to cover their front and flanks with skirmishers, who developed the enemy position and screened their own troops. Open order, moreover, was best suited for moving through the wooded countryside of America. That wooded terrain, so different from Europe's open fields, for which tactical doctrine was aimed, also affected tactical control. Army commanders, even corps commanders, could not control large, far-flung forces. Instead, army commanders concentrated on strategy. And corps commanders handled "grand tactics": the medium for translating theatre strategy into battlefield tactics, the art of manoeuvring large forces just outside the battlefield and bringing them onto that field. Once on the field, corps commanders provided overall tactical direction, but their largest practical units of tactical maneuver were divisions. More often, brigades, even regiments, formed those maneuver elements. Essentially, brigades did the fighting in the Civil War.

Besides affecting organization, difficult terrain helped relegate cavalry and artillery to lesser tactical roles. More influential there was the widespread use of long-range rifled shoulder arms. As recently as the Mexican War, when most infantry fired smoothbore muskets, cavalry and artillery had been key attacking arms. Attempting to continue such tactics in the Civil War proved disastrous, as infantry rifle power soon drove horsemen virtually off the battlefield and relegated artillery to defensive support. Rifle power devastated offensive infantry assaults, too, but senior commanders, who were so quick to understand its impact on cannon and cavalry, rarely grasped its effect on infantry. By 1864, infantry customarily did erect light field fortifications to strengthen its defensive battlefield positions and protect itself from enemy rifle power; but when attacking, whether against battle lines or fortifications, infantry continued suffering heavy casualties through clinging to tactical formations outmoded by technology. But if infantry was slow to learn, other arms swiftly found new tactical roles. The new mission of the artillery was to bolster the defensive, sometimes with 1 battery assigned to each infantry brigade, but more often with I battalion assigned to a Confederate infantry division and 1 brigade to a Federal infantry corps. With long-range shells and close-in canister, artillery became crucial in repulsing enemy attacks. But long-range shelling to support ones own attack had minimal effect, and artillery assaults were soon abandoned as suicidal. Throughout, artillery depended almost entirely on direct fire against visible targets.

Cavalry, in the meantime, served most usefully in scouting for tactical intelligence and in screening such intelligence from the foe. By midwar, moreover, cavalry was using its mobility to seize key spots, where it dismounted and fought afoot. Armed with breech-loading carbines, including Federal repeaters by 1864-65, these foot cavalry fought well even against infantry. Only rarely did mounted cavalry battle with saber and pistol. Rarer still were mounted pursuits of routed enemies.

Cavalry so infrequently undertook such pursuits chiefly because defeated armies were rarely routed. Size of armies, commitment to their respective causes by individual citizen-soldiers, difficult terrain, and impact of fortifications and technology all militated against the Napoleonic triumph, which could destroy an enemy army--and an enemy country--in just 1 battle. Raised in the aura of Napoleon, most Civil War commanders sought the Napoleonic victory, but few came close to achieving it. 60 years after Marengo and Austerlitz, warfare had so changed that victory in the Civil War would instead come through strategy. Yet within that domain of strategy, not just 1 battle but series of them--and the tactics through which they were fought--were the crucial elements in deciding the outcome of the Civil War.

7

Hitler and World War II

Because of his experiences in Vienna, World War One, the Münich putsch and in prison, Adolf Hitler dreamed of building a vast German Empire sprawling across Central and Eastern Europe. *Lebensraum* could only be obtained and sustained by waging a war of conquest against the Soviet Union: German security demanded it and Hitler's racial ideology required it. War, then, was essential. It was essential to Hitler the man as well as essential to Hitler's dream of a new Germany. In the end, most historians have reached the consensus that World War Two was Hitler's war. Unfortunately, although most western statesmen had sufficient warning that Hitler was a threat to a general European peace, they failed to rally their people and take a stand until it was too late. In this respect, you could argue that the responsibility for World War Two ought to remain on the shoulders of Britain, France and the United States.

Following 1933 — the year when Hitler consolidated his power as Chancellor through the Enabling Act — Hitler implemented his foreign policy objectives. These objectives clearly violated the provisions of the Versailles Treaty. Hitler's foreign policy aims accorded with the goals of Germany's traditional rulers in that the aim was to make Germany the most powerful state in all of Europe. For example, during World War One, German generals tried to conquer extensive regions in Eastern Europe. And with the Treaty of Brest-Litovsk (1918) between Germany and Russia, Germany took Poland, the Ukraine and the Baltic States from Russia. However, where Hitler departed from this traditional scenario was his obsession with racial supremacy. His desire to annihilate whole races of inferior peoples marked a break from the outlook of the old order. This old order never contemplated the restriction of the civil rights of the Jews. They wanted to Germanize German Poles, not enslave them.

But Hitler was an opportunist — he was a man possessed and driven by a fanaticism that saw his destiny as identical to Germany's. The propaganda machine that Hitler adopted, however, was perhaps the most important device at his disposal. With it he was able to successfully undermine his opponent's will to resist. And propaganda, after winning the minds of the German people, now became a most crucial instrument of German foreign policy as a whole. There were upwards of 27 million German people living outside the borders of the Reich. To force those 27 million into support for Hitler, the Nazis utilized their propaganda machine. For example, they made every effort to export anti-Semitism internationally, thus feeding off prejudices of other nations. Hitler also began to promote himself as Europe's best defence against Stalin, the Bolsheviks and the Soviet Union. In fact, the Nazi anti-Bolshevik propaganda convinced thousands of Europeans that Hitler was also Europe's best defence against all Communists.

Hitler was a shrewd statesman. He anticipated, for instance, that the British and French would back down the moment they were faced with his direct and willful violations of Versailles. He knew that any threat of war would drive the Anglo-French into a defensive posture. The reason for this should be pretty clear — Britain and France would have done anything to avoid another conflict and this defensive position managed to win a vote of confidence from public opinion.

The British believed that Germany had been treated too harshly by the provisions of Versailles and because of this, they were willing to make concessions to the Germans. The French, with the largest army on the Continent, refused to contemplate an offensive war, as was their position in World War One, and decided instead to protect their borders at all costs. The United States, meanwhile, stood aloof from any European conflict because they had their own problems to deal with, namely, the Great Depression. To top it all off, the British and French no longer trusted Russia, so the hopes of establishing an alliance along the lines which developed during the Great War was just not possible. So the British introduced their policy of appeasement. They hoped that by making concessions to Hitler, war would be avoided. They also held on to the illusion that Hitler was, once again, Europe's best defence against Soviet Russia. The British appeasers certainly missed the boat — even with *Mein Kampf* in their hands, they failed to understand Hitler's foreign policy aims. Hitler could be reasoned with, they argued. Meanwhile, Germany grew stronger and the German people began to look to Hitler as their messiah.

Hitler needed a strong army to realize his war aims. According to the provisions of the Versailles Treaty, the Germany army was to be limited to 100,000 soldiers. The size of the navy was limited as well. Germany was also forbidden to produce military aircraft, tanks and heavy artillery. The General Staff was dissolved. These were harsh provisions. How did Germany get by these conditions? Well, actually it was quite easy. In March 1935, Hitler declared that Germany was no longer bound by the provisions of the Versailles Treaty. He began conscription and built up the air force. France protested, weakly, and Britain negotiated a naval agreement with the Germans. One year later, on March 7, 1936, Hitler marched his troops into the Rhineland, a clear violation of Versailles. His generals cautioned Hitler that such a move would provoke an attack. Again, Hitler judged the Anglo-French response correctly. The British and French took no action. The British sat back. The French saw the remilitarization of the Rhineland as a grave threat to their security. With 22,000 German soldiers standing along the French border, why didn't the French act? The first reason was that France would not act alone and Britain offered no help at this point. Second, the French over-estimated German forces who marched into the Rhineland. Again, their posture was decidedly defensive. And lastly, French public opinion was strongly opposed to any confrontation with Hitler.

Meanwhile, European fascism was winning another war in Spain between 1936 and 1937. Mussolini and Hitler both supported Franco's right-wing dictatorship and as to be expected, the French refused to intervene. The Spanish Civil War was decisive for Hitler for it was here that he was able to test new weapons and new aircraft which would eventually make their appearance when World War Two finally broke out in 1939. And then in 1938, Hitler ordered his troops to march into Austria, which then became a province of Germany. The Austrians celebrated by ringing church bells, waving swastikas and attacking Jews. The *Anschluss* was yet another violation of Versailles. Why had so many people missed the boat? In *Mein Kampf*, Hitler had made it quite clear that Austria must be annexed to Germany, Did anyone listen? Did anyone make any effort to prevent *Anschluss*? No! Britain and France both informed the Chancellor of Austria that they would not help if invaded by Germany. Once again, non-intervention paved the way for Hitler's foreign policy aims.

Hitler used the threat of force to obtain Austria and a similar threat would give him the Sudetenland of Czechoslovakia. More than three-quarters of the population of the Sudetenland were ethnic Germans. The area also contained key industries and was vital to the protection of Czechoslovakia. Without this area heavily fortified Czechoslovakia could not hope to withstand German aggression. Sudentenland Germans, encouraged by the Nazis, began to denounce the Czech government. Meanwhile, Hitler's propaganda machine accused the Czech government of hideous crimes and warned of retribution. He ordered his generals to plan an invasion of Czechoslovakia. At this point, the British Prime Minister NEVILLE CHAMBERLAIN decided to intervene and Hitler agreed to a conference with him. The opinion of British statesmen was that the Sudetenland Germans were being deprived of their right to self-determination. The Sudetenland, like Austria, was not worth another war, they reasoned. Once the Germans were living under the German flag, the British argued, Hitler would be satisfied. And so the fate of Czechoslovakia was sealed in September 1938.

Chamberlain, Hitler, Mussolini and Daladier, the Prime Minister of France, signed the MÜNICH PACT and agreed that all Czech troops in the Sudetenland would be replaced by German troops. The British hailed Chamberlain — the French hailed Daladier. While Chamberlain returned to England with a piece of paper in his hand, Hitler was laughing. What Britain and France had shown was their own weakness and this weakness increased Hitler's appetite for even more territory. With the Sudetenland annexed, Hitler plotted to annihilate the independent existence of Czechoslovakia. And so, in March 1939, Czechoslovak independence came to an end. After Czechoslovakia, Germany turned to Poland. Hitler demanded that the Polish port town of Danzig be returned to Germany. Poland refused to hand over Danzig since it was vital to their economy. Meanwhile, France and Britain warned Hitler that they would come to the assistance of Poland. On May 22, 1939, Hitler and Mussolini signed the Pact of Steel and promised one another mutual aid. One month later, the German army presented Hitler with battle plans for the invasion of Poland.

While all this was going on, negotiations were under way between Britain, France and Russia. The Soviets wanted mutual aid — but they also demanded military bases in Poland and Romania. Britain would not give in to their demands. And of course, while all this is going on, Russia was conducting secret talks with Germany. The result of all this was that on August 23, 1939, Ribbentrop and Molotov signed the NAZI-SOVIET PACT of non-aggression. One section of this Pact — even more secret than the Nazi-Soviet Pact itself — called for the partition of Poland between Germany and Russia. The Nazi-Soviet pact served as the green light for the invasion of Poland and on September 1, 1939, German troops marched into Poland. Britain and France demanded that Hitler stop his forces but Hitler ignored them and so Britain and France declared war on Germany. Using the *Blitzkrieg* or lightening war, Poland succumbed to Germany on September 27, 1939.

The period of six months following the fall of Poland has been called "the phony war." Fighting was limited to minor skirmishes along the French and German borders. But in April

1940, Hitler struck at Denmark and Norway. Hitler needed to establish naval bases in these countries from which his submarines could attack England. Denmark surrendered in only one day and Norway soon followed. The following month, Hitler attacked Belgium, Holland and Luxembourg. Surrenders followed quickly. Meanwhile, French troops rushed to Belgium to prevent a German breakthrough. The German forces converged on the French port of Dunkirk, the last point of escape for the Allies. But Hitler called off his tanks and planned to use airstrikes to annihilate the Allies. As it turned out, fog and rain prevented Hitler from using the full force of his airplanes. 340,000 British and French forces were ferried across the English Channel to England while Germany bombed the beaches.

By late Spring 1940, there was every indication that France was about to fall to the Nazis. Numerous French divisions were cut off and in retreat. Millions of French refugees were making their way south and on June 10, 1940, Mussolini declared war on France. The French government sent out an appeal for armistice and so on June 22, 1940, French and German officials met in a railway car and signed the agreement. In a odd twist of fate, it was the same railway car used to sign the provisions of the Treaty of Versailles back in 1918.

With France fallen, Hitler assumed that Britain would make peace. The British rejected any overtures on the part of the Germans and so in August 1940, Hitler ordered his *Luftwaffe* to conduct massive airstrikes against Britain and the Battle of Britain had begun. The battle raged for almost five months. On September 15, the British RAF shot down sixty German aircraft and Hitler was forced to postpone his invasion of Britain. The Germans, however, continued their night time attacks on English cities and towns but British morale never broke during the *Blitz*. By the end of 1941, Hitler had also invaded Russia but Russia would not yield. By early 1942, Nazi Germany ruled virtually all of Europe. Territories were annexed, some were under German military authority while still others, such as France, collaborated with the Nazis. It was over this vast empire that Hitler intended to superimpose a New Order. The

Germans expropriated and exploited every country which they conquered. They took gold, art, machinery and food supplies back to Germany. Some foreign factories were confiscated — others produced what the Germans demanded. The bottom line is quite simple — the Germans took whatever it was they wanted.

Seven million people from all over occupied Europe were enslaved and transported to Germany where they lived and worked in forced labor camps. The Nazis rules by terror and fear. The New Order meant torture, prison, firing squads and concentration camps. For example, in Poland, priests and intellectuals were jailed and killed and most schools and churches were ordered closed. In Russia, political officials were immediately executed and prisoners of war were herded into camps and worked to death. Germany ended up taking 5.5 million Russian POWs, 3.5 million of which were killed or died in captivity.

The task of imposing what came to be known as "the final solution of the Jewish Problem," was outlined at a conference held on January 20, 1942. One result of the WANNSEE PROTOCOL, was that a portion of the responsibility for the extermination of European Jewry was given to HIMMLER'S SS. The SS responded with fanaticism and bureaucratic efficiency. The Jews were identified with Reason, Equality, Tolerance, Freedom and individualism. The Jews had no *Kultur*. Though perhaps German born, they were not a people of the *Volk*. The SS enjoyed their work a great deal. They regarded themselves as idealists who were writing the most glorious of chapters in the history of Germany. In Russia, special squads of the SS — the *Einsatzgruppen*, trained for genocide — entered captured towns and cities and rounded up Jewish men, women and children who were herded into groups and then shot en masse. About two million Russian Jews perished as a result. In Poland, Hitler established ghettoes where some 3.5 million Jews were forced to live, sealed off from the rest of the population.

To expedite the Final Solution, the Nazis began to use concentration camps. These camps were already in existence for the use of political prisoners. Jews from all over Europe were rounded up under the notion that they were about to be resettled. Although the Jews knew something about plans for their eventual extermination, they just could not believe that any 20th century nation would resort to such a crime against humanity. Of course, the Holocaust was a reality. Cattle cars full of Jews and other inferior races traveled days without food or water. When the doors opened, they found themselves in the unreal world of the concentration camp. SS doctors then inspected the "freight." Rudolf Hoess (1900-1947), commandant at Auschwitz described the procedure in the following way:

I estimate that at least 2,500,000 victims were executed and exterminated [at Auschwitz] by gassing and burning, and at least another half million succumbed to starvation and disease, making a total dead of about 3,000,000. This figure represents about 70% or 80% of all persons sent to Auschwitz as prisoners, the remainder having been selected and used for slave labor in the concentration camp industries....

The final solution of the Jewish Question meant the complete extermination of all Jews in Europe. I was ordered to establish extermination facilities at Auschwitz in June 1941. It took from three to fifteen minutes to kill people in the death chamber, depending upon climatic conditions. We knew when the people were dead because their screaming stopped. We usually waited about one-half hour before we opened the doors and removed the bodies. After the bodies were removed our special commandos took off the rings and extracted gold from the teeth of corpses....

The way we selected our victims was as follows.... Those who were fit to work were sent into the camp. Others were sent immediately to the extermination plants. Children of tender years were invariably exterminated since by reason of their youth they were unable to work.... We endeavored to fool the victims into thinking that they were to go through a delousing process. Of course, frequently they realized our true intentions, and we sometimes had riots and difficulties due to that fact. Very frequently women wide hide their children under clothes, but of course when we found them we would send the children in to be exterminated.

Auschwitz was more than a death factory. It also provided I. G. Farben with slave laborers, both Jew and non-Jew. Workers worked at a pace at which even the healthiest of workers would have found intolerable. And because Germany now had somewhat of an unlimited labor supply, working prisoners as fast as possible would solve two problems at the same time: increased production and the extermination of inmates. Auschwitz also allowed the SS, the elite members of the master race, to shape themselves according to Nazi ideology. The SS, for instance, amused themselves with pregnant women, women who were beaten with clubs, attacked by dogs, dragged by the hair and then thrown into the crematory, still alive. The SS systematically overworked, starved and beat their inmates. They made them live in filth and sleep in over-crowded rooms. The purpose of such inhuman behaviour was to rob the individual of any shred of human dignity. In this way, the SS and the Nazis could demonstrate — to themselves, of course — that the Jew was clearly an inferior race of people. After hours or weeks, exhausted, starving, diseased and beaten, these men and women were sent to the gas chamber.

Over the course of the last 3000 years or so, the Jews have been the focus of hostility, hatred and intolerance. The Egyptians, Greeks, Romans and medieval Christians all looked upon the Jew as an outsider, as a person who did not truly belong to or in the community in which they were living. What was unique about the HOLOCAUST was the Nazi's intention to murder, without exception, every single Jew they found. Also unique was the fanaticism and cruelty with which they pursued this goal. The Holocaust was the culmination of Nazi racial ideology. Using modern technology and bureaucratic machinery, the Nazis systematically killed at least six million Jews. This figure represents nearly 65% of Europe's Jewish population. 1.5 million of these were children. Another 6-7 million non-Jews were also exterminated meaning that the Holocaust resulted in the deaths of at least 13 million innocent souls. Could man ever return to the felicific idea of progress as advocated by the 18th or 19th centuries? Across occupied territories of the Third Reich there were Nazi collaborators who welcomed the fall of democracy and who still saw Hitler as the best defence against communism. But each country also produced a resistance movement that grew stronger as Nazi atrocities increased. The resistance movement rescued downed pilots, radioed military movements to London, and sabotaged German railway depots. The Danish underground managed to smuggle 8000 Jews into Sweden while the Polish resistance, estimated to number 300,000, reported on German positions and interfered with the movement of supplies. Russian partisans sabotaged railways, destroyed trucks and killed hundreds of Germans in ambush. The Yugoslav resistance army, led by Marshall Tito, was a disciplined fighting force which ultimately liberated the country from the Germans.

European Jews were specifically active in the French resistance movement. But in eastern Europe, the Jewish resisters received little or no support and were usually denounced to the Nazis. The Germans responded harshly to the Jewish resistance. For example, 200 Jews were killed for every one Nazi. However, in the Spring of 1943, the surviving Jews of the Warsaw ghetto managed to fight the Germans for several weeks. Also, in 1943, and after the Allies had landed in Italy, Italian resisters managed to liberate the country from the fascists and German occupation. And on July 20, 1944, Colonel Stauffenberg planted a bomb under Hitler's table at staff conference meeting — the bomb exploded but Hitler escaped serious injury. The Nazis responded by torturing and executing 5000 suspected anti-Nazis.

Although the European resistance was proof that some people refused to accept Hitler and the Nazis, their efforts did not bring an end to the war. Japan's imperialist endeavours from the early 1930s on and including the attack on PEARL Harbour on December 7, 1941, forced the United States to end its isolationist position and enter the war. Meanwhile, Hitler had made the same blunder as had Napoleon, by attacking Russia in winter. In February 1943, almost 300,000 soldiers died in the battle of Stalingrad and another 130,000 were taken prisoner. And in the fall of 1943, Allied forces liberated Italy. Mussolini was dismissed, and eventually shot and hung by his ankles in April 1945. Finally, on June 6, 1944 — D-Day — the Allies landed 2 million men on to the beach head at Normandy. By August, the Allies liberated Paris and then Brussels and Antwerp. Meanwhile, the Allies were conducting massive bombing raids on German industrial cities. The Russians drove across the Baltic states, Poland and Hungary and by February 1945, they were 100 miles from Berlin. By April, American, British and Russian troops were moving toward Berlin from all sides. On April 30, 1945, Hitler and Eva Braun committed suicide and one week later, May 7, a demoralized and near destroyed Germany surrendered unconditionally. Finally, on August 6, 1945, the United States dropped an atomic bomb on Hiroshima — 78,000 perished within fifteen minutes of the blast. Three days later, another bomb fell on Nagasaki and on August 14, Japan surrendered.

The legacy of World War Two was dramatic. 50 million lost their lives, 20 million Russians alone. The war also meant a vast number of people left Europe for either England or the United States in an exodus which has come to be known as the Great Sea Change. Hundreds of cities were destroyed, some of them centuries-old. Only 5% of Berlin remained intact, 70% of Dresden, Hamburg, Munich and Frankfurt were destroyed. The war also revealed the existence of two superpowers — the United States and the Soviet Union, countries which would determine the fate of Europe and the world for the next four decades. The world now had to atomic bomb. The world also had its Satan: Hitler. Vast imperialist empires were destroyed and then there was the Holocaust. In the intellectual realm and in the world of art, the European war created a Second Lost Generation with its own philosophy: existentialism.

WORLD WAR II AND POST-WAR (1939–47)

Molotov-Ribbentrop Pact (1939-41)

Soviet relations with the West further deteriorated when, one week prior to the start of the World War II, the Soviet Union and Germany signed the Molotov-Ribbentrop Pact, which included a secret agreement to split Poland and Eastern Europe between the two states. Beginning one week later, in September

1939, Germany and the Soviet Union divided Poland and the rest of Eastern Europe through invasions of the countries ceded to each under the Pact. For the next year and a half, they engaged in an extensive economic relationship, trading vital war materials until Germany broke the Molotov-Ribbentrop Pact with Operation Barbarossa, the invasion of the Soviet Union through the territories that the two countries had previously divided.

Allies against the Axis (1941-45)

During their joint war effort, which began thereafter in 1941, the Soviets suspected that the British and the Americans had conspired to allow the Soviets to bear the brunt of the fighting against Nazi Germany. According to this view, the Western Allies had deliberately delayed opening a second anti-German front in order to step in at the last moment and shape the peace settlement. Thus, Soviet perceptions of the West left a strong undercurrent of tension and hostility between the Allied powers.

WARTIME CONFERENCES REGARDING POST-WAR EUROPE

The Allies disagreed about how the European map should look, and how borders would be drawn, following the war. Each side held dissimilar ideas regarding the establishment and maintenance of post-war security. The western Allies desired a security system in which democratic governments were established as widely as possible, permitting countries to peacefully resolve differences through international organizations. Following Russian historical experiences with frequent invasions and the immense death toll (estimated at 27 million) and destruction the Soviet Union sustained during World War II, the Soviet Union sought to increase security by controlling the internal affairs of countries that bordered it. In April 1945, both Churchill and new American President Harry S. Truman opposed, among other things, the Soviets' decision to prop up the Lublin government, the Soviet-controlled rival to the Polish government-in-exile, whose relations with the Soviets were severed.

At the Yalta Conference in February 1945, the Allies failed to reach a firm consensus on the framework for post-war settlement in Europe. Following the Allied victory in May, the Soviets effectively occupied Eastern Europe, while strong US and Western allied forces remained in Western Europe. The Soviet Union, United States, Britain and France established zones of occupation and a loose framework for four-power control of occupied Germany. The Allies set up the United Nations for the maintenance of world peace, but the enforcement capacity of its Security Council was effectively paralyzed by individual members' ability to use veto power. Accordingly, the UN was essentially converted into an inactive forum for exchanging polemical rhetoric, and the Soviets regarded it almost exclusively as a propaganda tribune.

Beginnings of the Eastern Bloc

During the final stages of the war, the Soviet Union laid the foundation for the Eastern Bloc by directly annexing several countries as Soviet Socialist Republics that were initially (and effectively) ceded to it by Nazi Germany in the Molotov-Ribbentrop Pact. These included eastern Poland (incorporated into two different SSRs), Latvia (which became the Latvian SSR), Estonia (which became the Estonian SSR), Lithuania (which became the Lithuanian SSR), part of eastern Finland (which became the Karelo-Finnish SSR) and eastern Romania (which became the Moldavian SSR). British Prime Minister Winston Churchill was concerned that, given the enormous size of Soviet forces deployed in Europe at the end of the war, and the perception that Soviet leader Joseph Stalin was unreliable, there existed a Soviet threat to Western Europe. In April-May 1945, the British War Cabinet's Joint Planning Staff Committee developed Operation Unthinkable, a plan "to impose upon Russia the will of the United States and the British Empire". The plan, however, was rejected by the British Chiefs of Staff Committee as militarily unfeasible.

Potsdam Conference and defeat of Japan

At the Potsdam Conference, which started in late July after Germany's surrender, serious differences emerged over the future development of Germany and eastern Europe. Moreover, the participants' mounting antipathy and bellicose language served to confirm their suspicions about each others' hostile intentions and entrench their positions. At this conference Truman informed Stalin that the United States possessed a powerful new weapon. Stalin was aware that the Americans were working on the atomic bomb and, given that the Soviets' own rival program was in place, he reacted to the news calmly. The Soviet leader said he was pleased by the news and expressed the hope that the weapon would be used against Japan. One week after the end of the Potsdam Conference, the US bombed Hiroshima and Nagasaki. Shortly after the attacks, Stalin protested to US officials when Truman offered the Soviets little real influence in occupied Japan.

Tensions Build

In February 1946, George F. Kennan's "Long Telegram" from Moscow helped to articulate the US government's increasingly hard line against the Soviets, and became the basis for US strategy toward the Soviet Union for the duration of the Cold War. That September, the Soviet side produced the Novikov telegram, sent by the Soviet ambassador to the US but commissioned and "co-authored" by Vyacheslav Molotov; it portrayed the US as being in the grip of monopoly capitalists who were building up military capability "to prepare the conditions for winning world supremacy in a new war". On September 6, 1946, James F. Byrnes delivered a speech in Germany repudiating the Morgenthau Plan (a proposal to partition and de-industrialize post-war Germany) and warning the Soviets that the US intended to maintain a military presence in Europe indefinitely. As Byrnes admitted a month later, "The nub of our program was to win the German people [...] it was a battle between us and Russia over minds [...]"

A few weeks after the release of this "Long Telegram", former British Prime Minister Winston Churchill delivered his famous "Iron Curtain" speech in Fulton, Missouri. The speech called for an Anglo-American alliance against the Soviets, whom he accused of establishing an "iron curtain" from "Stettin in the Baltic to Trieste in the Adriatic".

CONTAINMENT THROUGH THE KOREAN WAR (1947–53)

After annexing several occupied countries as Soviet Socialist Republics at the end of World War II, other occupied states were added to the Eastern Bloc by converting them into puppet Soviet Satellite states, such as East Germany, the People's Republic of Poland, the People's Republic of Hungary, the Czechoslovak Socialist Republic, the People's Republic of Romania and the People's Republic of Albania. The Soviet-style regimes that arose in the Bloc not only reproduced Soviet command economies, but also adopted the brutal methods employed by Joseph Stalin and Soviet secret police to suppress real and potential opposition. In Asia, the Red Army had overrun Manchuria in the last month of the war, and went on to occupy the large swath of Korean territory located north of the 38th parallel.

In September 1947, the Soviets created Cominform, the purpose of which was to enforce orthodoxy within the international communist movement and tighten political control over Soviet satellites through coordination of communist parties in the Eastern Bloc. Cominform faced an embarrassing setback the following June, when the Tito–Stalin split obliged its members to expel Yugoslavia, which remained Communist but adopted a non-aligned position. As part of the Soviet domination of the Eastern Bloc, the NKVD, led by Lavrentiy Beria, supervised the establishment of Soviet-style secret police systems in the Bloc that were supposed to crush anti-communist resistance. When the slightest stirrings of independence emerged in the Bloc, Stalin's strategy matched that of dealing with domestic pre-war rivals: they were removed from power, put on trial, imprisoned, and in several instances, executed.

Containment and the Truman Doctrine

By 1947, US president Harry S. Truman's advisers urged him to take immediate steps to counter the Soviet Union's influence, citing Stalin's efforts (amid post-war confusion and collapse) to undermine the US by encouraging rivalries among capitalists that could precipitate another war. In February

1947, the British government announced that it could no longer afford to finance the Greek monarchical military regime in its civil war against communist-led insurgents. The American government's response to this announcement was the adoption of containment, the goal of which was to stop the spread of communism. Truman delivered a speech that called for the allocation of $400 million to intervene in the war and unveiled the Truman Doctrine, which framed the conflict as a contest between free peoples and totalitarian regimes. Even though the insurgents were helped by Josip Broz Tito's Yugoslavia, US policymakers accused the Soviet Union of conspiring against the Greek royalists in an effort to expand Soviet influence.

Enunciation of the Truman Doctrine marked the beginning of a US bipartisan defence and foreign policy consensus between Republicans and Democrats focused on containment and deterrence that weakened during and after the Vietnam War, but ultimately held steady. Moderate and conservative parties in Europe, as well as social democrats, gave virtually unconditional support to the Western alliance, while European and American Communists, paid by the KGB and involved in its intelligence operations, adhered to Moscow's line, although dissent began to appear after 1956. Other critiques of consensus politics came from anti-Vietnam War activists, the CND and the nuclear freeze movement.

Marshall Plan and Czechoslovak Coup d'état

In early 1947, Britain, France and the United States unsuccessfully attempted to reach an agreement with the Soviet Union for a plan envisioning an economically self-sufficient Germany, including a detailed accounting of the industrial plants, goods and infrastructure already removed by the Soviets. In June 1947, in accordance with the Truman Doctrine, the United States enacted the Marshall Plan, a pledge of economic assistance for all European countries willing to participate, including the Soviet Union. The plan's aim was to rebuild the democratic and economic systems of Europe and to counter perceived threats to Europe's balance of power, such as communist parties seizing control through revolutions or elections. The plan also stated that European prosperity was contingent upon German economic recovery. One month later, Truman signed the National Security Act of 1947, creating a unified Department of Defence, the Central Intelligence Agency (CIA), and the National Security Council. These would become the main bureaucracies for US policy in the Cold War.

Stalin believed that economic integration with the West would allow Eastern Bloc countries to escape Soviet control, and that the US was trying to buy a pro-US re-alignment of Europe. Stalin therefore prevented Eastern Bloc nations from receiving Marshall Plan aid. The Soviet Union's alternative to the Marshall plan, which was purported to involve Soviet subsidies and trade with eastern Europe, became known as the Molotov Plan (later institutionalized in January 1949 as the Comecon). Stalin was also fearful of a reconstituted Germany; his vision of a post-war Germany did not include the ability to rearm or pose any kind of threat to the Soviet Union.

In early 1948, following reports of strengthening "reactionary elements", Soviet operatives executed a coup d'état of 1948 in Czechoslovakia, the only Eastern Bloc state that the Soviets had permitted to retain democratic structures. The public brutality of the coup shocked Western powers more than any event up to that point, set in a motion a brief scare that war would occur and swept away the last vestiges of opposition to the Marshall Plan in the United States Congress.

The twin policies of the Truman Doctrine and the Marshall Plan led to billions in economic and military aid for Western Europe, and Greece and Turkey. With US assistance, the Greek military won its civil war, The Italian Christian Democrats defeated the powerful Communist-Socialist alliance in the elections of 1948. Increases occurred in intelligence and espionage activities, Eastern Bloc defections and diplomatic expulsions.

BERLIN BLOCKADE AND AIRLIFT

The United States and Britain merged their western German occupation zones into "Bizonia" (later "trizonia" with the addition of France's zone). As part of the economic rebuilding of Germany, in early 1948, representatives of a number of

Western European governments and the United States announced an agreement for a merger of western German areas into a federal governmental system. In addition, in accordance with the Marshall Plan, they began to re-industrialize and rebuild the German economy, including the introduction of a new Deutsche Mark currency to replace the old Reichsmark currency that the Soviets had debased.

Shortly thereafter, Stalin instituted the Berlin Blockade, one of the first major crises of the Cold War, preventing food, materials and supplies from arriving in West Berlin. The United States, Britain, France, Canada, Australia, New Zealand and several other countries began the massive "Berlin airlift", supplying West Berlin with food and other provisions. The Soviets mounted a public relations campaign against the policy change, communists attempted to disrupt the elections of 1948 preceding large losses therein, 300,000 Berliners demonstrated and urged the international airlift to continue, and the US accidentally created "Operation Vittles", which supplied candy to German children. In May 1949, Stalin backed down and lifted the blockade.

NATO BEGINNINGS AND RADIO FREE EUROPE

Britain, France, the United States, Canada and eight other western European countries signed the North Atlantic Treaty of April 1949, establishing the North Atlantic Treaty Organization (NATO). That August, Stalin ordered the detonation of the first Soviet atomic device. Following Soviet refusals to participate in a German rebuilding effort set forth by western European countries in 1948, the US, Britain and France spearheaded the establishment of West Germany from the three Western zones of occupation in May 1949. The Soviet Union proclaimed its zone of occupation in Germany the German Democratic Republic that October.

Media in the Eastern Bloc was an organ of the state, completely reliant on and subservient to the communist party, with radio and television organizations being state-owned, while print media was usually owned by political organizations, mostly by the local communist party. Soviet propaganda used Marxist philosophy to attack capitalism, claiming labor exploitation and war-mongering imperialism were inherent in the system.

Along with the broadcasts of the British Broadcasting Company and the Voice of America to Eastern Europe, a major propaganda effort begun in 1949 was Radio Free Europe/Radio Liberty, dedicated to bringing about the peaceful demise of the Communist system in the Eastern Bloc. Radio Free Europe attempted to achieve these goals by serving as a surrogate home radio station, an alternative to the controlled and party-dominated domestic press. Radio Free Europe was a product of some of the most prominent architects of America's early Cold War strategy, especially those who believed that the Cold War would eventually be fought by political rather than military means, such as George F. Kennan.

American policymakers, including Kennan and John Foster Dulles, acknowledged that the Cold War was in its essence a war of ideas. The United States, acting through the CIA, funded a long list of projects to counter the Communist appeal among intellectuals in Europe and the developing world. In the early 1950s, the US worked for the rearmament of West Germany and, in 1955, secured its full membership of NATO. In May 1953, Beria, by then in a government post, had made an unsuccessful proposal to allow the reunification of a neutral Germany to prevent West Germany's incorporation into NATO.

Chinese Revolution and SEATO

In 1949, Mao's Red Army defeated the US-backed Kuomintang (KMT) Nationalist Government in China, and the Soviet Union promptly created an alliance with the newly-formed People's Republic of China. Confronted with the Chinese Revolution and the end of the US atomic monopoly in 1949, the Truman administration quickly moved to escalate and expand the containment policy. In NSC-68, a secret 1950 document, the National Security Council proposed to reinforce pro-Western alliance systems and quadruple spending on defence.

US officials moved thereafter to expand containment into Asia, Africa, and Latin America, in order to counter revolutionary nationalist movements, often led by Communist parties financed by the USSR, fighting against the restoration of Europe's colonial empires in South-East Asia and elsewhere.

In the early 1950s (a period sometimes known as the "Pactomania"), the US formalized a series of alliances with Japan, Australia, New Zealand, Thailand and the Philippines (notably ANZUS and SEATO), thereby guaranteeing the United States a number of long-term military bases.

Korean War

One of the more significant impacts of containment was the outbreak of the Korean War. In June 1950, Kim Il-Sung's North Korean People's Army invaded South Korea. To Stalin's surprise, the UN Security Council backed the defence of South Korea, though the Soviets were then boycotting meetings to protest that Taiwan and not Communist China held a permanent seat on the Council. A UN force of personnel from South Korea, the United States, the United Kingdom, Turkey, Canada, Australia, France, the Philippines, the Netherlands, Belgium, New Zealand and other countries joined to stop the invasion.

Among other effects, the Korean War galvanised NATO to develop a military structure. Public opinion in countries involved, such as Great Britain, was divided for and against the war. British Attorney General Sir Hartley Shawcross repudiated the sentiment of those opposed when he said: I know there are some who think that the horror and devastation of a world war now would be so frightful, whoever won, and the damage to civilization so lasting, that it would be better to submit to Communist domination. I understand that view–but I reject it.

Even though the Chinese and North Koreans were exhausted by the war and were prepared to end it by late 1952, Stalin insisted that they continue fighting, and a cease-fire was approved only in July 1953, after Stalin's death. In North Korea, Kim Il Sung created a highly centralized and brutal dictatorship, according himself unlimited power and generating a formidable cult of personality.

CRISIS AND ESCALATION (1953–62)

Khrushchev, Eisenhower and De-Stalinization

In 1953, changes in political leadership on both sides shifted the dynamic of the Cold War. Dwight D. Eisenhower was inaugurated president that January. During the last 18 months of the Truman administration, the US defence budget had quadrupled, and Eisenhower moved to reduce military spending by a third while continuing to fight the Cold War effectively. In March, following the death of Joseph Stalin, Nikita Khrushchev became the Soviet leader following the deposition and execution of Lavrentiy Beria and the pushing aside of rivals Georgy Malenkov and Vyacheslav Molotov. On February 25, 1956, Khrushchev shocked delegates to the 20th Congress of the Soviet Communist Party by cataloguing and denouncing Stalin's crimes. As part of a campaign of de-Stalinization, he declared that the only way to reform and move away from Stalin's policies would be to acknowledge errors made in the past.

On November 18, 1956, while addressing Western ambassadors at a reception at the Polish embassy in Moscow, Khrushchev used his famous "Whether you like it or not, history is on our side. We will bury you" expression, shocking everyone present. However, he had not been talking about nuclear war, he later claimed, but rather about the historically determined victory of communism over capitalism. He then declared in 1961 that even if the USSR might indeed be behind the West, within a decade its housing shortage would disappear, consumer goods would be abundant, its population would be "materially provided for", and within two decades, the Soviet Union "would rise to such a great height that, by comparison, the main capitalist countries will remain far below and well behind". Eisenhower's secretary of state, John Foster Dulles, initiated a "New Look" for the containment strategy, calling for a greater reliance on nuclear weapons against US enemies in wartime. Dulles also enunciated the doctrine of "massive retaliation", threatening a severe US response to any Soviet aggression. Possessing nuclear superiority, for example, allowed Eisenhower to face down Soviet threats to intervene in the Middle East during the 1956 Suez Crisis.

Warsaw Pact and Hungarian Revolution

The Hungarian Revolution of 1956 occurred shortly after Khrushchev arranged the removal of Hungary's Stalinist leader Mátyás Rákosi. In response to a popular uprising, the new regime formally disbanded the secret police, declared its intention to withdraw from the Warsaw Pact and pledged to re-establish free elections. The Soviet Red Army invaded. Thousands of Hungarians were arrested, imprisoned and deported to the Soviet Union, and approximately 200,000 Hungarians fled Hungary in the chaos. Hungarian leader Imre Nagy and others were executed following secret trials.

From 1957 through 1961, Khrushchev openly and repeatedly threatened the West with nuclear annihilation. He claimed that Soviet missile capabilities were far superior to those of the United States, capable of wiping out any American or European city. However, Khrushchev rejected Stalin's belief in the inevitability of war, and declared his new goal was to be "peaceful coexistence". This formulation modified the Stalin-era Soviet stance, where international class struggle meant the two opposing camps were on an inevitable collision course where Communism would triumph through global war; now, peace would allow capitalism to collapse on its own, as well as giving the Soviets time to boost their military capabilities, which remained for decades until Gorbachev's later "new thinking" envisioning peaceful coexistence as an end in itself rather than a form of class struggle. US pronouncements concentrated on American strength abroad and the success of liberal capitalism. However, by the late 1960s, the "battle for men's minds" between two systems of social organization that Kennedy spoke of in 1961 was largely over, with tensions henceforth based primarily on clashing geopolitical objectives rather than ideology.

Berlin Ultimatum and European Integration

During November 1958, Khrushchev made an unsuccessful attempt to turn all of Berlin into an independent, demilitarized "free city", giving the United States, Great Britain, and France a six-month ultimatum to withdraw their troops from the sectors they still occupied in West Berlin, or he would transfer control of Western access rights to the East Germans. Khrushchev earlier explained to Mao Tse-tung that "Berlin is the testicles of the West. Every time I want to make the West scream, I squeeze on Berlin." NATO formally rejected the ultimatum in mid-December and Khrushchev withdrew it in return for a Geneva conference on the German question. More broadly, one hallmark of the 1950s was the beginning of European integration—a fundamental by-product of the Cold War that Truman and Eisenhower promoted politically, economically, and militarily, but which later administrations viewed ambivalently, fearful that an independent Europe would forge a separate détente with the Soviet Union, which would use this to exacerbate Western disunity.

Worldwide Competition

Nationalist movements in some countries and regions, notably Guatemala, Iran, the Philippines, and Indochina were often allied with communist groups—or at least were perceived in the West to be allied with communists. In this context, the US and the Soviet Union increasingly competed for influence by proxy in the Third World as decolonization gained momentum in the 1950s and early 1960s; additionally, the Soviets saw continuing losses by imperial powers as presaging the eventual victory of their ideology. The US government utilized the CIA in order to remove a string of unfriendly Third World governments and to support allied ones. The US used the CIA to overthrow governments suspected by Washington of turning pro-Soviet, including Iran's first democratically elected government under Prime Minister Mohammed Mosaddeq in 1953 and Guatemala's democratically elected president Jacobo Arbenz Guzmán in 1954. Between 1954 and 1961, the US sent economic aid and military advisors to stem the collapse of South Vietnam's pro-Western regime.

Many emerging nations of Asia, Africa, and Latin America rejected the pressure to choose sides in the East-West competition. In 1955, at the Bandung Conference in Indonesia, dozens of Third World governments resolved to stay out of the Cold War. The consensus reached at Bandung culminated with the creation of the Non-Aligned Movement in 1961. Meanwhile, Khrushchev broadened Moscow's'policy to establish ties with India and other key neutral states. Independence movements in the Third World transformed the post-war order into a more pluralistic world of decolonized African and Middle Eastern nations and of rising nationalism in Asia and Latin America.

Sino-Soviet split, space race, ICBMs

The period after 1956 was marked by serious setbacks for the Soviet Union, most notably the breakdown of the Sino-Soviet alliance, beginning the Sino-Soviet split. Mao had defended Stalin when Khrushchev attacked him after his death in 1956, and treated the new Soviet leader as a superficial upstart, accusing him of having lost his revolutionary edge.

After this, Khrushchev made many desperate attempts to reconstitute the Sino-Soviet alliance, but Mao considered it useless and denied any proposal. The Chinese and the Soviets waged an intra-Communist propaganda war. Further on, the Soviets focused on a bitter rivalry with Mao's China for leadership of the global communist movement, and the two clashed militarily in 1969. On the nuclear weapons front, the US and the USSR pursued nuclear rearmament and developed long-range weapons with which they could strike the territory of the other. In August 1957, the Soviets successfully launched the world's first intercontinental ballistic missile (ICBM) and in October, launched the first Earth satellite, Sputnik. The launch of Sputnik inaugurated the Space Race. This culminated in the Apollo Moon landings, which astronaut Frank Borman later described as "just a battle in the Cold War" with superior spaceflight rockets indicating superior ICBMs.

BERLIN CRISIS OF 1961

The Berlin Crisis of 1961 was the last major incident in the Cold War regarding the status of Berlin and post-World War II Germany. By the early 1950s, the Soviet approach to restricting emigration movement was emulated by most of the rest of the Eastern Bloc. However, hundreds of thousands of East Germans annually emigrated to West Germany through a "loophole" in the system that existed between East and West Berlin, where the four occupying World War II powers governed movement. The emigration resulted in a massive "brain drain" from East Germany to West Germany of younger educated professionals, such that nearly 20% of East Germany's population had migrated to West Germany by 1961. That June, the Soviet Union issued a new ultimatum demanding the withdrawal of allied forces from West Berlin. The request was rebuffed, and in August, East Germany erected a barbed-wire barrier that would eventually be expanded through construction into the Berlin Wall, effectively closing the loophole.

Cuban Missile Crisis and Khrushchev Ouster

The Soviet Union formed an alliance with Fidel Castro-led Cuba after the Cuban Revolution in 1959. In 1962, President John F. Kennedy responded to the installation of nuclear missiles in Cuba with a naval blockade. The Cuban Missile Crisis brought the world closer to nuclear war than ever before. It further demonstrated the concept of mutually assured destruction, that neither nuclear power was prepared to use nuclear weapons fearing total destruction via nuclear retaliation. The aftermath of the crisis led to the first efforts in the nuclear arms race at nuclear disarmament and improving relations, although the Cold War's first arms control agreement, the Antarctic Treaty, had come into force in 1961.

In 1964, Khrushchev's Kremlin colleagues managed to oust him, but allowed him a peaceful retirement. Accused of rudeness and incompetence, he was also credited with ruining Soviet agriculture and bringing the world to the brink of nuclear war. Khrushchev had become an international embarrassment when he authorised construction of the Berlin Wall, a public humiliation for Marxism-Leninism.

CONFRONTATION THROUGH DÉTENTE (1962–79)

In the course of the 1960s and '70s, Cold War participants struggled to adjust to a new, more complicated pattern of international relations in which the world was no longer divided into two clearly opposed blocs. From the beginning of the post-war period, Western Europe and Japan rapidly recovered from the destruction of World War II and sustained strong economic growth through the 1950s and '60s, with per capita GDPs approaching those of the United States, while Eastern Bloc economies stagnated. As a result of the 1973 oil crisis, combined with the growing influence of Third World alignments such as the Organization of Petroleum Exporting Countries (OPEC) and the Non-Aligned Movement, less-powerful countries had more room to assert their independence and often showed themselves resistant to pressure from either superpower. Moscow, meanwhile, was forced to turn its attention inward to deal with the Soviet Union's deep-seated domestic economic problems. During this period, Soviet leaders such as Alexey Kosygin and Leonid Brezhnev embraced the notion of détente.

Dominican Republic and French NATO withdrawal

President Lyndon B. Johnson landed 22,000 troops in the Dominican Republic in Operation Power Pack, citing the threat of the emergence of a Cuban-style revolution in Latin America. NATO countries remained primarily dependent on the US military for its defence against any potential Soviet invasion, a status most vociferously contested by France's Charles de Gaulle, who in 1966 withdrew from NATO's military structures and expelled NATO troops from French soil.

Czechoslovakia invasion

In 1968, a period of political liberalization in Czechoslovakia called the Prague Spring took place that included "Action Program" of liberalizations, which described increasing freedom of the press, freedom of speech and freedom of movement, along with an economic emphasis on consumer goods, the possibility of a multiparty government, limiting the power of the secret police and potentially withdrawing from the Warsaw Pact. The Soviet Red Army, together with most of their Warsaw Pact allies, invaded Czechoslovakia. The invasion was followed by a wave of emigration, including an estimated 70,000 Czechs initially fleeing, with the total eventually reaching 300,000.

The invasion sparked intense protests from Yugoslavia, Romania and China, and from Western European communist parties.

Brezhnev Doctrine

In September 1968, during a speech at the Fifth Congress of the Polish United Workers' Party one month after the invasion of Czechoslovakia, Brezhnev outlined the Brezhnev Doctrine, in which he claimed the right to violate the sovereignty of any country attempting to replace Marxism-Leninism with capitalism. During the speech, Brezhnev stated: When forces that are hostile to socialism try to turn the development of some socialist country towards capitalism, it becomes not only a problem of the country concerned, but a common problem and concern of all socialist countries.

The doctrine found its origins in the failures of Marxism-Leninism in states like Poland, Hungary and East Germany, which were facing a declining standard of living contrasting with the prosperity of West Germany and the rest of Western Europe.

THIRD WORLD ESCALATIONS

The US continued to spend heavily on supporting friendly Third World regimes in Asia. Conflicts in peripheral regions and client states—most prominently in Vietnam—continued. Johnson stationed 575,000 troops in Southeast Asia to defeat the National Front for the Liberation of South Vietnam (NLF) and their North Vietnamese allies in the Vietnam War, but his costly policy weakened the US economy and, by 1975, ultimately culminated in what most of the world saw as a humiliating defeat of the world's most powerful superpower at the hands of one of the world's poorest nations. Additionally, Operation Condor, employed by South American dictators to suppress leftist dissent, was backed by the US, which (sometimes accurately) perceived Soviet or Cuban support behind these opposition movements. Brezhnev, meanwhile, attempted to revive the Soviet economy, which was declining in part because of heavy military expenditures.

Moreover, the Middle East continued to be a source of contention. Egypt, which received the bulk of its arms and economic assistance from the USSR, was a troublesome client, with a reluctant Soviet Union feeling obliged to assist in both the 1967 Six-Day War (with advisers and technicians) and the War of Attrition (with pilots and aircraft) against US ally Israel; Syria and Iraq later received increased assistance as well as (indirectly) the PLO. During the 1973 Yom Kippur War, rumors of imminent Soviet intervention on the Egyptians' behalf brought about a massive US mobilization that threatened to wreck détente; this escalation, the USSR's first in a regional conflict central to US interests, inaugurated a new and more turbulent stage of Third World military activism in which the Soviets made use of their new strategic parity.

Sino-American Relations

As a result of the Sino-Soviet split, tensions along the Chinese-Soviet border reached their peak in 1969, and US President Richard Nixon decided to use the conflict to shift the balance of power towards the West in the Cold War. The Chinese had sought improved relations with the US in order to gain advantage over the Soviets as well. In February 1972, Nixon announced a stunning rapprochement with Mao's China by traveling to Beijing and meeting with Mao Zedong and Zhou Enlai. At this time, the USSR achieved rough nuclear parity with the US while the Vietnam War weakened US influence in the Third World and cooled relations with Western Europe). Although indirect conflict between Cold War powers continued through the late 1960s and early 1970s, tensions were beginning to ease.

Nixon, Brezhnev, and Détente

Following his China visit, Nixon met with Soviet leaders, including Brezhnev in Moscow. These Strategic Arms Limitation Talks resulted in two landmark arms control treaties: SALT I, the first comprehensive limitation pact signed by the two superpowers, and the Anti-Ballistic Missile Treaty, which banned the development of systems designed to intercept incoming missiles. These aimed to limit the development of costly anti-ballistic missiles and nuclear missiles. Nixon and Brezhnev proclaimed a new era of "peaceful coexistence" and established the groundbreaking new policy of *détente* (or cooperation) between the two superpowers. Between 1972 and 1974, the two sides also agreed to strengthen their economic ties, including agreements for increased trade. As a result of their meetings, *détente* would replace the hostility of the Cold War and the two countries would live mutually.

Meanwhile, these developments coincided with the "Ostpolitik" of West German Chancellor Willy Brandt. Other agreements were concluded to stabilize the situation in Europe, culminating in the Helsinki Accords signed at the Conference on Security and Co-operation in Europe in 1975.

LATE 1970S DETERIORATION OF RELATIONS

In the 1970s, the KGB, led by Yuri Andropov, continued to persecute distinguished Soviet personalities such as Aleksandr Solzhenitsyn and Andrei Sakharov, who were criticising the Soviet leadership in harsh terms. Indirect conflict between the superpowers continued through this period of détente in the Third World, particularly during political crises in the Middle East, Chile, Ethiopia and Angola.

Although President Jimmy Carter tried to place another limit on the arms race with a SALT II agreement in 1979, his efforts were undermined by the other events that year, including the Iranian Revolution and the Nicaraguan Revolution, which both ousted pro-US regimes, and his retaliation against Soviet intervention in Afghanistan in December.

Second Cold War (1979–85)

The term *second Cold War* has been used by some historians to refer to the period of intensive reawakening of Cold War tensions and conflicts in the late 1970s and early 1980s. Tensions greatly increased between the major powers with both sides becoming more militaristic.

Afghanistan War

During December 1979, approximately 75,000 Soviet troops

invaded Afghanistan in order to support the Marxist government formed by ex-Prime-minister Nur Muhammad Taraki, assassinated that September by one of his party rivals. As a result, US President Jimmy Carter withdrew the SALT II treaty from the Senate, imposed embargoes on grain and technology shipments to the USSR, demanded a significant increase in military spending, and further announced that the United States would boycott the 1980 Moscow Summer Olympics. He described the Soviet intervention in Afghanistan as "the most serious threat to the peace since the Second World War".

Reagan and Thatcher

In 1980, Ronald Reagan defeated Jimmy Carter in the US presidential election, vowing to increase military spending and confront the Soviets everywhere. Both Reagan and new British Prime Minister Margaret Thatcher denounced the Soviet Union and its ideology. Reagan labeled the Soviet Union an "evil empire" and predicted that Communism would be left on the "ash heap of history".

Polish Solidarity Movement

Pope John Paul II provided a moral focus for anti-communism; a visit to his native Poland in 1979 stimulated a religious and nationalist resurgence centered on the Solidarity movement that galvanized opposition and may have led to his attempted assassination two years later. Reagan also imposed economic sanctions on Poland to protest the suppression of Solidarity. In response, Mikhail Suslov, the Kremlin's top ideologist, advised Soviet leaders not to intervene if Poland fell under the control of Solidarity, for fear it might lead to heavy economic sanctions, representing a catastrophe for the Soviet economy.

SOVIET AND US MILITARY AND ECONOMIC ISSUES

Moscow had built up a military that consumed as much as 25 percent of the Soviet Union's gross national product at the expense of consumer goods and investment in civilian sectors. Soviet spending on the arms race and other Cold War commitments both caused and exacerbated deep-seated structural problems in the Soviet system, which saw at least a decade of economic stagnation during the late Brezhnev years. Soviet investment in the defence sector was not driven by military necessity, but in large part by the interests of massive party and state bureaucracies dependent on the sector for their own power and privileges. The Soviet Armed Forces became the largest in the world in terms of the numbers and types of weapons they possessed, in the number of troops in their ranks, and in the sheer size of their military–industrial base. However, the quantitative advantages held by the Soviet military often concealed areas where the Eastern Bloc dramatically lagged behind the West.

By the early 1980s, the USSR had built up a military arsenal and army surpassing that of the United States. Previously, the US had relied on the qualitative superiority of its weapons, but the gap had been narrowed. Ronald Reagan began massively building up the United States military not long after taking office. This led to the largest peacetime defence buildup in United States history. Tensions continued intensifying in the early 1980s when Reagan revived the B-1 Lancer program that was canceled by the Carter administration, produced LGM-118 Peacekeepers, installed US cruise missiles in Europe, and announced his experimental Strategic Defence Initiative, dubbed "Star Wars" by the media, a defence program to shoot down missiles in mid-flight.

With the background of a buildup in tensions between the Soviet Union and the United States, and the deployment of Soviet RSD-10 Pioneer ballistic missiles targeting Western Europe, NATO decided, under the impetus of the Carter presidency, to deploy MGM-31 Pershing and cruise missiles in Europe, primarily West Germany. This deployment would have placed missiles just 10 minutes' striking distance from Moscow. After Reagan's military buildup, the Soviet Union did not respond by further building its military because the enormous military expenses, along with inefficient planned manufacturing and collectivized agriculture, were already a heavy burden for the Soviet economy. At the same time, Reagan persuaded Saudi

Arabia to increase oil production, even as other non-OPEC nations were increasing production. These developments contributed to the 1980s oil glut, which affected the Soviet Union, as oil was the main source of Soviet export revenues. Issues with command economics, oil prices decreases and large military expenditures gradually brought the Soviet economy to stagnation.

On September 1, 1983, the Soviet Union shot down Korean Air Lines Flight 007, a Boeing 747 with 269 people aboard, including sitting Congressman Larry McDonald, when it violated Soviet airspace just past the west coast of Sakhalin Island—an act which Reagan characterized as a "massacre". This act increased support for military deployment, overseen by Reagan, which stood in place until the later accords between Reagan and Mikhail Gorbachev. The Able Archer 83 exercise in November 1983, a realistic simulation of a coordinated NATO nuclear release, has been called most dangerous moment since the Cuban Missile Crisis, as the Soviet leadership keeping a close watch on it considered a nuclear attack to be imminent. US domestic public concerns about intervening in foreign conflicts persisted from the end of the Vietnam War. The Reagan administration emphasized the use of quick, low-cost counter-insurgency tactics to intervene in foreign conflicts. In 1983, the Reagan administration intervened in the multisided Lebanese Civil War, invaded Grenada, bombed Libya and backed the Central American Contras, anti-communist paramilitaries seeking to overthrow the Soviet-aligned Sandinista government in Nicaragua. While Reagan's interventions against Grenada and Libya were popular in the US, his backing of the Contra rebels was mired in controversy.

Meanwhile, the Soviets incurred high costs for their own foreign interventions. Although Brezhnev was convinced in 1979 that the Soviet war in Afghanistan would be brief, Muslim guerrillas, aided by the US and other countries, waged a fierce resistance against the invasion. The Kremlin sent nearly 100,000 troops to support its puppet regime in Afghanistan, leading many outside observers to dub the war "the Soviets' Vietnam". However, Moscow's quagmire in Afghanistan was far more disastrous for the Soviets than Vietnam had been for the Americans because the conflict coincided with a period of internal decay and domestic crisis in the Soviet system.

A senior US State Department official predicted such an outcome as early as 1980, positing that the invasion resulted in part from a "domestic crisis within the Soviet system.... It may be that the thermodynamic law of entropy has... caught up with the Soviet system, which now seems to expend more energy on simply maintaining its equilibrium than on improving itself. We could be seeing a period of foreign movement at a time of internal decay". The Soviets were not helped by their aged and sclerotic leadership either: Brezhnev, virtually incapacitated in his last years, was succeeded by Andropov and Chernenko, neither of whom lasted long. After Chernenko's death, Reagan was asked why he had not negotiated with Soviet leaders. Reagan quipped, "They keep dying on me".

END OF THE COLD WAR (1985–91)

Gorbachev Reforms

A second Reykjavík Summit was held in Iceland. Talks went well until the focus shifted to Reagan's proposed Strategic Defence Initiative, which Gorbachev wanted eliminated: Reagan refused. The negotiations failed, but the third summit in 1987 led to a breakthrough with the signing of the Intermediate-Range Nuclear Forces Treaty (INF). The INF treaty eliminated all nuclear-armed, ground-launched ballistic and cruise missiles with ranges between 500 and 5,500 kilometers (300 to 3,400 miles) and their infrastructure.

East–West tensions rapidly subsided through the mid-to-late 1980s, culminating with the final summit in Moscow in 1989, when Gorbachev and George H. W. Bush signed the START I arms control treaty. During the following year it became apparent to the Soviets that oil and gas subsidies, along with the cost of maintaining massive troops levels, represented a substantial economic drain. In addition, the security advantage of a buffer zone was recognised as irrelevant and the Soviets officially declared that they would no longer intervene in the affairs of allied states in Eastern Europe. In 1989, Soviet forces withdrew from Afghanistan and by 1990 Gorbachev consented to German reunification, the only alternative being a Tiananmen scenario. When the Berlin Wall came down, Gorbachev's "Common European Home" concept began to take shape.

On December 3, 1989, Gorbachev and Reagan's successor, George H. W. Bush, declared the Cold War over at the Malta Summit; a year later, the two former rivals were partners in the Gulf War against longtime Soviet ally Iraq.

Faltering Soviet System

By 1989, the Soviet alliance system was on the brink of collapse, and, deprived of Soviet military support, the Communist leaders of the Warsaw Pact states were losing power. In the USSR itself, *glasnost* weakened the bonds that held the Soviet Union together and by February 1990, with the dissolution of the USSR looming, the Communist Party was forced to surrender its 73-year-old monopoly on state power.

At the same time freedom of press and dissent allowed by *glasnost* and the festering "nationalities question" increasingly led the Union's component republics to declare their autonomy from Moscow, with the Baltic states withdrawing from the Union entirely. The 1989 revolutionary wave that swept across Central and Eastern Europe overthrew the Soviet-style communist states, such as Poland, Hungary, Czechoslovakia and Bulgaria, Romania being the only Eastern-bloc country to topple its communist regime violently and execute its head of state.

Soviet Dissolution

Gorbachev's permissive attitude toward Eastern Europe did not initially extend to Soviet territory; even Bush, who strove to maintain friendly relations, condemned the January 1991 killings in Latvia and Lithuania, privately warning that economic ties would be frozen if the violence continued. The USSR was fatally weakened by a failed coup and as a growing number of Soviet republics, particularly Russia, threatened to secede the USSR was declared officially dissolved on December 25, 1991.

Legacy

Created on December 21, 1991, the Commonwealth of Independent States is viewed as a successor entity to the Soviet Union but according to Russia's leaders its purpose was to "allow a civilized divorce" between the Soviet Republics and is comparable to a loose confederation. Following the Cold War, Russia cut military spending dramatically, but the adjustment was wrenching, as the military-industrial sector had previously employed one of every five Soviet adults and its dismantling left millions throughout the former Soviet Union unemployed. After Russia embarked on capitalist economic reforms in the 1990s, it suffered a financial crisis and a recession more severe than the US and Germany had experienced during the Great Depression. Russian living standards have worsened overall in the post-Cold War years, although the economy has resumed growth since 1999.

The legacy of the Cold War continues to influence world affairs. After the dissolution of the Soviet Union, the post-Cold War world is widely considered as unipolar, with the United States the sole remaining superpower. The Cold War defined the political role of the United States in the post-World War II world: by 1989 the US held military alliances with 50 countries, and had 1.5 million troops posted abroad in 117 countries. The Cold War also institutionalized a global commitment to huge, permanent peacetime military-industrial complexes and large-scale military funding of science.

Military expenditures by the US during the Cold War years were estimated to have been $8 trillion, while nearly 100,000 Americans lost their lives in the Korean War and Vietnam War. Although the loss of life among Soviet soldiers is difficult to estimate, as a share of their gross national product the financial cost for the Soviet Union was far higher than that of the US.

In addition to the loss of life by uniformed soldiers, millions died in the superpowers' proxy wars around the globe, most notably in Southeast Asia. Most of the proxy wars and subsidies for local conflicts ended along with the Cold War; the incidence of interstate wars, ethnic wars, revolutionary wars, as well as refugee and displaced persons crises has declined sharply in the post-Cold War years. No separate campaign medal has been authorized for the Cold War; however, in 1998, the United State Congress authorized Cold War Recognition Certificates "to all members of the armed forces and qualified federal government civilian personnel who faithfully and honorably served the United States anytime during the Cold War era, which is defined as Sept. 2, 1945-to Dec. 26, 1991."

The legacy of Cold War conflict, however, is not always easily erased, as many of the economic and social tensions that were exploited to fuel Cold War competition in parts of the Third World remain acute. The breakdown of state control in a number of areas formerly ruled by Communist governments has produced new civil and ethnic conflicts, particularly in the former Yugoslavia. In Eastern Europe, the end of the Cold War has ushered in an era of economic growth and a large increase in the number of liberal democracies, while in other parts of the world, such as Afghanistan, independence was accompanied by state failure.

Historiography

As soon as the term "Cold War" was popularized to refer to post-war tensions between the United States and the Soviet Union, interpreting the course and origins of the conflict has been a source of heated controversy among historians, political scientists, and journalists. In particular, historians have sharply disagreed as to who was responsible for the breakdown of Soviet–US relations after the Second World War; and whether the conflict between the two superpowers was inevitable, or could have been avoided. Historians have also disagreed on what exactly the Cold War was, what the sources of the conflict were, and how to disentangle patterns of action and reaction between the two sides.

Although explanations of the origins of the conflict in academic discussions are complex and diverse, several general schools of thought on the subject can be identified. Historians commonly speak of three differing approaches to the study of the Cold War: "orthodox" accounts, "revisionism", and "post-revisionism".

"Orthodox" accounts place responsibility for the Cold War on the Soviet Union and its expansion into Eastern Europe. "Revisionist" writers place more responsibility for the breakdown of post-war peace on the United States, citing a range of US efforts to isolate and confront the Soviet Union well before the end of World War II. "Post-revisionists" see the events of the Cold War as more nuanced, and attempt to be more balanced in determining what occurred during the Cold War. Much of the historiography on the Cold War weaves together two or even all three of these broad categories.

8

Perspective of Modern Strategy and Civil War Tactics

Do prominent Civil War historians also research and write about the Napoleonic era, the eighteenth century, or other wars of the 19th century? Almost none-but the rare men who do are the ones who give us the greatest insight into Civil War combat. How can you understand Civil War tactics without perspective, without studying what Civil War generals studied, without comparing Civil War weapons to those that came before and after? You cannot! How can you understand Civil War tactics by looking solely at the infantry? Many Civil War historians attempt just that, getting bogged down in the minutiae of battles instead of gaining perspective by researching other eras. Because of this, many historians don't fully understand why Civil War combat was indecisive. And because of their lack of background, when historians specializing in the Civil War have seen Civil War generals write of "Napoleonic" tactics, firstly-they may not have understood what Napoleonic tactics were-something more than men fighting shoulder to shoulder-and secondly, it didn't occur to them that "Napoleonic" might refer to another Napoleon, Napoleon III. (The Bloody Crucible of Courage, Brent Nosworthy)

THE AUSTRO-PRUSSIAN WAR-THE FIRST MODERN WAR

The Civil War featured a number of new innovations-ironclads, land mines, and so forth. It is often represented that the new rifle musket was one of these great innovations-that it made the old tactics obsolete, that thousands of lives were wasted by using 50 year old tactics. Although the tactics used weren't exactly Napoleonic in a Napoleon I sense, they were NOT modern either-an evolution not a revolution.

Major tactical change in the mid 19th century was pioneered by the Prussian army. Only they dared to make radical change. Developed in 1848, the Prussian Dreyse needle gun was a quick firing, bolt-action, breech-loading rifle that infantrymen could load and fire in a prone position. In 1863, the Prussians estimated that three hundred of their men armed with the needle gun were superior to 900 of the enemy armed with muzzle loaders. In a small engagement at Lundby in the 1864 Denmark War, 124 Prussians repulsed 180 attacking Danes, inflicted 88 casualties on them as they advanced from 250 meters to 150 meters. In 1866, Prussian troops armed with needle guns easily defeated an Austrian army equipped with muzzle-loading Lorenz rifles, weapons also used in the Civil War. Instead of using a long thin line of men to blast away at an opposing long thin line of men at close range, the Prussians used small company columns that sent men forward into skirmish lines to gain fire superiority. The skirmish line would take advantage of the terrain, and the men, who had had extensive target practice, would take careful note of the range to the enemy and adjust their sights accordingly. The skirmish line was now the main effort, and the column existed primarily to lend support and to send troops forward to the skirmish line. These methods easily defeated the Austrians, who used columns of infantry for shock attacks. At Podol, 400 Prussians defeated 2,000 Austrians, losing only 100 men compared to over 1,000 killed, wounded, and captured Austrians. (Austro p134) At Trautenau, an Austrian "victory", 5,000 Austrians were lost compared to 1,300 Prussians. (Austro p150) Austrian artillery was effective out to 5,000 meters, but the gunners were vulnerable to fire from the needle gun. One Austrian battery at Koniggratz lost 54 men and 68 horses to rifle fire in the course of several minutes, (Austro p 252) something the likes of which had not seen in the American Civil War. Although only one Prussian bullet out of 250 fired actually hit anyone-little different from the past-the Austrians lost 5 men to every one the Prussians lost-plus the rapid fire had an immense psychological impact on the enemy. (The Franco-Prussian War, Geoffrey Wawro p51) Prussian cavalry, despite facing rifled muskets, were effectively used against fleeing infantry and even successfully captured an enemy artillery battery. (Austro p262) Had Civil War armies faced the Prussians, they too would have been slaughtered.

Prussian Needle Gun

In response to these developments, the French army fielded the breech-loading Chassepot rifle which could fire 8 to 15 rounds per minute compared to the 4 to 5 rounds of the Prussian needle gun. (Franco p52) The Chassepot had a longer range as well. In the early skirmishes of the war, it was clear that the Chassepot was superior. In one instance, a French platoon held off a company, and in another, three Frenchmen stopped a column of Prussians. (Franco 87, 93) In addition to quick firing, breech loading rifles, the Franco-Prussian War in 1870 also featured breech-loading artillery, effective out to 3,800 meters, and the mitrailleuse, a crude machine gun mounted on an artillery carriage. The mitrailleuse mowed men down at a range of 1,200 yards firing 100 to 200 rounds per minute. (Franco 53) All of these weapons lead to a genuine tactical revolution. Prussian weapons and tactics were matched against even superior French small arms, and Prussian frontal attacks consistently failed. Newer, more lethal weapons had forced new tactics, and combat was less decisive. By the Franco-Prussian War, artillery and infantry could still co-operate in battle, but cavalry co-operating with infantry in the attack was no longer practical. Its use was now limited to screening the army. (Franco 61) Infantry fighting exclusively as skirmishers had made infantry fire even more deadly and the men more steady than if they were in closed order. Jean Colin in his classic "Transformations of Warfare" explains:

"Comparative isolation is good for the morale of a man from the time he finds himself in the zone of fire. If men are close to each other emotions are transmitted and hyper-excitement is reciprocally induced-this is very bad for the steadiness of the combatant.... If the intervals are large, the man who falls has plenty of room, is seen by a less number of people, and drags no one down in his fall; the moral(e) impression made on his comrades is slighter, their courage is less shaken."

French Chassepot

So all factors conspired to make combat less decisive. Much more so than during the American Civil War, the defence was now supreme, and an army with an average of one man per yard of front could be expected to hold its position. Shallow flanking moves became the key to success on the battlefield. In comparison, even behind entrenchments, Lee's army at Spotsylvania averaged 5 men per yard, and Civil War armies on occasion averaged 8 men per yard of front.

As weapons technology continued to advance, the indecisive trench warfare of the First World War was the next logical step. In 1914 the battle line stretched so far that there was no flank remaining to attack. Infantry units were still armed exclusively with rifles. To break this deadlock, rifle units were replaced with units armed with a mix of weapons down to the squad level-grenades, flame throwers, mortars, and squad automatics, all used together for the purpose of fire suppression-keeping the enemy's head down. This allowed the infantry to move forward for the kill. This was the beginning of modern tactics like those still used today. The family tree of these modern tactics goes back to mid 19th century Europe-not to the American Civil War, which had no children.

Casualty Figures

Further proof that Civil War weapons were not as deadly as they are often portrayed can be found in casualty figures. Historians charting the lethality of weapons discovered a counter-intuitive trend. As the lethality of weapons increased, the percentage casualties for a constant unit of time has decreased. So while battles in the linear era produced casualties in the range of 10 to 40% per day, by World War II, casualties on the order of 1% per day were considered heavy. Let's take a look at some battles over a range of time periods to compare the losses-killed and wounded only-not captured or missing. (generally, figures are from David Chandler's Guide to the Battlefields of Europe)

A Rifled Musket Revolution?

But why compare Civil War tactics to those of the eighteenth century and Napoleon's time? After all, the rifled musket had changed everything. Right? That's what almost everyone says, and the majority is never wrong, now is it? John Hennessey, in his excellent book "Return to Bull", gives the conventional version of the effect of the rifled musket. He writes:

"Civil War tactics were largely the product of Napoleon Bonaparte. That meant, most particularly, that their theory was predicated in large part on the use of the bayonet. But in 1862, after First Manassas, Shiloh and Gaines Mill, the rifle musket, now in vogue on both sides, had rendered the bayonet charge impractical. While Napoleon's charging lines at Waterloo or Austerlitz had been exposed to musket fire for a hundred yards, the rifle muskets could ravage a charging line with accuracy from 350 yards in, and do damage at more than 500 yards. By 1862, most battle lines never made it close enough to engage in a classic hand-to-hand fight. Most soldiers found their bayonets more useful as candle holders or pot hooks than as weapons of death."

Not to pick on Mr. Hennessey, but he misunderstands Napoleonic tactics and the use of bayonet. In Napoleon's time, as well as in the Civil War, the bayonet was a psychological weapon-and a powerful one. With few exceptions, the bayonet charge was conducted only after achieving fire superiority-which created morale superiority. When the enemy line looked shaky was the time for a bayonet attack. An advance with cold steel would convince him that he had a pressing engagement further to the rear. The fact that bayonet wounds have always been rare does not prove that the bayonet was an ineffective weapon. It proves the exact opposite.

As we will see, Civil War rifle-muskets aren't all that they're cracked up to be. A major advance in small arms during the half century before was actually the percussion cap, which, unlike flints, were consistently reliable. A much higher percentage of shots after the first volley were fired successfully, and the infantryman could pay more attention to his aim without gunpowder burning near his eyes.

Rifled bullets also flew a straighter, more predictable course. But in one important respect the rifled musket was actually inferior to its predecessor. A bullet traveling down a smoothbore barrel would bounce around, with its final trajectory determined by its final bounce. But at fairly short range, 100 yards or less, the smoothbore was quite good, though, with between 40-75% of shots hitting a simulated line of cavalry in various peacetime experiments. At 200 yards, 18-30% of shots hit the target. The rifling in the new rifled muskets gave the bullet a much truer course, but they also created much more friction than in smoothbores, which lowered the muzzle velocity significantly. This meant that the bullet traveled a more parabolic course. So even though the bullet flew a *truer* course, its relatively slow speed meant that at long range the shooter had to estimate the range accurately to within a few yards in order to hit his target.

Jack Coggins writes, "A bullet fired by a kneeling man at the belt buckle of a man running toward him at an estimated range of 300 yards would pass over the head of a man 250 yards away. Thus, if the shooter had overestimated the range by as little as 50 yards he would have missed." In addition, the bullet would fall at the feet of a man 350 yards away. The further the range, the more vital the estimate of range was, and the more difficult the task became. Twentieth century studies show that people are quite bad at estimating ranges, with errors usually around 30%. (Ohio Dept of Natural Resources, Division of Wildlife website) Modern rifles are much better longer range weapons. While the rifled musket bullet would rise 43 inches over the line of sight, a World War II era M-1 rifle bullet would rise just 7.2 inches above the line of sight, making accurate range estimation much less important. (Coggins 38-9) Despite the flatter trajectory of modern bullets, even today, firefights rarely occur at ranges over 400 yards. The human eye is the reason for this. In fact, at 500 yards, a human face can only be made out as a light spot. (Hughes 26) Take a look across a football field. Do you think you could hit anything at 100 yards? What if someone was shooting at YOU? Brent Nosworthy's "Bloody Crucible of Courage" says that the Union army quit making adjustable sights for their rifle muskets because the men were too frightened in battle to remember to adjust them. Perhaps it wouldn't have mattered even if men could keep their wits in battle.

Many men were too frightened to even tell whether their weapon had fired. Not even noting the absence of a kick to their shoulder, a strong enough force to leave a bruise, men simply loaded one round on top of the other. SLA Marshall, in a flawed but important study of Korean War combat, found that a substantial portion of infantrymen in battle never fired their weapons; the fear of death simply overcame them. It is expecting a great deal for an infantryman to accomplish the simple task of loading and aiming a musket in battle. People are not designed to face that sort of danger. They are designed to run for their lives.

When you also figure that after some artillery fire and a volley or two of musketry there may have be so much smoke that men couldn't even see the enemy, how can you expect them to hit anything? It should be no surprise that Paddy Griffith in "Battle Tactics of the Civil War" calculated an average first volley of around 140 yards, little different from previous wars, and with little difference in lethality. When you consider that each man was eager to open fire, to do something seemingly constructive against the threat facing him, 140 yards was too far away for an effective volley.

So although rifle-muskets were an improvement over smoothbores, the advantage appears slight. Grady McWhiney's thesis that there was a rifle revolution and that the Confederates wasted their manpower in futile frontal assaults is dead wrong. The technology of rifled muskets didn't make combat indecisive. Other factors may have, however.

Napoleonic Tactics and Civil War Tactics

If you understand how Napoleon fought, you will see that Civil War tactics were different in a number of important ways.

These differences perhaps explain the indecisive nature of Civil War combat.

In the gunpowder age, battle was rarely decisive; Napoleonic combat, the ultimate development of linear tactics, is the exception. To understand Napoleonic tactics, you first have to understand how and why they developed. To do that, you have to go back one hundred years before even Napoleon's time to the invention of the socket bayonet. Before then, an infantry battalion was an unwieldy and vulnerable combination of musketeers and pikemen, with the pikemen protecting the musketeers from enemy pikemen and cavalry. When the socket bayonet replaced the plug bayonet, musketeers shed themselves of pikemen because they could now protect themselves and still fire their muskets. Musketeers stretched themselves thinner, first into six ranks, then four, then three, and finally just two. It was still an awkward system in some ways, with difficulty deploying an army from the march into line of battle. In Marlborough's day, in the early 1700s, it took most of the day to prepare for battle, and it was impossible to surprise an enemy on the march. When battle began, the whole of the infantry would typically attack together simultaneously in two lines. The logical place for cavalry was still on the flanks. In battle, the cavalry would defeat the opposing enemy horsemen then attack the rear of the enemy infantry just like in the 1600s-but also much like during the Civil War, at least in theory. By Napoleon's time, however, this would change-thanks to advances in infantry tactics.

With the use of thinner battle lines-two or three ranks-a quicker system was developed to deploy from marching column into line of battle. Battle was becoming more practical, no longer a rare and consensual event. Frederick the Great perfected this system, marching and deploying on the enemy's flank for a devastating attack. If you have read about Frederick at Leuthen, you will see the similarities with Jackson's attack on the XI Corps at Chancellorsville, Early's attack at Cedar Creek, and Warren's attack at Five Forks. And if you have heard of Rossbach, then you might be skeptical of Longstreet's hoped-for turning movement at Gettysburg. Indeed, in many ways the Civil War looks more like the Seven Years War than it does the Napoleonic Wars. Let's take a look at change in the 18th century and the development of Napoleonic tactics, one feature at a time.

Artillery

There was plenty of room to improve upon mid-18th century tactics, and the defeated and humiliated French army lead the way with reform. The Austrians had already made great strides in reducing the weight of their guns, with their new pieces weighing only half as much as their predecessors.

The French adopted these concepts with the Gribeauval system. Frederick had already complaining in the Seven Years' War that the new Austrian artillery was killing off his highly trained infantry, who were re-known for their discipline and quick rate of fire. The new lighter field artillery had the potential to revolutionize warfare. There was no choice for a monarch but to enter into an artillery arms race-or else have his army slaughtered. Masses of the new mobile guns could be brought to bear against the enemy, blowing holes in his line and demoralizing his men.

Skirmishers

Frederick was also whining that Austrian light infantrymen sent ahead of their main line were picking off officers and men while taking cover behind trees and terrain features. With an army made in many cases of forcibly recruited Euro-trash held in bondage only by the threat of severe punishment, Frederick couldn't trust his men to go forward and skirmish. With the prospect of freedom, they might run away and never be seen again.

Frederick resisted this change, at least for a while. Other armies developed highly trained and motivated special units of light infantry too. Although skirmishers of the French Revolutionary Wars and Napoleonic times are often stereotyped as ill-trained levies good for nothing more than swarming in dense masses in front of the enemy line, modern historians dispute this. Whenever possible, skirmishers of the era were highly motivated, well trained, and good shots. Their calm, slow, well-aimed fire, combined with artillery, gradually wore down the enemy and un-nerved the survivors before the main attack.

Columns

A misunderstanding of early English-speaking historians has distorted our understanding of a major aspect of Napoleonic warfare-the use of columns. Focusing on the Peninsula War and relying almost exclusively on British sources, some historians came to the misguided conclusion that the French primarily used battalions of infantry for shock action in columns of attack. As early as the mid 1700s the French were keeping their second line in column formation to allow for a flexible response to problems or opportunities on the first line. During the 1777 Battle of Brandywine, the British army, generally thought of as conservative, advanced on the rebels in maneuver columns then deployed into line. By Napoleonic times French infantry, preceded by skirmishers, advanced toward the enemy in battalion-sized columns for more flexibility and maneuverability on the battlefield, allowing them to adjust to enemy deployments, better seize opportunities, or to attempt to flank the enemy line. Before contact with the enemy, however, the columns would *deploy* into line for the firefight. A bayonet charge in column formation was only done after gaining firepower superiority when the enemy troops looked shaky and on the verge of breaking. Against most armies, this method worked very well. The infantry's increased flexibility helped in other ways. The infantry columns also allowed much closer cooperation with the artillery, which was better able to mass against a portion of the enemy line or even move forward with the infantry. More importantly, closer co-operation with the cavalry was also possible. Unlike in the 18th century, cavalry could advance right along with the infantry.

Cavalry

While 18th century cavalry was placed exclusively on the flanks, the new infantry columns allowed the mounted arm to advance in columns directly in support of the infantry, and even change places with them to lead the attack. To protect themselves. enemy infantry would form squares, but in so doing they deprived themselves of much of their firepower and their ability to maneuver. If artillery could be brought forward, the enemy squares would be blasted out of existence. Either way, a massive hole was formed in the enemy line, and decisive victory was assured.

In terms of grand tactics, Napoleon would typically threaten the enemy's flank, forcing him to commit his reserve. He always kept a large reserve available, a vitally important part of his system, to either exploit success of stave off defeat. Most often, with the enemy reserve committed, Napoleon would send his own reserve into the weak point in the enemy line and secure a decisive victory. Co-operation among all three combat arms was key to Napoleon's system, and the reserve decided the battle. Does this sound like Civil War tactics to you? No! Civil War armies kept few reserves, and Civil War combat featured little in the way of combined arms cooperation. Civil War tactics were NOT Napoleonic.

The new French tactics in Spain and Portugal didn't work out so well, and their old school British opponents may have never understood their intent. Rough terrain complicated the system considerably. It was difficult to mass artillery batteries, and it was difficult for cavalry to support the infantry. Wellington sometimes sent as much as one third of his men forward as skirmishers, and the French could never gain superiority over them. Since Wellington kept his infantry hidden behind the reverse slope, the French maneuver columns blundered upon the British line and were surprised. Struggling to deploy into line and disorganized and shocked by the surprise encounter, the French received one or two close range volleys from their British opponents who then let out a cheer and charged. The British system worked consistently, except at Albeura-and at Waterloo, where the open terrain suited Napoleon's methods. Terrain explains much of the British success against the French. In part, terrain also explains why combined arms tactics were so rare during the Civil War, but we'll discuss that later. Perhaps because of the British success, and because of the bloody nature of Napoleon's later battles, post-Napoleonic military theorists became somewhat reactionary and supported tactics which looked backward to the 18th century.

CIVIL WAR TACTICS LOOK LIKE A POOR MAN'S 18TH CENTURY

The first American army, the Continental Army, was based on its British opponent during the Revolution; even then, the British were known for a brief musketry exchange followed by a charge. Civil War tactics don't resemble this, or British Peninsula tactics, or Napoleonic tactics. But Civil War tactics do resemble the 18th century in that infantry was typically formed in two lines flanked by cavalry. Civil War battles sometimes even featured a Frederican oblique order attack.

Although Gettysburg featured a Napoleonic concentration of artillery, genuine Napoleonic tactics for example, would have involved cavalry supporting Pickett's Charge-and Union cavalry charging in pursuit-in short, combat with the potential for decisiveness. The technology of rifled muskets didn't make this sort of thing impossible. Koniggratz in 1866 shows this as do some later Civil War battles. Because combined arms attacks weren't regularly attempted, battle was predictably indecisive.

Unlike Napoleonic and eighteenth century battle, all too often, Civil War combat degraded into a confused infantry firefight with officers gradually losing control, with any hope for maneuver lost. After the onset of confusion, shock action with the bayonet was not practical. Perhaps due to lack of training and discipline-an inevitability to some degree with a democratic government-it was always difficult to get men to close with the enemy. Once an infantry advance stopped in order to fire, it could rarely be made to continue forward. Prussian observer Justus Scheibert believed that a deficiency in lower level officers, who showed "ignorance of military things", explained why the brigade became the tactical unit of the war, "hence stiffness in the lines and clumsiness in management and direction of troops". Poor performance on the battlefield was the result, and "the loss of an upper-level commander would cripple (the) advance". He described an attacking infantry division as "like ghosts of days and ways of Frederick the Great.", in essence a poor man's version of mid 18th century methods. (Scheibert 49) He described a typical attack;

"The nearer to the enemy, the more faulty the lines and the more ragged the first (line) until it crumbled and mixed with the skirmishers. Forward went this muddle leading the wavy rest. Finally the mass obtruded upon the point of attack. In a sustained, stubborn clash, even the third would join the melee. Meanwhile the usually weak reserve tried to be useful on the flanks, or stiffened places that faltered, or plugged holes. In sum it had been a division neatly drawn up. Now its units, anything but neat, vaguely coherent, resembled a swarm of skirmishers." (Scheibert 41)

In contrast, Scheibert writes:

"Prussian tactics freed (officers) to use their own minds... Liberated battalion and even company commanders could be the heads of tactical units, their own, and make them fight as right-thinking officers saw fit and as well-trained troops best could. The flexible line at the forward edge resembles a chain, then with detachable links under independent guidance. At crisis they can dismember into smaller and even the smallest units without disfunction... Our Prussian tactics thus gave our line officers energy, elasticity, and speed-to the entire army's benefit... Furthermore, diligent peacetime training provided our troops an abundance of formations, something to fit any circumstance... Lee, the first American to acknowledge this superiority, replied in the thick of Chancellorsville when I spoke with amazement at the bravery of Jackson's corps: 'Just give me Prussian formations and Prussian discipline along with it-you'd see things turn out differently here!" (Scheibert 49)

An extreme example of how potentially decisive combat degraded into chaos is Brawner Farm. Jackson had the opportunity to attack and crush an isolated and much smaller Union division with his corps, but an indecisive firefight resulted, and because of Jackson's peculiarities, his subordinates feared to take the initiative and stood idly by while the opportunity to destroy a Union division was lost.

Could Civil War battles have been decisive?

Maybe. Skirmishers weren't consistently well used. In the French Revolutionary Wars and the Napoleonic Wars, skirmishers could all but decide a battle, but we don't see that in the Civil War. The Confederate army improved in this respect through the war, forming elite sharpshooter battalions in each brigade, but the Union army allowed its light infantry to decline over time.

Why couldn't the Union army have formed units similar to the Confederate brigades' sharpshooter battalions and one-upped them by giving their skirmishers repeating rifles to instead of to the cavalry? Union skirmishers with repeaters firing rapidly from a prone position could have easily dominated Southern light infantrymen-and possibly even repulse full scale attacks. Could the cavalry have advanced with and supported infantry like in Napoleon's time? If you accept the argument that rifled muskets were little better than smoothbores, then maybe they could. Although admittedly an occurrence of the smoothbore era, Jeb Stuart successfully attacked Union infantry at 1st Manassas. Later examples were not as successful. At Gaines Mill and at Cedar Mountain Union cavalry unsuccessfully attacked infantry, but these failures should come as no surprise since these were desperate attacks against unbroken advancing infantry.

Perhaps the fences and broken terrain with numerous woodlots made cavalry attacks on infantry impractical. At Chancellorsville, for example, a Union cavalry regiment attacked down a narrow road, unable to change direction. Failure was the predictable result. Lack of training and experience in the cavalry arm may also have made it impractical. Horses were expensive, and it was difficult to find forage for them in the sparsely populated country. European cavalry was the product of years of training, a horse alone requiring three years to train. Further, Union cavalry were armed with repeating rifles, and in many cases served as mounted infantry, which meant that they largely abandoned the full potential of shock attack, their traditional battlefield role. The Union cavalry mounted shock attacks against infantry and conducted after-battle pursuit only late in the war- at Third Winchester and Cedar Creek for example. We may never know what could have been.

An Artillery Revolution?

We have seen that the effectiveness of rifled muskets wasn't as great as is often portrayed. So far, we haven't said much about Civil War artillery. The supposed threat that rifled muskets posed to artillerymen is largely an illusion. Artillery units suffered lower casualty rates than the infantry, in line with experience in previous wars. New rifled artillery pieces were accurate at long range, making columns vulnerable. At ranges less than 1,000 yards, brass Napoleon guns were more useful. (Fratt 50) Civil War brass guns were nowhere near as effective as the artillery of the 1866 and 1870 wars in Europe. The guns do look much like their Napoleonic predecessors, but appearances can be deceiving. The 12 pounder Napoleon guns were actually a great improvement over their predecessors.

Another beneficial advance of the 12-pounder Napoleon was far and away the most important and dramatic. Before and during the Napoleonic Wars, guns, which are direct fire weapons, were limited to firing round shot or canister. Howitzers, for indirect fire at a higher trajectory, fired a shell, a hollow projectile filled with explosive detonated by a fuse which was set alight during firing. Around 1800, Henry Shrapnel invented the round that bears his name, a shell filled with powder and small round balls, a much more lethal round than the simple shell that it made obsolete. When it was invented, the shrapnel round could only be fired by howitzers, a small fraction of the artillery pieces in use. With advances in metal technology, however, and with a reduction in the powder charge from 1/3 to 1/4 of the weight of the projectile, the shrapnel round could be fired from a standard piece styled a "gun-howitzer", the famed Napoleon gun-howitzer. Seventy eight bullets were contained in a single 12 pounder shrapnel round. (Coggins 67) No longer was the artilleryman limited to roundshot at long range. Now he could deliver killing power said to approach that of canister at nearly a mile's range. In British peacetime experiments, around 10% of the bullets in a shrapnel round hit a target. (Hughes 38) Both enemy infantry and cavalry were made more vulnerable. Brent Nosworthy notes that during the 1859 Italian War, artillery disrupted a cavalry unit from over a mile away, preventing it from forming and attacking. Confirming that this thinking was prevalent during the Civil War, in 1865, Francis Lippitt wrote in "A Treatise on the Tactical Use of the Three Arms, Infantry, Artillery and Cavalry",

> Since the introduction of the new rifled arms, exposing cavalry masses to a deadly fire at far greater distances than ever before known, a fire often reaching to the reserves, it seemed doubtful whether the manoeuvring and charging in heavy compact masses, which formerly rendered cavalry of the line so formidable, would any longer be practical.

So more than any other cause, advances in artillery technology made the combined use of cavalry and infantry for decisive combat a difficult proposition.

Despite all this, many historians still believe that artillery wasn't important during the war. Casualties caused by artillery fire were negligible-or so they say. A frequently cited example is the Wilderness, where artillery was said to account for only about 6% of all casualties. Paddy Griffith points out that many casualties attributed to small arms fire may in fact have been caused by artillery, specifically by the small round balls in Shrapnel rounds. Griffith suggests that the percentage of casualties caused by artillery in this battle were probably in proportion to the percentage of artillerymen in the armies. Because of the terrain, this battle, and this result, represent an extreme case. Lee knew that he was deficient in artillery, and he fought in the Wilderness in order to negate the Union advantage. The relative ineffectiveness of artillery in this battle is clearly an aberration. Chancellorsville was also fought in the Wilderness. In this battle, perhaps only the Confederate guns at Hazel Grove allowed Lee to capture Fairview Heights and defeat the Union army. Look at Spotsylvania a year later, also fought in the Wilderness. The massive Union attack on the Mule Shoe broke through because Lee had withdrawn his artillery the night before. Several days later, a Union attack on the base of the salient failed quickly and decisively due to

Confederate artillery fire. And we must remember that most ground was NOT as unfavorable as the Wilderness. Take a look at Malvern Hill, Antietam, Fredericksburg, and Gettysburg and the importance of artillery is obvious. Clearly artillery *was* important or army commanders wouldn't have eagerly added to their stocks of guns up until the last year of the war. In fact, Paddy Griffith suggests that in some battles, artillery accounted for 20 to 50% of casualties. Those who over-estimate the advantages of the rifled musket say that it threatened to make the artilleryman obsolete, but perhaps the opposite was more true. Although many historians do not stress this point, or even acknowledge it, advances in the artillery arm had made Napoleonic combined arms tactics difficult to impossible.

C-CUBED AND STAFFS

Civil War generals, especially Lee, are often criticized for creating inadequate staffs, and these criticisms are entirely justified. An authority on Napoleonic warfare, Scott Bowden in "Last Chance for Victory" says that Napoleon had more staff officers in a division than Lee did in his entire army at Gettysburg. Unable to coordinate the army effectively, on July 2nd Lee launched an en echelon attack, a favourite technique of Frederick the Great, largely because it was impossible to get all of his divisions to attack simultaneously.

When division commander Gen. Pender was hit, the attack broke down, perhaps saving the Union army. McClellan's attacks at Antietam are another example of poor coordination. Possibly planned as an en echelon attack for similar reasons, the Union army was instead committed piecemeal, one corps at a time, and each one was defeated in turn.

Despite the incompetence of the Union command, Lee's army was near the breaking point, and had McClellan committed the reserve, a Napoleon-like act that you might expect from someone known as the "Young Napoleon", the Confederate army would surely have been destroyed. Unlike the Napoleonic Wars, and more like the 18th century, reserves were a rarity in the Civil War, and a commander had few options once a battle "developed".

Command Style

Lee is often criticized for using discretionary orders, but this was actually one of the great strengths of his army. Particularly considering the terrain, his inadequate staff, and the difficulty of getting timely and accurate information, Lee giving his subordinates latitude was to his advantage. For example, Ewell is condemned for failing to take Cemetery Hill and Culps Hill on the first day of Gettysburg, which, it is said, Jackson surely would have done. The effects of this failure are clear-140 years later. However Ewell had good reasons for his actions. His corps was disorganized, and a large Union force was on his flank, right at the foot of Benner's Hill. Had he been attacked in his flank, the wisdom of his decision wouldn't be questioned. The Prussian observer Scheibert quotes Lee as saying, "You have to realize how things stand with us. Recognize that my orders then would do more harm than good. I rely on my division and brigade commanders. How terrible if I could not. I plan and work as hard as I can to bring my troops to the right place at the right time. I have done my duty then. The moment I order them forward, I put the battle and the fate of my army in the hands of God." (Scheibert 42)

In addition to the Army of the Potomac's many political problems, unlike the Army of Northern Virginia, it suffered from a top-down command mentality, something which had also hindered Napoleon's opponents. At Wagram in 1809, for example, a French corps marched along the front of the Austrian army, vulnerable to attack. The Austrian commanders, however, did not take the initiative and remained in passive defence. Similar things happened in the Civil War. Let's take a look at the Grant/Meade era, when subordinates were given little latitude to think for themselves. At the Wilderness, one of Warren's divisions was sent forward to Saunder's Field without support on its flanks. Another division with the opportunity to remain on the high ground at the Chewning Farm was ordered to pull back. At Spotsylvania, Warren was ordered to attack when this was an obvious waste of human life. Having not been given simple, common sense discretion, by the time of the battle at Cold Harbour, Union troops-from corps commander to private-were *taking* discretion. Instead of wasting lives in suicidal attacks, many units instead made only token attacks. This sabotaged any hopes of success that neighbouring units had, resulting in yet another waste of human life.

Subordinates must be encouraged to think for themselves-told what to do, but not how to do it. Their input and ideas must be sought. This prepares them for higher command. This was Napoleon's way, and this would be the way of the German Army in World War II, which is the model for the current US Army system of "operational analysis". To deprive commanders of discretion invites the many failings of a top-down system, just like in a totalitarian government-or a business where the CEO doesn't want to hear bad news. Lee's Confederate army was far from perfect- but at least in this way it was clearly superior.

The Civil War was not modern tactically, but it was not fought using Napoleonic tactics either. Regardless of the reasons-technology, tactics, terrain, command and control problems-or more likely a mixture of all these things-circumstances tended toward making Civil War combat less decisive than Napoleonic combat. Whether Napoleonic combined arms cooperation was still possible on a large scale during the Civil War is debatable. But the advent of rifled muskets doesn't explain this failure. Advances in artillery technology had more effect, but even these changes don't offer a complete explanation. Command, control, and communications problems, along with difficult terrain, made decisive battle more difficult to achieve. Numerous are the examples of Civil War battles on the verge of decisiveness-but without that final step that would have annihilated the enemy-Shiloh, Second Manassas, Antietam, Gettysburg, Chickamauga. Perhaps this failure to achieve decisive results encouraged the late-war custom of entrenching, although there are other explanations. The Prussian observer Justus Scheibert argued that breastworks were "safeguards against panic". (Scheibert 50) Modern historian Earl Hess argues that troops entrenched as a reaction to the shock of battle. Others point out that entrenching freed up troops to turn or flank the enemy-so entrenching was essentially a method to facilitate maneuver-one which had the opposite effect. Only one side had to entrench in order to force their opponent to do so. To do otherwise was just too risky, and there was no turning back. All of these explanations have validity. The 1864 campaigns little resemble those of 1862 or 1863. Battle lines were stretched thinner, putting commanders even more out of touch with the situation, and making armies even more difficult to control than before. At any rate, battle tactics had failed. Perhaps the use of entrenchments was inevitable, with a bloody attritional struggle like the Overland and Petersburg Campaigns being the predictable result.

STRATEGY AND TACTICS, MILITARY

Military strategy and tactics are essential to the conduct of warfare. Broadly stated, strategy is the planning, coordination, and general direction of military operations to meet overall political and military objectives. Tactics implement strategy by short-term decisions on the movement of troops and employment of weapons on the field of battle. The great military theorist Carl von Clausewitz put it another way: "Tactics is the art of using troops in battle; strategy is the art of using battles to win the war." Strategy and tactics, however, have been viewed differently in almost every era of history.

The change in the meaning of these terms over time has been basically one of scope as the nature of war and the shape of society have changed and as technology has developed. Strategy, for example, literally means "the art of the general" (from the Greek *strategos*) and originally signified the purely military planning of a campaign. Thus until the 17th and 18th centuries strategy included to varying degrees such problems as fortification, maneuver, and supply. In the 19th and 20th centuries, however, with the rise of mass ideologies, vast conscript armies, global alliances, and rapid technological change, military strategy became difficult to distinguish from "grand strategy," that is, the proper planning and utilization of the entire resources of a society —military, technological, economic, and political. The change in the scope and meaning of tactics over time has been largely due to enormous changes in technology. Tactics have always been difficult — and have become increasingly difficult — to distinguish in reality from strategy because the two are so interdependent. (Indeed, in the 20th century, tactics have been termed *operational strategy.*) Strategy is limited by what tactics are possible; given the size, training, and morale of forces, type and number of weapons available, terrain, weather, and quality and location of enemy forces, the tactics to be used are dependent on strategic considerations.

Strategic and Tactical Principles of Warfare

Military commanders and theorists throughout history have formulated what they considered to be the most important strategic and tactical principles of war. Napoleon I, for example, had 115 such principles. The Confederate general Nathan Bedford Forrest had but one: "Get there first with the most men." Some of the most commonly cited principles are the objective, the offensive, surprise, security, unity of command, economy of force, mass, and maneuver. Most are interdependent.

Military forces, whether large-scale or small-scale, must have a clear objective that is followed despite possible distractions. Only offensive operations — seizing and exploiting the initiative — however, will allow the choice of objectives; the offense also greatly increases the possibility of surprise (stealth and deception) and security (protection against being surprised or losing the possibility of surprising the enemy). Unity of command, or cooperation, is essential to the pursuit of objectives, the ability to use all forces effectively (economy of force), and the concentration of superior force at a critical point (mass). Maneuver consists of the various ways in which troops can be deployed and moved to obtain offensive, mass, and surprise. A famous example that illustrates most of these principles occurred during World War II when the Allied forces eventually agreed on the objective of defeating Germany first with a direct offensive against the European continent. Under a combined command headed by Gen. Dwight D. Eisenhower, they effectively massed their forces in England, deceived Germany regarding the point of invasion, collected intelligence on the disposition of German forces, and set the vast maneuver called Operation Overlord into motion.

Unthinking rigid attention to a principle of war, however, can be unfortunate. In the face of two Japanese naval forces, Adm. William Halsey's decision at the Battle of Leyte Gulf not to divide the fleet (the principle of mass) led to the pitting of the entire enormous American naval force against a decoy Japanese fleet. Division of the fleet (maneuver) would still have left Halsey superior to both Japanese forces.

Strategic and Tactical Maneuvers

Classification of actual military types of maneuvers and their variations have long been a part of military science. New technology and weapons have not drastically altered some of the classical types of offensive maneuver: penetration, envelopment, defensive-offensive maneuvers, and turning movements.

The penetration — one of the oldest maneuvers — is a main attack that attempts to pierce the enemy line while secondary attacks up and down the enemy line prevent the freeing of the enemy reserves. A favourite maneuver of the Duke of Marlborough (early 18th century), it was also used by Gen. Bernard Montgomery at El Alamein (1942).

The envelopment is a maneuver in which a secondary attack attempts to hold the enemy's centre while one (single envelopment) or both flanks (double envelopment) of the enemy are attacked or overlapped in a push to the enemy's rear in order to threaten the enemy's communications and line of retreat. This forces the enemy to fight in several directions and possibly be destroyed in position. New variations include vertical envelopments (airborne troops or airmobile troops) and amphibious envelopments. Noted single envelopments were accomplished by Alexander the Great at Arbela (or Gaugamela, 331 BC), Robert E. Lee at the Battle of Chancellorsville (1863), and Erwin Rommel at Gazala (1942; leading to the capture of Tobruk); famous double envelopments include those of Hannibal at the Battle of Cannae (216 BC), the American Revolution War Battle of Cowpens (1781), and the destruction of the 7th German

Army at the Falaise Gap (1944). Defensive-offensive maneuvers include attack from a strong defensive position after the attacking enemy has been sapped in strength, as in two battles of the Hundred Years' War, the Battle of Crécy (1346) and the Battle of Agincourt (1415), or feigned withdrawals that attempt to lure the enemy out of position as performed by William the Conqueror at the Battle of Hastings (1066) and by Napoleon at the Battle of Austerlitz (1805).

Turning maneuvers are indirect approaches that attempt to swing wide around an enemy's flank to so threaten an enemy's supply and communication lines that the enemy is forced to abandon a strong position or be cut off and encircled. Napoleon was a master of the turning movement, using it many times between 1796 and 1812. Robert E. Lee used the maneuver at the Second Battle of Bull Run (1862); the German drive to the French coast in 1940 was another example.

Theoretical Development of Strategy and Tactics

The historical roots of strategy and tactics date back to the origins of human warfare and the development of large-scale government and empire. The dense tactical infantry formation of overlapping shields called the phalanx, for example, existed in an early form in ancient Sumer (*c.*3000 BC). The development of strategy and tactics parallels to some extent the growth, spread, and clash of civilizations; technological discoveries and refinements; and the evolution of modern state power, ideology, and nationalism.

Early Strategy and Tactics. The Mediterranean basin saw the dawn of modern military strategy and tactics. It was under such leaders as Philip II (382–336 BC) and Alexander the Great (356–323 BC) of Macedonia and Hannibal (247–183 BC) of Carthage that the first great strides were made in military science. Philip combined infantry, cavalry, and primitive artillery into a trained, organized, and maneuverable fighting force backed up by engineers and a rudimentary signaling system. His son Alexander became an accomplished strategist and tactician with his concern for planning, keeping open lines of communication and supply, security, relentless pursuit of foes, and the use of surprise. Hannibal was a supreme tactician whose crushing victories taught the Romans that the flexible attack tactics of their legions needed to be supplemented by unity of command and an improved cavalry. The Romans eventually replaced their citizen-soldiers with a paid professional army whose training, equipment, skill at fortification, road building, and siege warfare became legendary. The Byzantine emperors studied Roman strategy and tactics and wrote some of the first essays on the subject.

The Middle Ages saw a decline in the study and application of strategy — with the exception of the great Mongol conqueror Genghis Khan. Medieval tactics began with an emphasis on defensive fortifications, siegecraft, and armoured cavalry. The introduction, however, of such new developments as the crossbow, longbow, halberd, pike, and, above all, gunpowder began to revolutionize the conduct of war.

The Emergence of Modern Warfare. Gustav II Adolf, king of Sweden (r. 1611-32), has been called the father of modern tactics because he reintroduced maneuver into military science. His disciplined national standing army — differing from the common use of mercenaries — was organized into small, mobile units armed with highly superior, maneuverable firepower and supplemented by mounted dragoons (his creation) armed with carbine and saber. Frederick II (the Great) of Prussia (r. 1740-86), the master of initiative and mass, conducted war in an age of limited warfare — armies were small and expensive; road and supply systems were inadequate. In the Seven Years' War (1756-63), Frederick faced a coalition whose various forces almost surrounded Prussia. Using a strategy of interior lines, Frederick — supported by a highly disciplined army and horse artillery (his creation) — would quickly maneuver, assemble a superior force at some decisive point along the line of encirclement, and, with massed howitzer fire, strike hard against an enemy flank before moving to another point.

With Napoleon I, however, the age of modern warfare was born. The French Revolution had produced a mass patriot army organized into loose divisional formations. Napoleon carefully planned his campaigns and quickly maneuvered his troops by forced marches to a selected field of battle. His battles began with skirmishing and cannonading, followed by an overwhelming concentration of forces in shock bayonet attacks against enemy flanks in turning and enveloping movements designed to utterly destroy opposing forces. Because of the greater complexities of warfare, a rudimentary general staff began to emerge under Napoleon.

The 19th Century: Theory and Technological Change. Napoleonic strategy and tactics were closely studied by the first great theorists of war, the Prussian general Carl von Clausewitz (1780–1831) and the French general Antoine Jomini (1779–1869). Clausewitz's *On War* (1832–34; Eng. trans., 1908) emphasized the close relationship between war and national policy and the importance of the principles of mass, economy of force, and the destruction of enemy forces. Jomini, on the other hand, emphasized occupying enemy territory through carefully planned, rapid, and precise geometric maneuvers. Whereas Jomini's theories had influence in France and North America, Clausewitz's teachings in particular were influential on the great Prussian military strategists of the 19th century, Helmuth von Moltke — architect of victory in the Franco-Prussian War (1870) — and Alfred von Schlieffen — creator of the Schlieffen plan (defence against Russia and envelopment of France), which Germany applied in a modified form at the beginning of World War I.

The 19th century was an era of far-reaching technological change that vastly altered the scope of tactics and strategy, an alteration seen in what has been called the first total war, the U.S. Civil War. Railroads and steamships increased the volume, reach, and speed of mobilization and of conscription. The consistent support of war industry became critical. The growth in range and accuracy of rifle firepower created new tactical problems: artillery had to be placed farther behind the lines, massed charges became ineffective if not disastrous, cavalry became limited to reconnaissance and skirmish, and troops began to fight from trenches and use grenades and land mines. Telegraph communications linked widening theaters of war and made large-scale strategy and tactics possible. During the

U.S. Civil War the large-scale strategy of the North (blockade, division of the Confederacy, destruction of the Confederate armies and supplies) backed by superior industry and manpower were the key factors in its victory. The development of the machine gun late in the 19th century would have its most telling effect in World War I.

World Wars: Trench Tactics to Nuclear Strategy. World War I began with immense, rapid, national mobilizations and classical offensive maneuvers, but after mutual attempts at envelopment at and after the Battle of the Marne, stationary trench warfare ensued across a wide battlefront. A war of attrition set in that called for total national involvement in the war effort. Two key technological developments in the war were to fashion the strategic and tactical debates of the 1920s and 1930s. The use of airpower was advocated by such theorists as Giulio Douhet (1869–1930), Billy Mitchell, Henry ("Hap") Arnold, and Hugh Trenchard (1873–1956). They insisted that airpower alone could win wars, not only by striking at enemy forces but by strategic bombing —the massive attack on cities, industries, and lines of communication and supply that characterized part of Allied strategy during World War II. The other World War I development was that of motorized armoured vehicles such as the tank. The use of the tank as the new cavalry of the modern age was advocated by B. H. Liddell Hart, Charles de Gaulle, and J. F. C. Fuller (1878–1966) in the interwar period. The Germans were the first to effectively use the tactical offensive combination of air and tank power in the field of battle in the blitzkriegs, under such commanders as Heinz Guderian and Erwin Rommel, which conquered much of Europe in World War II.

The primary tactical advance in World War II may have been that of amphibious warfare. The principal significance of that war, however, was in the first application of truly global strategies wielded by massive coalitions dedicated once again to the offensive. The development of nuclear weapons, which continued after the war, introduced the new science of nuclear strategy and tactics. The immense destructive nature of these weapons, however, meant that warfare of limited strategic goals, using conventional tactics and conventional but technologically advanced weapons, would predominate in the "limited" wars that followed World War II. The very need to keep wars limited has produced a new strategic form: the small, mobile special forces, armed with light but sophisticated weapons and trained in guerrilla tactics, that can be rapidly deployed and as rapidly withdrawn from hostile territory.

MODERN STRATEGY AND TACTICS

Total War and Mechanized War

The first modern total war, fought with mass armies and modern firearms, was the U.S. Civil War. It demonstrated the importance of industrial mobilization; modern communications (especially railroads and the telegraph), and the deadly effect of new small arms, such as the rifled musket, on mass formations of attacking infantry. Beginning as a contest between armies, it grew into a conflict between two societies; before its termination almost the entire resources of both North and South were engaged.

The lessons of the U.S. Civil War were little noticed in Europe, where strategy and tactics continued to be thought of in terms of mid-19th-century practice. European theorists also ignored the extensive and effective use of machine guns, artillery, and rifles in the colonial wars of the 19th cent. As a result, the bloody stalemate of World War I came as a surprise to most generals.

It was characterized by trench warfare and by bloody frontal attacks, which were usually stopped at great cost to the attackers by massed small arms and artillery fire. In an effort to break the stalemate, both sides turned to new technical devices, such as the tank, the airplane, the submarine, and poison gas. The importance of the tank was stressed in theories of mechanized warfare formulated in the 1920s and 30s in the writings of B. H. Liddell Hart, Charles de Gaulle, and J. F. C. Fuller; they proved prophetic when the Nazi blitzkrieg marked World War II as a war of mobility, characterized by vast movements of mechanized armies.

Airpower, Nuclear Weapons, and Beyond

The introduction of aircraft in World War I gave rise to theories of airpower that have dominated strategic and tactical thinking ever since. The basis of airpower was set down by such men as Giulio Douhet, H. M. Trenchard, and William Mitchell, who believed that future wars would be won by air forces. Their theory of strategic bombing called for aerial attacks on the enemy's population and industrial centres to destroy the enemy's will and ability to continue fighting. In World War II that strategy was carried out in massive form by British and U.S. air forces in attacks on Germany and Japan. It was found, however, that aerial bombardment did not cut off industrial production and, in fact, strengthened the enemy's will to continue. In order to win the war the Allies had to conduct a number of campaigns with ground forces and, in the case of Germany, occupy the enemy's homeland.

The introduction and development of nuclear weapons and the guided missile have not changed the basic strategic theory of airpower, but these new weapons have revolutionized airpower itself. The replacement of high-explosive bombs by nuclear bombs and the change from propeller-driven manned aircraft to rocket-powered guided missiles meant that a force armed with these weapons could destroy almost any target on the planet. From the dropping of the first atomic bomb a new school of military theory, nuclear strategy, developed. In the 1950s, the United States evolved the theory of "massive retaliation," to be used against the USSR as a response to acts of aggression.

In the early 1960s the threat of nuclear war did not prevent many successful nationalist revolutions and Communist people's wars as advocated by Mao Zedong, Ernesto "Che" Guevara, and Vo Nguyen Giap. The result was a greater stress on conventional weapons and on increased tactical and strategic flexibility, as well as an interest in the long history and practice of counterinsurgency. That military strategy has become national strategy, involving complex assessments of technological resources, politics, and national priorities, was made clear in the Vietnam War and Afghanistan War where superior strategies and tactics allowed small nations to defeat great powers armed with the latest weaponry.

Outer space has also become a crucial strategic issue. President Ronald Reagan's Strategic Defence Initiative raised the possibility of the use of space-based weapons and satellites to combat an nuclear attack involving ballistic missiles, as the popular term for the program—"Star Wars"—made clear. Space is also important strategically for intelligence gathering using reconnaissance satellites and for coordination of military forces using the Global Positioning System, as was done successfully during the Persian Gulf War.

NAVAL STRATEGY AND TACTICS

Naval strategy and tactics have been shaped by the forms and capabilities of naval warships. Geography is also an important factor in shaping naval thinking. In the Mediterranean, and for islands such as Britain, strong navies were crucial. For the many empires of the Middle East, the Central Asian steppes, or India, naval power was less important or superfluous. Not until Alfred T. Mahan wrote *The Influence of Sea Power upon History* in the last decade of the 19th cent. was the central theme of naval strategy formulated in universal terms, although the British had been practicing it for hundreds of years. The main strategy of sea power was defined as "command of the sea," i.e., the ability to deny use of the sea as a means of transportation to an enemy while simultaneously protecting one's own merchant shipping, and the ability to use the sea to project power ashore while denying that capability to the enemy. Despite the introduction of new weapons such as steam warships, armoured ships, heavy ordnance, submarines, and aircraft, "command of the sea" remained a fundamental objective of naval strategy. Another important naval strategy is "overseas presence," i.e., the visible display of seapower as a deterrent to intervention by opposing powers in key areas of international tension.

The development of airpower has led to a host of changes, including the emergence of aircraft carriers and naval air fleets and the development of submarine-based retaliatory missile forces. The employment of land-based and carrier-based aircraft during World War II showed that command of the seas rested in great part on control of the air above it. The submarine, introduced in World War I, greatly changed naval strategy and led to the development of many new weapons and tactics. In both world wars the submarine was employed mainly as a commerce destroyer and, as such, could not by itself gain command of the sea. However, the use of long-range guided missiles on nuclear-powered submarines in the 1960s transformed the submarine into a major weapon of strategic bombardment. Nuclear-powered submarines carrying guided missiles are almost invulnerable to attack.

LAWS OF WAR

The law of war is a body of law concerning acceptable justifications to engage in war (*jus ad bellum*) and the limits to acceptable wartime conduct (*jus in bello*). The law of war is considered an aspect of public international law (the law of nations) and is distinguished from other bodies of law, such as the domestic law of a particular belligerent to a conflict, that may also provide legal limits to the conduct or justification of war.

Among other issues, modern laws of war address declarations of war, acceptance of surrender and the treatment of prisoners of war, military necessity along with *distinction* and *proportionality*, and the prohibition of certain weapons that may cause unnecessary suffering.

Early Sources and History

Attempts to define and regulate the conduct of individuals, nations, and other agents in war and to mitigate the worst effects of war have a long history. The earliest known instances are found in the Hebrew Bible (Old Testament). For example, Deuteronomy 20:19-20 limits the amount of acceptable collateral and environmental damage:

When thou shalt besiege a city a long time, in making war against it to take it, thou shalt not destroy the trees thereof by forcing an axe against them: for thou mayest eat of them, and thou shalt not cut them down (for the tree of the field is man's life) to employ them in the siege: Only the trees which thou knowest that they be not trees for meat, thou shalt destroy and cut them down; and thou shalt build bulwarks against the city that maketh war with thee, until it be subdued.

Similarly, Deuteronomy 21:10-14 requires that female captives who were forced to marry the victors of a war could not be sold as slaves. In the early 7th century, the first Caliph, Abu Bakr, whilst instructing his Muslim army, laid down the following rules concerning warfare:

Stop, O people, that I may give you ten rules for your guidance in the battlefield. Do not commit treachery or deviate from the right path. You must not mutilate dead bodies. Neither kill a child, nor a woman, nor an aged man. Bring no harm to the trees, nor burn them with fire, especially those which are fruitful. Slay not any of the enemy's flock, save for your food. You are likely to pass by people who have devoted their lives to monastic services; leave them alone.

These rules were put into practice during the early Muslim conquests of the 7th and 8th centuries. After the expansion of the Caliphate, Islamic legal treatises on international law from the 9th century onwards covered the application of Islamic military jurisprudence to international law, including the law of treaties; the treatment of diplomats, hostages, refugees and prisoners of war in Islam; the right of asylum; conduct on the battlefield; protection of women, children and non-combatant civilians; contracts across the lines of battle; the use of poisonous weapons; and devastation of enemy territory. These laws were put into practice by Muslim armies during the Crusades, most notably by Saladin and Sultan al-Kamil. For example, after al-Kamil defeated the Franks, Oliverus Scholasticus praised the Islamic laws of war, commenting on how al-Kamil supplied the defeated Frankish army with food:

Who could doubt that such goodness, friendship and charity come from God? Men whose parents, sons and daughters, brothers and sisters, had died in agony at our hands, whose lands we took, whom we drove naked from their homes, revived us with their own food when we were dying of hunger and showered us with kindness even when we were in their power.

In medieval Europe, the Roman Catholic Church also began promulgating teachings on just war, reflected to some extent in movements such as the Peace and Truce of God. The impulse to restrict the extent of warfare, and especially protect the lives and property of non-combatants continued with Hugo Grotius and his attempts to write laws of war.

Modern Sources

The modern law of war is derived from two principal sources:

- *Lawmaking treaties* (or *conventions*) — sec the section below called "International treaties on the laws of war".
- *Custom*. Not all the law of war derives from or has been incorporated in such treaties, which can refer to the continuing importance of customary law. Such customary international law is established by the general practice of nations together with their acceptance that such practice is required by law.

Positive international humanitarian law consists of treaties (international agreements) which directly affect the laws of war by binding consenting nations and achieving widespread consent—see the section below called "International treaties on the laws of war". The opposite of positive laws of war is customary laws of war, many of which were explored at the Nuremberg War Trials. These laws define both the *permissive* rights of states as well as *prohibitions* on their conduct when dealing with irregular forces and non-signatories.

Historian Geoffrey Best has called the period from 1856 to 1909 the law of war's "epoch of highest repute." The defining aspect of this epoch was the establishment, by states, of a positive legal or legislative foundation (i.e., written) superseding a regime based primarily on religion, chivalry, and customs. It is during this "modern" era that the international conference became the forum for debate and agreement between states and the "multilateral treaty" served as the positive mechanism for codification.

In addition, the Nuremberg War Trial judgment on "The Law Relating to War Crimes and Crimes Against Humanity" held, under the guidelines Nuremberg Principles, that treaties like the Hague Convention of 1907, having been widely accepted by "all civilised nations" for about half a century, were by then part of the customary laws of war and binding on all parties whether the party was a signatory to the specific treaty or not.

Interpretations of international humanitarian law change over time and this also affects the laws of war. For example Carla Del Ponte, the chief prosecutor for the International Criminal Tribunal for the former Yugoslavia pointed out in 2001 that although there is no specific treaty ban on the use of depleted uranium projectiles, there is a developing scientific debate and concern expressed regarding the effect of the use of such projectiles and it is possible that, in future, there may be a consensus view in international legal circles that use of such projectiles violate general principles of the law applicable to use of weapons in armed conflict. This is because in future it may be the consensus view that depleted uranium projectiles breaches one or more of the following treaties: The Universal Declaration of Human Rights; the Charter of the United Nations; the Genocide Convention; the United Nations Convention Against Torture; the Geneva Conventions including Protocol I; the Convention on Conventional Weapons of 1980; the Chemical Weapons Convention; and the Convention on the Physical Protection of Nuclear Material.

Purposes of the Laws

Some of the central principles underlying laws of war are:

- Wars should be limited to achieving the political goals that started the war (e.g., territorial control) and should not include unnecessary destruction;
- Wars should be brought to an end as quickly as possible;
- People and property that do not contribute to the war effort should be protected against unnecessary destruction and hardship;

To this end, laws of war are intended to mitigate the evils of war by:

- Protecting both combatants and noncombatants from unnecessary suffering;
- Safeguarding certain fundamental human rights of persons who fall into the hands of the enemy, particularly prisoners of war, the wounded and sick, and civilians;
- Facilitating the restoration of peace.

Example Substantive Laws of War

To fulfil the purposes noted above, the laws of war place substantive limits on the lawful exercise of a belligerent's power. Generally speaking, the laws require that belligerents refrain from employing violence that is not reasonably necessary for military purposes and that belligerents conduct hostilities with regard for the principles of humanity and chivalry. However, because the laws of war are based on consensus, the content and interpretation of such laws are extensive, contested, and ever-changing. The following are particular examples of some of the substance of the laws of war, as those laws are interpreted today.

Declaration of War

Some treaties, notably the UN charter (1945) Article 2, and some other articles in the charter, seek to curtail the right of member states to declare war; as does the older Kellogg-Briand Pact of 1928 for those nations who ratified it.

Lawful Conduct of Belligerent Actors

Modern laws of war regarding conduct during war (*jus in bello*), such as the 1949 Geneva Conventions, provide that it is unlawful for belligerents to engage in combat without meeting certain requirements, among them the wearing of a distinctive uniform or other distinctive signs visible at a distance, and the carrying of weapons openly. Impersonating soldiers of the other side by wearing the enemy's uniform is allowed, though fighting in that uniform is unlawful *perfidy*, as is the taking of hostages.

The Red Cross, Red Crescent, & The White Flag

Modern laws of war, such as the 1949 Geneva Conventions,

also include prohibitions on attacking doctors, ambulances or hospital ships displaying a Red Cross, a Red Crescent or other emblem related to the International Red Cross and Red Crescent Movement. It is also prohibited to fire at a person or vehicle bearing a white flag, since that indicates an intent to surrender or a desire to communicate.

In either case, persons protected by the Red Cross/Crescent or white flag are expected to maintain neutrality, and may not engage in warlike acts; in fact, engaging in war activities under a protected symbol is itself a violation of the laws of war known as perfidy. Failure to follow these requirements can result in the loss of protected status and make the individual violating the requirements a lawful military target.

Applicability to States and Individuals

The law of war is binding not only upon States as such but also upon individuals and, in particular, the members of their armed forces. Parties are bound by the laws of war to the extent that such compliance does not interfere with achieving legitimate military goals. For example, they are obliged to make every effort to avoid damaging people and property not involved in combat, but they are not guilty of a war crime if a bomb mistakenly hits a residential area.

By the same token, combatants that *intentionally* use protected people or property as shields or camouflage are guilty of violations of laws of war and are responsible for damage to those that should be protected.

Remedies for Violations

During conflict, punishment for violating the laws of war may consist of a specific, deliberate and limited violation of the laws of war in reprisal.

Soldiers who break specific provisions of the laws of war lose the protections and status afforded as prisoners of war, but only after facing a "*competent tribunal*" (GC III Art 5). At that point they become an unlawful combatant but they must still be "*treated with humanity and, in case of trial, shall not be deprived of the rights of fair and regular trial*", because they are still covered by GC IV Art 5. For example in 1976 foreign soldiers fighting for FNLA were captured by the MPLA in the civil war that broke out when Angola gained independence from Portugal in 1975. In the Luanda Trial, after "*a regularly constituted court*" found them guilty of being mercenaries, three Britons and an American were shot by a firing squad on July 10, 1976. Nine others were imprisoned for terms of 16 to 30 years.

Spies and terrorists may be subject to civilian law or military tribunal for their acts and in practice have been subjected to torture and/or execution. The laws of war neither approve nor condemn such acts, which fall outside their scope. However, nations that have signed the *UN Convention Against Torture* have committed themselves not to use torture on anyone for any reason. Citizens and soldiers of nations which have not signed the Fourth Geneva Convention are also not protected by it (Article 4: "*Nationals of a State which is not bound by the Convention are not protected by it*".), whether they are spies or terrorists. Also, citizens and soldiers of nations which have not signed and do not abide by the Third and Fourth Geneva Conventions are not protected by them. (Common Article 2: "*[The High Contracting Parties] shall furthermore be bound by the Convention in relation to [a Power which is not a contracting party], if the latter accepts and applies the provisions thereof*" (emphasis added).)

If someone is (or is suspected to be) a citizen or soldier of a nation which has signed or abides by the Fourth Geneva Convention, or is (or is suspected to be) a "prisoner of war" (POW) per the definitions of such "*protected persons*" in the Third Geneva Convention, the following applies: A POW who breaks specific provisions of the laws of war may be penalized, but not penalized worse than the tribunal would penalize its own soldiers for the same offense (and usually a disciplinary, not judicial, punishment if its own soldiers normally wouldn't be brought to trial for a particular offense) and POW's may not be penalized based on rank or gender, nor with corporal punishment, collective punishments for individual acts, lack of daylight, or torture/cruelty (GC IV, Art. 82 through Art. 88).

After a conflict has ended, persons who have committed or ordered any breach of the laws of war, especially atrocities, may be held individually accountable for war crimes through process of law. Also, nations which signed the Geneva Conventions are required to search for, then try and punish, anyone who has committed or ordered certain "*grave breaches*" of the laws of war.

History has shown that the laws of war are traditionally more strictly applied to those defeated, as the victorious faction are placed in the role of policing themselves. While it can be argued that the victors may be less strict on their own forces, it can also be argued that the signing of the treaties involved in the laws of war implies a good-faith promise to adhere to them equally. As with many facets of war, the aftermath and subsequent legal proceedings depend heavily on circumstance, and are different for each conflict.

There is an emerging trend in the US to hold private corporations civilly liable for aiding and abetting in war crimes, by knowingly providing substantial assistance in the commission of the crimes. Under international law, the mens rea element is knowledge, not intent that the crimes be carried out. This opens the door not only to hold private security contractors liable, but also other kinds of corporations which employ violent mercenary or terrorist groups as private security forces. Although conflict zones often lack functioning legal systems, and government may even have passed laws immunizing private mercenaries from criminal liability, aiding and abetting a war crime can still be the basis for civil liability in a foreign court with jurisdiction over the defendant corporation.

Role of the United States

While many point correctly to the Lieber Code, which was promulgated by the Union during the American Civil War, as critical in the development of the laws of land warfare, one researcher who analysed the evolution of these laws concludes that "following the publication of Lieber's code as General Orders 100 in 1863, the United States did not effectively contribute anything to The Hague Laws relating to land warfare as they evolved during this period." This was probably because the United States considered itself a sea power (with corresponding significant participation and contributions to the law of the sea) and did not plan on getting entangled in continental (European) land wars.

International Treaties on the Laws of War

List of declarations, conventions, treaties and judgements and on the laws of war:

- 1856 Paris Declaration Respecting Maritime Law abolished privateering
- 1864 First Geneva Convention "for the Amelioration of the Condition of the Wounded and Sick in Armed Forces in the Field"
- 1868 St. Petersburg Declaration Renouncing the Use, in Time of War, of Explosive projectiles Under 400 grams Weight
- 1874 Project of an International Declaration concerning the Laws and Customs of War (Brussels Declaration). Signed in Brussels 27 August. This agreement never entered into force, but formed part of the basis for the codification of the laws of war at the 1899 Hague Peace Conference.
- 1880 Manual of the Laws and Customs of War at Oxford. At its session in Geneva in 1874 the Institute of International Law appointed a committee to study the *Brussels Declaration* of the same year and to submit to the Institute its opinion and supplementary proposals on the subject. The work of the Institute led to the adoption of the Manual in 1880 and it went on to form part of the basis for the codification of the laws of war at the 1899 Hague Peace Conference.
- 1899 Hague Conventions consisted of four main sections and three additional declarations (the final main section is for some reason identical to the first additional declaration):

    I. Pacific Settlement of International Disputes

II. Laws and Customs of War on Land

III. Adaptation to Maritime Warfare of Principles of Geneva Convention of 1864

IV. Prohibiting Launching of Projectiles and Explosives from Balloons

- o Declaration I-On the Launching of Projectiles and Explosives from Balloons
- o Declaration II-On the Use of Projectiles the Object of Which is the Diffusion of Asphyxiating or Deleterious Gases
- o Declaration III-On the Use of Bullets Which Expand or Flatten Easily in the Human Body

- 1907 Hague Conventions had thirteen sections, of which twelve were ratified and entered into force and two declarations

I. The Pacific Settlement of International Disputes

II. The Limitation of Employment of Force for Recovery of Contract Debts

III. The Opening of Hostilities

IV. The Laws and Customs of War on Land

V. The Rights and Duties of Neutral Powers and Persons in Case of War on Land

VI. The Status of Enemy Merchant Ships at the Outbreak of Hostilities'

VII. The Conversion of Merchant Ships into War-Ships

VIII. The Laying of Automatic Submarine Contact Mines

IX. Bombardment by Naval Forces in Time of War

X. Adaptation to Maritime War of the Principles of the Geneva Convention

XI. Certain Restrictions with Regard to the Exercise of the Right of Capture in Naval War

XII. The Creation of an International Prize Court [Not Ratified]*

XIII. The Rights and Duties of Neutral Powers in Naval War

Declaration I-extending Declaration II from the 1899 Conference to other types of aircraft

Declaration II-on the obligatory arbitration

- 1909 London Declaration concerning the Laws of Naval War largely reiterated existing law, although it showed greater regard to the rights of neutral entities. Never went into effect.
- 1922 The Washington Naval Treaty, also known as the *Five-Power Treaty* (6 February)
- 1923 Hague Draft Rules of Aerial Warfare
- 1925 Geneva protocol for the Prohibition of the Use in War of Asphyxiating, Poisonous or Other Gases, and of Bacteriological Methods of Warfare
- 1927-1930 Greco-German arbitration tribunal
- 1928 Kellogg-Briand Pact (also known as the *Pact of Paris*)
- 1929 Geneva Convention, Relative to the treatment of prisoners of war
- 1929 Geneva Convention on the amelioration of the condition of the wounded and sick
- 1930 Treaty for the Limitation and Reduction of Naval Armament (London Naval Treaty 22 April)
- 1935 Roerich Pact
- 1936 Second London Naval Treaty (25 March)
- 1938 Amsterdam Draft Convention for the Protection of Civilian Populations Against New Engines of War.
- 1938 League of Nations declaration for the "Protection of Civilian Populations Against Bombing From the Air in Case of War"
- 1945 United Nations Charter (entered into force on October 24, 1945)
- 1946 Judgment of the International Military Tribunal at Nuremberg
- 1947 Nuremberg Principles. formulated under UN General Assembly Resolution 177 21 November 1947

- 1948 United Nations Convention on the Prevention and Punishment of the Crime of Genocide.
- 1949 Geneva Convention I for the Amelioration of the Condition of the Wounded and Sick in Armed Forces in the Field
- 1949 Geneva Convention II for the Amelioration of the Condition of Wounded, Sick and Shipwrecked Members of Armed Forces at Sea
- 1949 Geneva Convention III Relative to the Treatment of Prisoners of War
- 1949 Geneva Convention IV Relative to the Protection of Civilian Persons in Time of War
- 1954 Hague Convention for the Protection of Cultural Property in the Event of Armed Conflict
- 1971 Zagreb Resolution of the Institute of International Law on Conditions of Application of Humanitarian Rules of Armed Conflict to Hostilities in which the United Nations Forces May be Engaged
- 1977 United Nations Convention on the Prohibition of Military or Any Other Hostile Use of Environmental Modification Techniques
- 1977 Geneva Protocol I Additional to the Geneva Conventions of 12 August 1949, and Relating to the Protection of Victims of International Armed Conflicts
- 1977 Geneva Protocol II Additional to the Geneva Conventions of 12 August 1949, and Relating to the Protection of Victims of Non-International Armed Conflicts
- 1978 Red Cross Fundamental Rules of International Humanitarian Law Applicable in Armed Conflicts
- 1980 United Nations Convention on Prohibitions or Restrictions on the Use of Certain Conventional Weapons Which May be Deemed to be Excessively Injurious or to Have Indiscriminate Effects (CCW)
  - 1980 Protocol I on Non-Detectable Fragments

- o 1980 Protocol II on Prohibitions or Restrictions on the Use of Mines, Booby-Traps and Other Devices
- o 1980 Protocol III on Prohibitions or Restrictions on the Use of Incendiary Weapons
- o 1995 Protocol IV on Blinding Laser Weapons
- o 1996 Amended Protocol II on Prohibitions or Restrictions on the Use of Mines, Booby-Traps and Other Devices
- o Protocol on Explosive Remnants of War (Protocol V to the 1980 Convention), 28 November 2003, entered into force on 12 November 2006

- 1994 San Remo Manual on International Law Applicable to Armed Conflicts at Sea.
- 1994 ICRC/UNGA Guidelines for Military Manuals and Instructions on the Protection of the Environment in Time of Armed Conflict
- 1994 UN Convention on the Safety of United Nations and Associated Personnel
- 1996 The International Court of Justice advisory opinion on the Legality of the Threat or Use of Nuclear Weapons
- 1997 Convention on the Prohibition of the Use, Stockpiling, Production and Transfer of Anti-Personnel Mines and on their Destruction (Ottawa Treaty)
- 1998 Rome Statute of the International Criminal Court entered into force on 1 July 2002.
- 2000 Optional Protocol on the Involvement of Children in Armed Conflict, entered into force on 12 February 2002.

9

Antiquity: India, Persia and Alexander the Great

There is uncertainty as to when elephant warfare first began. The earliest Indian Vedic religious hymns, the Rigveda, dating from the late 2nd and early 1st millennia BCE, make reference to the use of elephants for transport-especially Indra and his divine white elephant, Airavata-but make no reference to the use of elephants in war, focusing instead on Indra's role in leading horse cavalry. The later stories of the Mahabharata, dating from around the 8th century BCE in their earliest forms, and the Ramayana, dating from around the 4th century BCE, do however mention elephant warfare, suggesting its introduction during the intervening period. The ancient Indian kings certainly valued the elephant in war, some stating that 'an army without elephants is as despicable as a forest without a lion, a kingdom without a king or as valour unaided by weapons.'

From India, military thinking on the use of war elephants spread westwards to the Persian Empire, where they were used in several campaigns and in turn came to influence the campaigns of Alexander the Great. The first confrontation between Europeans and the Persian war elephants occurred at the Alexander's Battle of Gaugamela (331 BCE), where the Persians deployed fifteen elephants. These elephants were placed at the centre of the Persian line and made such an impression on the Macedonian troops that Alexander felt the need to sacrifice to the God of Fear the night before the battle-but according to some sources the elephants ultimately failed to deploy in the final battle owing to their long march the day before. Alexander won resoundingly at Gaugamela, but was deeply impressed by the enemy elephants and took these first fifteen into his own army, adding to their number during his capture of the rest of Persia.

By the time Alexander reached the borders of India five years later, he had a substantial number of elephants under his own command. When it came to defeating Porus, who ruled in the Punjab region of modern day Pakistan, Alexander found himself facing a considerable force of between 85 and 100 war elephants at the Battle of the Hydaspes River. Preferring stealth and mobility to sheer force, Alexander manoeuvered and engaged with just his infantry and cavalry, ultimately defeating Porus' forces, including his elephant corps, albeit at some cost. Looking further east again, however, Alexander could see that the kings of the Nanda Empire and Gangaridai could deploy as between 3,000 and 6,000 war elephants. Such a force was many times larger than the number employed by the Persians and Greeks, which discouraged Alexander's small band of men and effectively halted their advance into India. On his return, Alexander established a force of elephants to guard his palace at Babylon, and created the post of *elephantarch* to lead his elephant units.

The successful military use of elephants spread further. The successors to Alexander's empire, the Diadochi, used hundreds of Indian elephants in their wars, with the Seleucid empire being particularly notable for their use of the animals, still being largely brought from India. Indeed, the campaign between the Seleucids and Chandragupta Maurya (Sandrokottos), founder of the Maurya empire in 305 BCE ended with the Seleucids ceding vast eastern territories in exchange for 500 war elephants-a small part of the Maurya forces, which included up to 9,000 elephants by some accounts. The Seleucids put their new elephants to good use at the battle of Ipsus four years later. Later in its history, the Seleucid Empire used elephants in its efforts to crush the Maccabean Revolt in Judea. The elephants were terrifying to the lighter-armed Jewish warriors, and the youngest of the Hasmonean brothers, Eleazar Maccabeus, famously defeated one of the creatures in the Battle of Beth Zechariah, sticking a spear under the belly of an elephant he mistakenly believed to be carrying Seleucid king Antiochus V, killing the elephant at the cost of Eleazar's own life.

Antiquity: the Mediterranean

The Egyptians and the Carthaginians began acquiring African elephants for the same purpose, as did the Numidians and the Kushites. The animal used was the North African forest elephant which would become extinct from over-exploitation. These animals were smaller than the Asian elephants used by the Seleucids on the east of the Mediterranean region, particularly those from Syria, which stood 2.5-3.5 meters (8–10 ft) at the shoulder. It is likely that at least some Syrian elephants were traded abroad-the favourite elephant of Hannibal was an impressive animal named *Surus* ("the Syrian"), for example, and may have been of Syrian stock, though the evidence remains ambiguous.

Since the late 1940s a strand of scholarship has argued that the African forest elephants used by Numidian, Ptolemaic and Punic armies did not carry howdahs or turrets in combat, perhaps owing to the physical weakness of the species. Some allusions to turrets in ancient literature are certainly anachronistic or poetic invention, but other references are less easily discounted. There is explicit contemporary testimony that the army of Juba I of Numidia included turreted elephants in 46 BCE. This is confirmed by the image of a turreted African elephant used on the coinage of Juba II. This also appears to be the case with Ptolemaic armies: Polybius reports that at the battle of Raphia in 217 BCE the elephants of Ptolemy IV carried turrets; these beasts were significantly smaller than the Asian elephants fielded by the Seleucids and so presumably African forest elephants. There is also evidence that Carthaginian war elephants were furnished with turrets and howdahs in certain military contexts.

Farther south, tribes would have had access to the African Savanna elephant. Although much larger than either the African forest elephant or the Asian elephant, these proved difficult to tame for war purposes and were not used extensively. Some Asian elephants were traded westwards to the Mediterranean markets; Pliny the Elder stated that the Sri Lankan elephants, for example, were larger, fiercer and better for war than local elephants. This superiority, as well as the proximity of the supply to seaports, made Sri Lanka's elephants a lucrative trading commodity.

Although the use of war elephants in the Mediterranean is most famously associated with the wars between Carthage and Rome, the introduction of war elephants was primarily the result of the Greek kingdom of Epirus. King Pyrrhus of Epirus brought twenty elephants to attack the Romans at the battle of Heraclea in 280 BCE, leaving some fifty additional animals, on loan from Pharaoh Ptolemy II, on the mainland. The Romans were unprepared for fighting elephants, and the Greek forces routed the Romans. The next year, the Greeks again deployed a similar force of elephants, attacking the Romans at the battle of Asculum. This time the Romans came prepared with flammable weapons and anti-elephant devices: these were ox-led chariots, equipped with long spikes to wound the elephants, pots of fire to scare them, and accompanying screening troops who would hurl javelins at the elephants to drive them away. A final charge of Greek elephants won the day again, but this time Pyrrhus had suffered very heavy casualties-a Pyrrhic victory.

Inspired by these victories, Carthage developed its own use of war elephants and deployed them extensively during the First Punic War. The results were not inspiring. At Adyss in 255 BCE, the Carthaginian elephants were ineffective due to the terrain, whilst at the battle of Panormus in 251 BCE the Romans were able to terrify the Carthaginian elephants, which fled from the field. During the Second Punic War, Hannibal famously led an army of war elephants across the Alps-although unfortunately most of them perished in the harsh conditions. The Romans had developed effective anti-elephant tactics, leading to Hannibal's defeat at his final battle of Zama in 202 BCE; his elephant charge was ineffective because the disciplined

Roman maniples simply made way for them to pass. Rome brought back many elephants at the end of the Punic Wars, and used them in its campaigns for many years afterwards. The conquest of Greece saw many battles in which the Romans deployed war elephants, including the invasion of Macedonia in 199 BCE, the battle of Cynoscelphalae 197 BCE, the battle of Thermopylae, and the battle of Magnesia in 190 BCE, during which Antiochus III's fifty-four elephants took on the Roman force of sixteen. In later years the Romans deployed twenty-two elephants at Pydna in 168 BCE. They also featured throughout the Roman campaign against the Celtiberians in Hispania and against the Gauls. Famously, the Romans used a war elephant in the invasion of Britain, one ancient writer recording that 'Caesar had one large elephant, which was equipped with armor and carried archers and slingers in its tower. When this unknown creature entered the river, the Britons and their horses fled and the Roman army crossed over',-although he may have confused this incident with the use of a similar war elephant in Claudius' final conquest of Britain. At least one elephant skeleton with flint weapons that has been found in England was initially misidentified as these elephants, but later dating proved it to be a mammoth skeleton from the stone age.

By the time of Claudius, however, such animals were being used by the Romans in single numbers only-the last significant use of war elephants in the Mediterranean was against the Romans at the battle of Thapsus, 46 BCE, where Julius Caesar armed his fifth legion (*Alaudae*) with axes and commanded his legionaries to strike at the elephant's legs. The legion withstood the charge, and the elephant became its symbol. Thapsus was the last significant use of elephants in the West. The Parthian dynasty of Persia occasionally used war elephants in their battles against the Roman Empire but elephants were of substantial importance in the army of the subsequent Sassanid dynasty. The Sassanids employed the animals in many of their campaigns against their western enemies. One of the most memorable engagements was the Battle of Vartanantz in 451 AD, at which the Sassanid elephants terrified the Armenians.

Another example is the Battle of al-Qadisiyyah of 636 AD, in which a unit of thirty-three elephants were used, albeit less successfully, against the invading Arab forces. The Sassanid elephant corps held primacy amongst the Sassanid's cavalry forces and was recruited from India. The elephant corps was under a special chief, known as the *Zend"hapet*, or "Commander of the Indians," either because the animals came from that country, or because they were managed by natives of Hindustan. The Sassanid elephant corps was never on the same scale as other further east, however, and after the fall of the Sassanid empire the use of war elephants died out in the region.

War with Alexander the Great

Alexander had inherited both masterful tactics from his father, Phillip of Macedonia, and the world's best military force. He also inherited rule over the martially powerful Greeks and Macedonians. After Alexander consolidated his kingdom and defeated some warlike Thracian tribes on his Northern border he began to conquer the "known world". Alexander defeated the world's largest empire of the time, the Persians in two pitched battles. He then defeated the defiant Phoenician cities on the Eastern Mediterranean and Egypt before returning to finish off the Persians in yet another massive pitched battle. After that he marched East, fighting the tough tribes of modern Afghanistan, there he lost more men in battle then in his war with the vast Persian Empire! Once he had established control of Afghanistan through brutal, genocidal war he aimed his army at the indo-gangetic plains where the hundreds of small kingdoms that had stretched across it had consolidated into sixteen different kingdoms.

In 326 BC Alexander the Great began his invasion of the India. He moved East intent on conquering all the lands to the "Great Out Sea", which he believed to be on the other side of India. Alexander and his forces crossed the Indus river but where halted at the Hydapes River by a large army on the other side. Porus, ruler of the Punjab Region, had positioned a large army on the other bank complete with war elephants, archers, infantry and chariots. The infantry were armed with bamboo cane framed hide shields and bamboo spears with iron heads. The Indian archers employed an effective 6 ft long bow also made out of bamboo that shot long cane arrows. However the most frightening aspect of the Indian army was the war elephants. These massive beasts were something the Greeks and Macedonians hadn't faced and they would soon wreak havoc on the battle field.

Alexander out maneuvered Porus and was able to cross up river with an elite part of his army. The Indian chariots that Porus sent to counter the crossing became stuck in the mud, and Porus' son who was leading the counter attack was killed. As Porus turned his army to face Alexander the remaining part of Alexanders forces crossed the river forcing a confrontation on two fronts. Porus lined up his army to counter Alexander and sent his infantry and elephants against him. Alexander's forces, formed into to formidable Macedonian phalanx, advanced in an echelon. A tactic Alexander had learned from his father, Phillip, who had in turn learned it from the great Greek general and strategist, Epaminondas.

As the two armies approached each other they must have both been intimidated by the sight of their exotic opponents. Confronting the tightly packed and well armoured Macedonian phalanx was a terrifying sight that had sent Persian armies fleeing before even engaging them. While the Indian war elephants with their bronze reinforced trunks terrified the Macedonians and panicked their horses. As the armies collided the elephants killed many Macedonians but the lightly armoured Indian infantry was unable to compete with the Greek and Macedonian phalanxes who where the world's best heavy infantry at the time. The Indian infantry huddled near the elephants for protection, however the great beasts having suffered many wounds, became enraged trampling anyone around them. Alexander's cavalry then slammed into the back of the Indian army, delivering the deathblow.

Porus was outclassed by Alexander's refined combined arms tactics and the professionalism of his force, the panicle of hundreds of years of evolution in the Greek style of war. However, Porus himself fought on with such bravery and tenacity that he gained the respect and admiration of Alexander. Alexander made him a satrap, a regional governor but in practice he would be a subordinate king in his own right. Alexander would need the support of the local nobility to administer his far flung empire when he returned to the West. Interestingly, Alexander also encountered poisoned projectiles during his invasion of India, probably dipped in the venom of the Russell's viper.

After the Battle of Hydapes Alexander's army, home sick and tired after over a decade of campaigning mutinied, refusing to march further to the East fearing even greater Indian armies that were said to have thousands of war elephants. Alexander reluctantly agreed and returned to Persia where he died in 323 BC while planning an invasion of Arabia. At age 32 he had conquered most of the know world creating the greatest empire it had ever seen, but it would not survive his death.

Maurya Empire and Military

The Maurya Empire, ruled by the Mauryan dynasty, was the first empire that was able to unite all of India. The Empire was founded in 322 BC by Chandragupta Maurya. Chandragupta was a general who overthrew the ruling Dynasty of the Nanda kingdom, a state to the East of the straps created by Alexander. The Maurya Empire expanded rapidly westwards across central and western India in the wake of the withdrawing armies of Alexander's quarrelling successors. Chandragupta's successors continued his policies of expansion through war, creating the world's largest empire at that time. The Greeks that remained merged cultures with the Indians over the following centuries creating an Indo-Greek identity.

The Mauryan military reqruited people from all over the subcontinent and from all Castes creating a diverse army.

The core of the army was composed of warriors from Uttarapathian in central and western India. Uttarapatha had many warlike peoples, including the Kambojas, Yavanas, and Sakas. Other groups that provided levy troops in times of war were the Maghadas, Assamese, and Cheras. While the Tamil (Dravidian) kingdoms in the Southern tip only paid tribute.

One interesting group that was requrited into the Mauryan armies was the Nagas, which translate to 'serpents', a mystical people from Eastern India that worshiped cobras.

Like the Vendic armies, Muaryan armies were formed out of four parts, the Chariot, Elephant, Infantry and Archers, the largest part of the force. At its height the Maurya Empire had 750,000 soldiers and made advances in the weapons and armor of their military. War elephants were even armoured and fitted with sword like attachments on their trunks. Small forts were also put on their backs where soldiers would attack from with javelins and bows or long spears, tridents or other polearms at close range. The Mauryan military was reported to have over 9000 war elephants.

After several week rulers the Muaryan Dynasty collapsed in 185 BC. The fall of the Mauryas left the Khyber Pass between Bactria and India unguarded, and a wave of foreign invasion followed. The Greco-Bactrian king, Demetrius, capitalized on the situation and invaded with his Greek army conquering the North East of the subcontinent around 180 BC. While the Greeks formed the Indo-Greek Kingdom the Muarya Empire broke up into smaller kingdoms, which then broke up into smaller Kingdoms again.

Status Quo in Ancient Indian Warfare

The Indo-Greeks were then conquered by an invading force of Scythians around 70 BC. The Scythians were a nomadic Indo-European people who then established the Indo-Scythian Empire in Northwest India. They fought as mounted horse archers, using the powerful composite bow. They were followed by the Yuezhi, Tocharian tribes who also invaded from the great Asian landmass and displaced the Scythians. The Yuezhi were then followed by yet another Indo-European group (this time from the Iranian branch) of nomadic horse archers, the Parthians. The Parthians then from Indo-Parthian kingdoms in Northwest of India while the Indo-Scythians had been pushed into central India. The Indo-Parthians in turn where concuered by the Kushans, another tribal confederation of Tocharian origins. The Tocharians were the most Easterly branch of the

Indo-Europeans and had been being pushed out of central Asia. The Kushan Empire originally formed in the 1st century CE in and would eventually fall into decline and collapse under pressure from the Sassanid empire to the West and the emerging Gupta Empire to the East.

While these events unfolded in Northwest, West and at times the central portions of the subcontinent other Indian Kingdoms formed in Eastern and Southern India. Examples include Pandyan, Cholas, and Chera. The Satavahana empire formed in the Southeast and later the kingdoms of Kalabhras, Kadamba and the Tamil Kingdom of Pallava formed in the South of India.

The kingdoms that dominated the Northwest could never conquer the Southern and Eastern Kingdoms due to military factors. First of all their horses would succumb to the tropical climate of Southern and central India, even if they could operate effectively in the forested or mountainous regions. Furthermore the powerful, but expensive (they could take ten years to construct) compound bow was susceptible to warping in the humid climate unlike the bamboo longbow. Inversely, when the empires of the South and East advanced into the planes of Western or Northwestern India they would be out maneuvered and out shot by the mobile horse archers.

Antiquity: The Far East

In China, the use of war elephants was relatively rare compared to other locations. Their earliest recorded use took place as late as 554 AD when the Western Wei deployed two armoured war elephants from Lingnan in battle, guided by Malay slaves, and equipped with wooden towers, and swords fastened onto their trunks. The elephants were turned away by archers' arrows. The Han Dynasty of the 2nd century BCE fought against Yue kingdoms of South East Asia (ancient Vietnamese) that did employ war elephants. Common tactics used to repel these elephants included massed crossbow or artillery fire, and digging pits or trenches filled with spikes.

By comparison, neighbouring states significantly embraced the use of war elephants. Sri Lankan history records indicate elephants were used as mounts for kings leading their men in the battle field, with individual mounts being recorded in history. The elephant Kandula was King Dutugamunu's mount and Maha Pambata, 'Big Rock', the mount of King Elara during their historic encounter on the battlefield in 200 BCE, for example. In Southeast Asia, along the borders of in modern day Vietnam, the Champan army employed up to 602 war elephant against the Sui Chinese. The Sui troops led the elephants into a trap of falling into deep pits dug by them, also making extensive use of crossbows.

Middle Ages

In the Middle Ages, elephants were seldom used in Europe. Charlemagne took his elephant, Abul-Abbas, when he went to fight the Danes in 804, and the Crusades gave Holy Roman Emperor Frederick II the opportunity to capture an elephant in the Holy Land, the same animal later being used in the capture of Cremona in 1214, but the use of these individual animals was more symbolic than practical.

Farther east, elephants continued to be used in warfare. The Mongols faced war-elephants in Khorazm, Burma, Vietnam and India throughout the 13th century. Despite their unsuccessful campaigns in Vietnam and India, the Mongols defeated the war elephants outside Samarkand by using catapults and mangonels, and in Burma by showering arrows from their famous composite bow. Genghis and Kublai both retained captured elephants as part of their entourage. Another central Asian invader, Timur faced similar challenges a century later. In 1398 Timur's army faced more than one hundred Indian elephants in battle and almost lost because of the fear they caused amongst his troops. Historical accounts say that the Timurids ultimately won by employing an ingenious strategy: Timur tied flaming straw to the back of his camels before the charge. The smoke made the camels run forward, scaring the elephants, who crushed their own troops in their efforts to retreat. Another account of the campaign reports that Timur used oversized caltrops to halt the elephants' charge. Later, the Timurid leader used the captured animals against the Ottoman Empire.

It is recorded that King Rajasinghe I, when he laid siege to the Portuguese fort at Colombo, Sri Lanka in 1558, had an army of 2200 elephants. The Sri Lankans had continued their proud traditions in capturing and training elephants from ancient times. The officer in charge of the royal stables, including the capture of elephants, was called the *Gajanayake Nilame*, whilst the post of *Kuruve Lekham* controlled the Kuruwe or elephant men-the training of war elephants was the duty of the Kuruwe clan who came under their own Muhandiram, a Sri Lankan administrative post.

In the Southeast Asia, the powerful Khmer Empire had come to regional dominance by the 9th century AD, drawing heavily on the use of war elephants. Uniquely, the Khmer military deployed double cross-bows on the top of their elephants.

With the collapse of Khmer power in the 15th century, the successor region powers of Burma (now Myanmar) and Siam (now Thailand) also adopted the widespread use of war elephants. In many battles of the period it was the practice for leaders to fight each other personally on elephants. One famous battle occurred when the Burmese army attacked Siam's Kingdom of Ayutthaya. The war was concluded when the Burmese crown prince Minchit Sra was killed by Siamese King Naresuan in personal combat on elephant in 1593.

Farther north, the Chinese continued to reject the use of war elephants throughout the period, with the notable exception of the Southern Han during the 10th century AD-the "only nation on Chinese soil ever to maintain a line of elephants as a regular part of its army". This anomaly in Chinese warfare is explained by the geographical proximity and close cultural links of the southern Han to Southeast Asia. The military officer who commanded these elephants was given the title "Legate Digitant and Agitant of the Gigantic Elephants." Each elephant supported a wooden tower that could allegedly hold ten or more men.

For a brief time, war elephants played a vital role in Southern Han victories such as the invasion of Chu in 948 AD, but the Southern Han elephant corps were ultimately soundly defeated at Shao in 971 AD, decimated by crossbow fire from troops of the Song Dynasty. As one academic has put it, "thereafter this exotic introduction into Chinese culture passed out of history, and the tactical habits of the North prevailed."

Modern Era

With the advent of gunpowder warfare in the late 15th century, the balance of advantage for war elephants on the battlefield began to change. Whilst muskets had limited impact on elephants, which could withstand numerous volleys, cannon fire was a different matter entirely-an animal could easily be knocked down by a single shot. With elephants still being used to carry commanders on the battlefield, they became even more tempting targets for enemy artillery.

Nonetheless, in southeast Asia the use of elephants on the battlefield continued up until the end of the 19th century. One of the major difficulties in the region was terrain, and elephants could cross difficult terrain in many cases more easily than horse cavalry. The Siamese Army was utilising war elephants armed with jingals up until the Franco-Siamese War of 1893, whilst the Vietnamese used them in battle as late as 1885, during the Sino-French War. Into the 20th century, non-battle-trained elephants were used for other military purposes as late as World War II, particularly because the animals could perform tasks in regions that were problematic for modern vehicles. Sir William Slim, commander of the XIVth Army wrote about elephants in his introduction to "Elephant Bill": *They built hundreds of bridges for us, they helped to build and launch more ships for us than Helen ever did for Greece.*

Without them our retreat from Burma would have been even more ardous and our advance to its liberation slower and more difficult.

Elephants are now more valuable to many armies in failing states for their ivory than as transport, and many thousands of elephants have died during civil conflicts due to poaching. They are classed as a pack animal in a U.S. Special Forces field manual issued as recently as 2004, but their use by US personnel is discouraged because elephants are an endangered species. The last recorded use of elephants in war occurred in 1987 when Iraq was alleged to have used them to transport heavy weaponry for use in Kirkuk.

Tactical use

There were many military purposes for which elephants could be used. In battle, war elephants were usually deployed in the centre of the line, where they could be useful to prevent a charge or to conduct one of their own. Their sheer size and their terrifying appearance made them valued heavy cavalry. Off the battlefield, they could carry heavy material and provided a useful means of transport before mechanized vehicles rendered them mostly obsolete.

An elephant charge could reach about 30 km/h (20 mph), and unlike horse cavalry, could not be easily stopped by an infantry line setting spears. Such a charge was based on pure force: elephants crashing into an enemy line, trampling and swinging their tusks. Those men who were not crushed were at least knocked aside or forced back. Moreover, elephants could inspire terror in an enemy unused to fighting them-even the very disciplined Romans-and could cause the enemy to break and flee. Horses unaccustomed to the smell of elephants also panicked easily. The elephants' thick hide gave them considerable protection, whilst their height and mass offered considerable protection for their riders. Some elephants were even equipped with their own armor to further protect them. Many generals preferred to base themselves from elephants so as to get a better view of the battlefield.

In addition to charging, the elephants could provide a safe and stable platform for archers to fire arrows in the middle of the battlefield, from which more targets could be seen and engaged. The archery evolved into more advanced weapons, and several Khmer and Indian kings used giant crossbow platforms (similar to the ballista) to fire long armor-piercing shafts to kill other enemy war elephants and cavalry. The late 16th century AD also saw the use of culverin and jingals on elephants, an adaptation to the gunpowder age that would ultimately drive elephants from the battlefield. Elephants were further enhanced with their own weaponry and armour. In Sri Lanka, heavy iron chains with steel balls at the end were tied to the trunks of war elephants, which the animals were trained to swirl menacingly and with great skill. Numerous cultures designed elephant Armour, aiming to protect the body and legs of the animal whilst leaving his trunk free to attack the enemy. Larger animals could also carry a protective tower on their backs, called a howdah.

In the Punic wars a crew of three men were used in battle: archers and potentially men armed with sarissas (six metre long pikes). Further east, large numbers of men were carried, with the senior commander either utilising the howdah or leading from his seat on the elephant's neck. The driver, called a mahout, was responsible for controlling the animal. In many armies, the mahout also carried a chisel-blade and a hammer to cut through the spinal cord and kill the animal if the elephant went berserk.

War elephants had tactical weaknesses, however, that enemy forces often learnt to exploit. Elephants had a tendency to panic themselves: after sustaining painful wounds or when their driver was killed they would run amok, indiscriminately causing casualties as they sought escape. Their panicked retreat could inflict heavy losses on either side. Experienced Roman infantry often tried to sever their trunks, causing an instant panic, and hopefully causing the elephant to flee back into its own lines. Fast skirmishers armed with javelins were also used to drive them away, as javelins and similar weapons could madden an elephant. Elephants were often unarmoured and vulnerable to blows to their flanks, so Roman infantry armed some sort of flaming object or with a stout line of pikes, such as Triarii would often attempt to make the elephant turn to expose its flank to the infantry, making the elephant susceptible to a pike thrust or a Skirmisher's javelin. The cavalry sport of tent pegging grew out of training regimes for horsemen to incapacitate or turn back war elephants. One famous historical method for disrupting elephant units was the war pig. Ancient writers believed that "elephants are scared by the smallest squeal of a pig", and the vulnerability was exploited. At the Megara during the Diadochi wars, for example, the Megarians reportedly poured oil on a herd of pigs, set them alight, and drove them towards the enemy's massed war elephants. The elephants bolted in terror from the flaming squealing pigs.

The value of war elephants in battle remains a contested issue. In the 19th century, it was fashionable to contrast the western, Roman focus on infantry and discipline with the eastern, exotic use of war elephants that relied merely on fear to defeat their enemy. One writer commented that war elephants "have been found to be skittish and easily alarmed by unfamiliar sounds and for this reason they were found prone to break ranks and flee." Nonetheless, the continued use of war elephants for several thousand years speaks to their enduring value to the historical battlefield commander.

Bibliography

Alger, John, *The Quest for Victory: The History of the Principles of War;* New York, 1982.

Arend, A.: *International Law and the Use of Force*, London, Routledge, 1993.

Bellamy, C.: *Knights in White Armour: The New Art of War and Peace*, London, Random House, 1997.

Black, Jeremy, *Introduction to Global Military History: 1775 to the present day*, Routledge Press, 2005

Carpenter, Stanley D. M., *Military Leadership in the British Civil Wars, 1642-1651: The Genius of This Age*, Routledge, 2005

Chaliand, Gérard, *The Art of War in World History: From Antiquity to the Nuclear Age*, University of California Press, 1994

D'Aguilar, G.C., *Napoleon's Military Maxims*, free ebook, Napoleon's Military Maxims

DuBois, Edmund L., Wayne P. Hughes, and Lawrence J. Low. *A Concise Theory of Combat*. Institute for Joint Warfare Analysis, Monterey, CA. 1997.

Fuller, John F. C., *Foundations of the Science of War*. London, 1925.

Gartner, Scott Sigmund, *Strategic Assessment in War*, Yale University Press, 1999

Heuser, Beatrice, *The Evolution of Strategy: Thinking War from Antiquity to the Present,* Cambridge University Press, 2010.

Holt, Thaddeus, *The Deceivers: Allied Military Deception in the Second World War*, Simon and Schuster, June, 2004.

Lider, Julian, *Military Theory: Concept, Structure, Problems,* Swedish Studies in International Relations, Aldershot, 1983.

Mary, W.: *Asian Power and Politics: the Cultural Dimensions of Authority*, Cambridge, Belknap Press, 1985.

Matloff, Maurice, *American Military History: 1775-1902,* Combined Books, 1996

Posen, B.R.: *The Sources of Military Doctrine*, Ithaca, 1984, Cornell Univ. Press.

Rosen, P.: *Societies and Military Power: India and its Armies*, Ithaca, Cornell University Press, 1996.

Savkin, V. Y., *Basic Principles of Operational Art and Tactics,* Moscow, 1972.

Sun-tzu, *The Art of War*, Oxford, 1963.

Tiede, Herbert R. "Principles of War." *Marine Corps Gazette,* April 1995.

Tomes, Robert R., *US Defense Strategy from Vietnam to Operation Iraqi Freedom: Military Innovation and the New American Way of War, 1973–2003*, Routledge Press, 2007

Vaughn, Thomas B. "Morale: *The 10th Principle of War?*" May 1983.

Wilden, Anthony, *Man and Woman, War and Peace: The Strategist's Companion*, Routledge, 1987

Index

□□□